FESTIVE FOLDING

★ ★ ★ ★ ★

Decorative origami for parties and celebrations

PAUL JACKSON

NORTH LIGHT BOOKS

A QUINTET BOOK

First published in the USA by North Light Books,
an imprint of F & W Publications, Inc.
1507 Dana Avenue
Cincinnati, Ohio 45207

ISBN 0–89134–402–0

This book was designed and produced by
Quintet Publishing Limited
6 Blundell Street
London N7 9BH

Creative Director: Terry Jeavons
Designer: Stuart Walden
Project Editor: Judith Simons
Editor: Henrietta Wilkinson
Illustrator: David Kemp
Photographer: Paul Forrester

Typeset in Great Britain by
Central Southern Typesetters, Eastbourne
Manufactured in Singapore by
Chroma Graphics (Overseas) Pte Ltd, (Singapore)
Printed in Singapore by Kim Hup Lee Printing Co. Pte. Ltd.

CONTENTS

INTRODUCTION

★ ★ ★ ★ ★

FOREWORD

Why do people fold paper? Most do so because they enjoy making something out of nothing. A sheet of paper is so ordinary to us that to transform it into a beautiful object can seem miraculous. But another reason is its simplicity. Folding paper needs no tools, no specialized equipment, no machinery – just the paper and your hands. It is relaxing, involving, and rewarding.

The first papers capable of being folded were made in China about 2,000 years ago, although there is no evidence that the Chinese folded paper in a decorative way at that time. A few dozen ancient Japanese designs have survived into the modern era, but since the secret of making paper did not actually cross to Japan until several centuries after its invention in China, the exact origins of the craft are obscure.

Traditional Japanese designs have been the inspiration for the recent flood of new creative work from Japan and the West, and the Japanese word for paper folding – origami – has been adopted worldwide. Today, there are many thousands of designs in an astonishing range of styles and techniques. What must have once seemed a trivial diversion has proven to be a craft, or art, of extraordinary richness. There are now societies of paper folders in most major Western countries, who organize exhibitions and courses, and publish a growing number of high-quality specialized publications. Origami has come of age.

Please read the next few pages before attempting any of the designs. They will give you all the information you need to understand the instructions for the projects and to choose the right papers.

Good luck and happy festive folding!

PAPER

Most types of paper are suitable for folding, but the trick behind successful folding is matching the right paper to the right design. Avoid using papers that do not crease sharply, such as newspaper, tissue or paper towels, unless these are particularly specified.

Specialist Japanese shops usually sell square origami paper in packets, but these outlets are few and far between, and local art and craft suppliers do not always sell it. In any case, origami paper is often expensive and the colors can be harsh, although having different colors or designs on the two sides can be very useful for certain projects.

Good papers for trying out a design include typing paper, writing paper, photocopy paper and computer paper. These are all inexpensive, easily available and crease very well. If nothing else is around, a page cut from a glossy magazine will also fold well.

When folding a design for a festive occasion, a special paper will always make a design look more attractive. Special papers may be bought from two main sources: shops which supply materials to artists, and those which supply materials to graphic artists and designers. Large cities sometimes have shops which specialize in selling paper, but they are disappointingly few in number. Patterned giftwrap paper, sold by stationers, is useful for decorative designs.

In the case of designs which need to be sturdy, such as the Easter *Egg Basket*, use thick artists' papers which can absorb moisture without warping, such as Ingres paper or watercolor paper. This will allow you to employ the so-called "wet folding" process: before folding a suitable paper, stroke both sides with a lightly dampened – not wet – cloth, then fold; the paper will dry rigid into its folded shape. Even the thickest watercolor paper becomes pliable when wet and will fold into a design of remarkable strength. Other papers, such as drawing paper or thin card, are suitable for general folding but are not suitable for this "wet folding" process, because they warp and shred when wet.

Some of the designs, such as the *Witch on a Broomstick*, are best made from a sheet which has different colors on its two sides. If you cannot find such papers, use two thin sheets of different colors and fold them, back-to-back, as one·

Stationery shops often sell sheets or rolls of metallic foil backed with paper. This material is very malleable for folding, but has a harsh, crude surface which can look rather unattractive. Use it selectively, perhaps for festive decorations such as the *Bauble* or the *Bell*. To soften the reflective surface but to keep the folding properties of foil, try covering the foil-side with a layer of soft-colored tissue. The effect can be very beautiful.

The introductory paragraphs to each design suggest what weight of paper to use. Lightweight paper is the weight of typing paper, computer paper or lighter papers, such as airmail paper. Mediumweight paper is the weight of drawing paper. Heavy paper is the weight of watercolor paper. It is advisable to use the weight suggested, but it is only a guide. A paper of another weight may work equally well, so feel free to experiment.

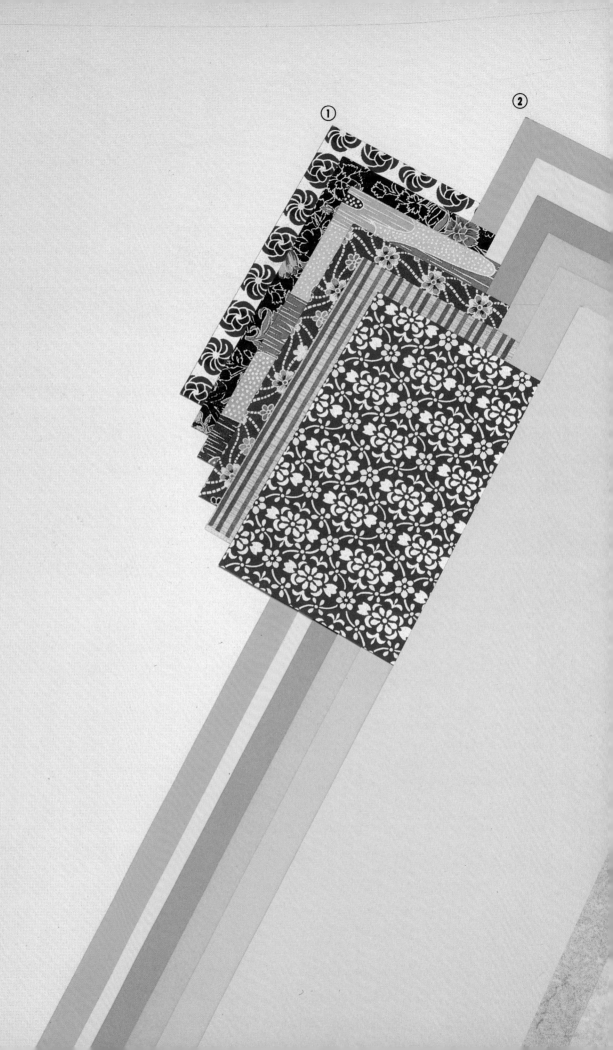

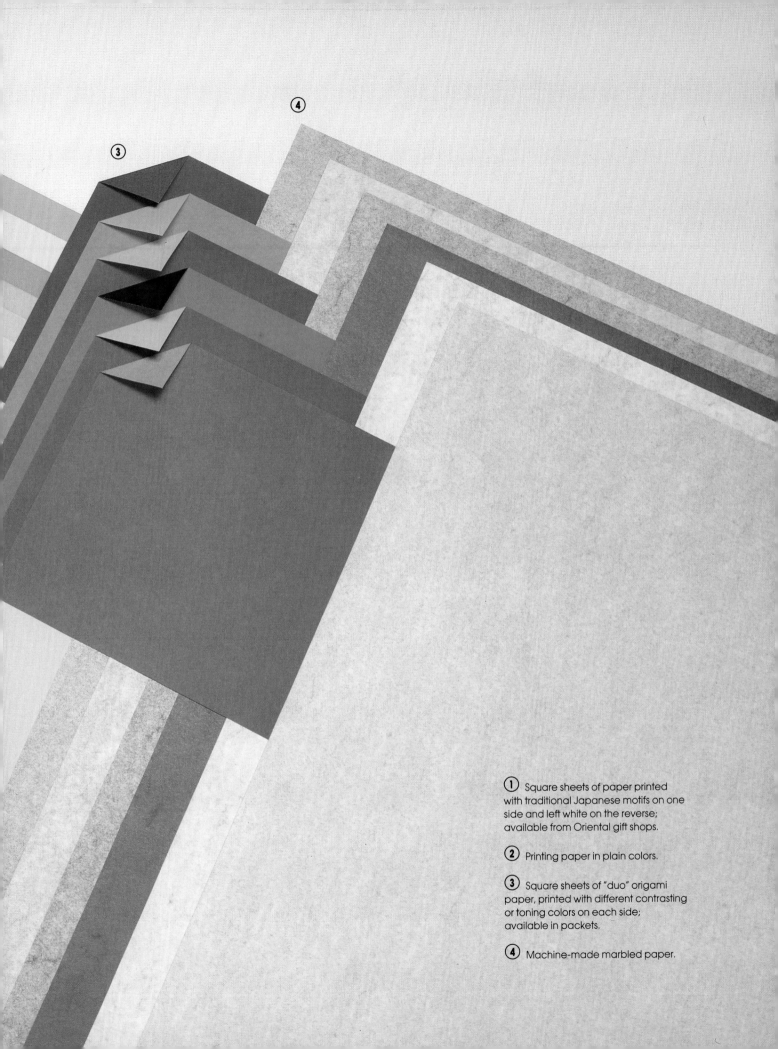

① Square sheets of paper printed with traditional Japanese motifs on one side and left white on the reverse; available from Oriental gift shops.

② Printing paper in plain colors.

③ Square sheets of "duo" origami paper, printed with different contrasting or toning colors on each side; available in packets.

④ Machine-made marbled paper.

(5) Metallic foil, plain and printed, backed with white paper; available from Oriental gift shops.

(6) Thick, heavyweight paper printed with a cloud-effect design; widely available from graphic equipment suppliers.

(7) Origami paper in plain colors with white flares down the center of each sheet; suitable for decorations.

(8) Thick, heavyweight paper printed with a mottled design; widely available from graphic equipment suppliers.

(9) Traditional square origami paper, printed in plain colors on one side and left white on the reverse.

SYMBOLS

Refer to this table when folding. Make sure that you follow all the symbols on all the steps

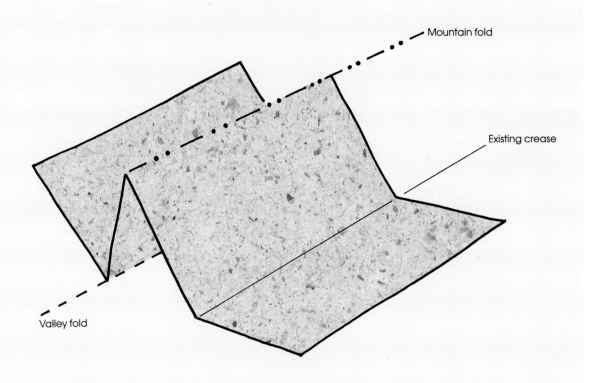

Mountain fold

Existing crease

Valley fold

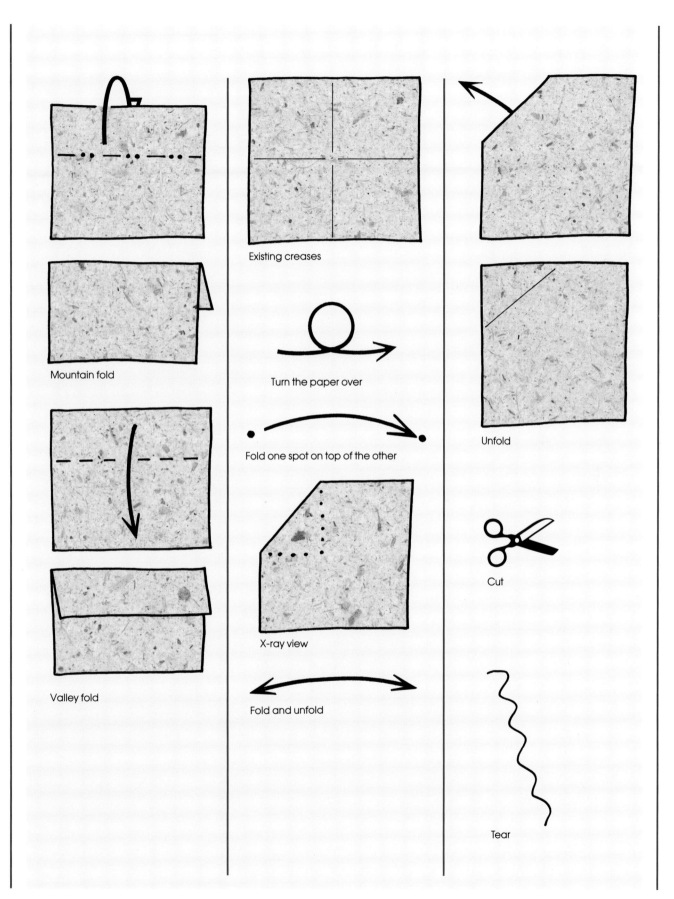

Mountain fold

Existing creases

Valley fold

Turn the paper over

Fold one spot on top of the other

X-ray view

Fold and unfold

Unfold

Cut

Tear

TIPS ON FOLDING

Folding paper is not difficult, but it can become difficult if you fold in an incorrect way. To help you fold properly, here are some tips:

● Fold against a hard, level surface such as a table top or hardback book. Experts fold entirely in the air, but this is awkward for beginners. Nevertheless, there will be occasions, particularly when folding the last stages of a design, when you will need to pick up the paper and fold it in the air, but do so only when necessary.

● Fold slowly; do not rush! Folding needs to be done carefully and neatly. A few sloppy creases here and there can throw everything else out of alignment, so check and double-check the accuracy of your folds.

● Fold crisply and firmly.

● Look at the diagrams and read all the instructions. All too often mistakes are made by looking at one without reference to the other. Look at *all* the symbols (see pages 14 and 15) on a step, checking whether a crease is a valley or a mountain, which corner or edge is at the top of the paper, whether you should turn the paper over, how the lettered corners move about from step to step, and so on.

● The symbols and written instructions for each step will make a shape which looks like the next illustration. So it is important to keep looking ahead to the next diagram to see what shape you are trying to make. Never look at one step in isolation from the others, but look ahead, then back, then ahead and so on.

● Before folding a design, check that the paper you are using is *exactly* square, *exactly* a 2 ×1 rectangle, or whatever the shape specified, and that it is not too small, too large, too thick or too thin for that design.

● Wash your hands!

STAR RATING

To help you judge the difficulty of a design, a graded star rating has been included with each project.

★ elementary
★★ fairly simple
★★★ not too difficult
★★★★ fairly difficult

FOLDING TECHNIQUES

It is a simple matter to make a valley or mountain crease, but techniques become more complex when more than one crease is made at a time, such as when a corner or edge is opened out and pushed into itself. This procedure is known as either the "inside reverse fold" (commonly known simply as the "reverse fold"), or its opposite, the "outside reverse fold." Before folding a design which contains this procedure, try it out a few times first by folding the examples below.

INSIDE REVERSE FOLDS

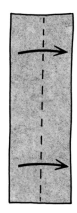

1 Using an oblong scrap of paper, fold the paper in half lengthwise.

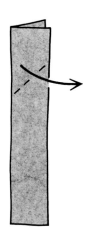

2 Valley fold as shown.

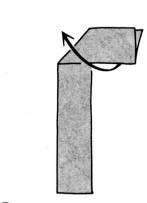

3 Unfold . . .

4 . . . like this.

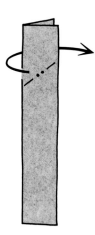

5 Mountain fold along the line of the valley fold, making a flexible crease.

6 Unfold.

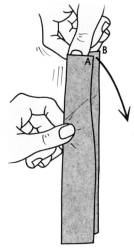

7 Hold the paper as shown, thumb inside the paper between A and B. Move the top hand down and to the right . . .

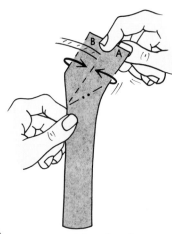

8 . . . separating A from B and making mountain and valley folds as shown, collapsing the paper . . .

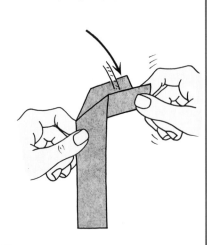

9 . . . like this.

10 The inside reverse fold complete.

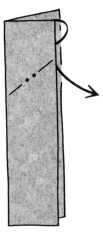

11 This diagram denotes an inside reverse fold.

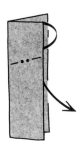

12 Reverse folds can be at any angle, such as this . . .

13 . . . which is almost folded in half.

14 This is a small reverse fold, in which a corner is pushed in . . .

15 . . . like this. Practice these reverse folds.

OUTSIDE REVERSE FOLDS

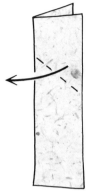

1 Start with Step 2 of the inside reverse fold, then valley fold as shown.

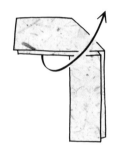

2 Unfold . . .

3 . . . like this.

4 Mountain fold along the line of the valley fold, making a flexible crease.

5 Unfold.

6 Hold carefully as shown. With the left thumb, push into the paper at the top of the V-shaped crease, while pulling edge BA towards you . . .

7 . . . like this. Crease mountains and valleys as shown. Bring edge BA to the front while moving the hands backwards . . .

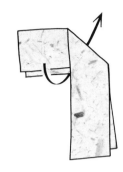

8 . . . like this. Collapse further.

9 The outside reverse fold complete.

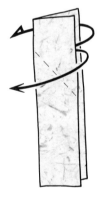

10 This diagram denotes an outside reverse fold.

1

CHRISTMAS

★ ★ ★ ★ ★

SIX-POINTED STAR

TRADITIONAL

One of the simplest and most attractive of all folded decorations, the six-pointed star uses the most basic folding techniques. Steps 1–4 show how to make an equilateral triangle (one with all its sides of equal length) from a square. If you know another method of doing this by all means use it, although the one shown here is accurate and pleasing.

Make several stars, in an array of bright colors, and hang them from the Christmas tree for extra sparkle.

STAR RATING ★★

PAPERS

Use a square of paper of any weight or size. The best paper to use for this decoration is paper-backed metallic foil, which reflects the light and will make the star stand out against the dark foliage of a natural Christmas tree.

OTHER EQUIPMENT

Scissors; needle and thread.

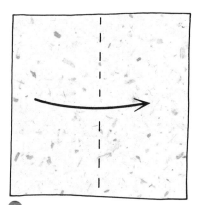

1 Fold in half, left to right.

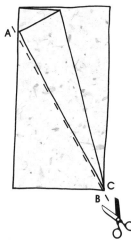

3 Cut along edge BA. Open out the bottom left-hand triangle and discard the remainder of the paper. Add creases which run into corners B and C to locate the center of the triangle.

2 Turn in the top layer corner to exactly touch the crease made in Step 1, at such a point that the new crease will run exactly down to the bottom corner. Take your time lining it up – this is the most important crease in the whole design. Badly placed, it will spoil the shape of the star.

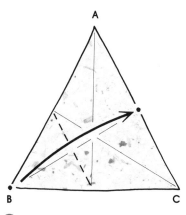

4 Fold B across to the opposite edge.

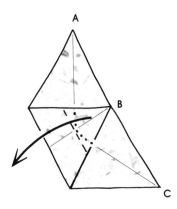

5 Fold B back along a crease which passes over the center of the triangle.

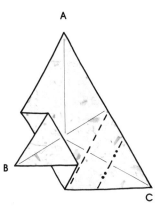

6 Repeat Steps 4 and 5 with C.

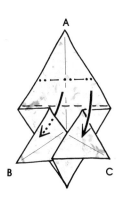

7 Repeat Steps 4 and 5 with A. Tuck the left-hand part of the pleat under B to lock A, B and C together in a symmetrical pattern . . .

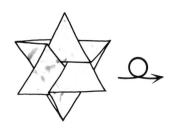

8 . . . like this. Turn over.

9 The Six-Pointed Star complete. To suspend, attach a loop to the star with needle and thread. The star looks most effective when hung in groups.

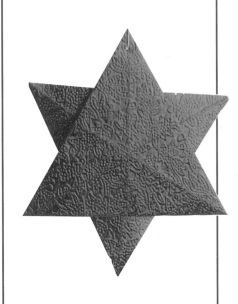

BAUBLE

ORIGIN UNKNOWN

Here is another stunning decoration for the Christmas tree. This may seem like a complex design, but it is little more than a simple crease pattern repeated many times along the paper. The secret of success is to crease with care and accuracy.

1 With the paper right side up, valley fold twice to form three equal sections.

2 Make valley creases midway between each section, creating six equal divisions.

3 Make valley creases midway between the existing creases, creating 12 equal divisions.

4 Make valley creases midway between each of the existing creases, creating 24 equal divisions. Keep the folds accurate.

5 Fold the sheet in half along its length. Unfold.

6 Fold the sides into the middle of the sheet, creasing right along its length. Unfold.

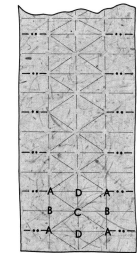

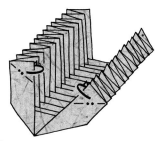

7 Look at the crease pattern so far. All the existing creases are valleys, the new ones will be mountains.

9 Along the two outer edge sections, re-crease alternate valley creases to make them mountains as shown. This will produce a pleated effect along the edges, with diamonds across the middle. Locate As, Bs, Cs, and Ds.

12 Mountain fold the single layer corners inside at both front ends.

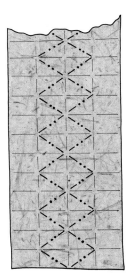

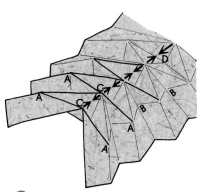

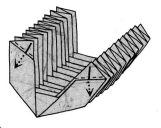

10 Now squeeze the pleats together on both edges so that the side and end points (C and A) of the diamond rise up, and the middle point (D) of the diamond and pleat (B) cave in.

13 Valley fold the double layer corners on the inside edges, as shown. Repeat all the way down the row of pleats, neatly folding in each corner in turn.

8 Now make careful diagonal *mountain* folds across the middle, as shown, making sure your folds exactly connect at the intersections of existing creases. It may help to draw the line of the new folds with a pencil before creasing. This is a tricky step. Make sure the creases do not stray toward the outer edges of the sheet, and make them firm.

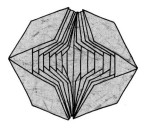

11 Compress the pleats all along the strip, concertina fashion. Press firmly to reinforce all the creases, and then turn over.

14 Bring the ends around and together to form the bauble shape.

15 Tuck the left-hand edge under the right, as shown, locking the bauble.

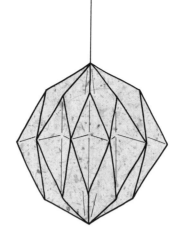

16 The Bauble complete. To hang it, simply use a needle and thread to fix a loop to the top of the bauble. Alternatively, before locking the ends of the bauble together (see Step 15), attach a blob of modeling clay to the free ends of a loop of thread and position it inside the body of the bauble, allowing the loop to issue from the top. The locking action will enclose the modeling clay and hold the thread firmly in place.

ANGEL

DESIGNED BY DAVE BRILL, UK

This elegant, semi-abstract design is far removed from the literal style of representation seen in some models. It succeeds well in capturing the likeness of a subject with just a few folds – just as difficult as using many. The Angel can be used to decorate the front of a Christmas card, or attached to the top of the Christmas tree with a loop of adhesive tape.

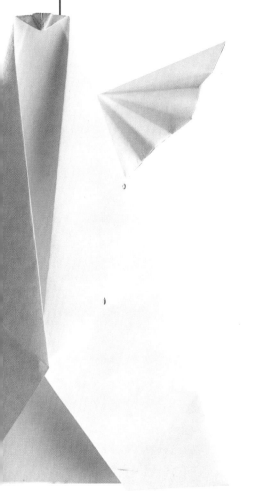

STAR RATING ★★

PAPERS

A rectangle of mediumweight paper or foil, proportioned 3:2, an 8 x 12 in (20 x 30 cm) sheet is suitable for this piece.

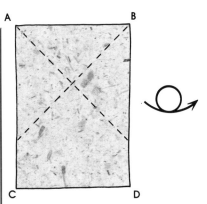

1 Fold A over to the right so that it lies on edge BD. Crease and unfold. Repeat, folding B over to the left to lie on edge AC. Crease, unfold, and turn over.

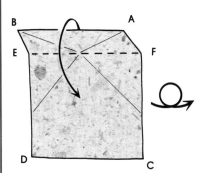

3 Make a horizontal valley fold which passes through the centerpoint of the mountain "cross." Turn back over.

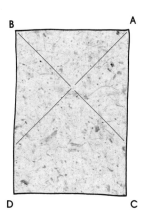

2 The creases now rise toward you.

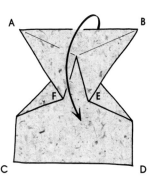

4 Holding the sides of the paper at E and F, let A and B rise up as the sides are brought inward . . .

27

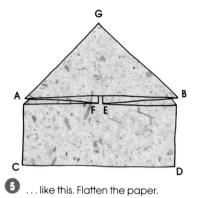

5 ... like this. Flatten the paper.

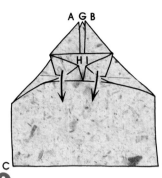

8 Hold G, A and B and swing them back up to where G used to be at the top. Keep a firm hold of them. The paper does not lie flat in the middle.

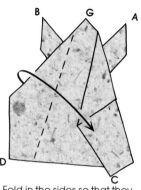

11 Fold in the sides so that they overlap in the center (see next drawing). Note that they do not quite meet at G. C has already been folded.

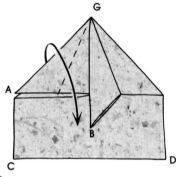

6 Imagine a center crease from the top point (G) down the middle of the paper. Fold in A and B to lie along that imaginary crease. Keep it neat at G. B has already been folded.

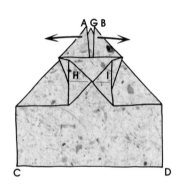

9 Flatten the paper to form triangles H and I. Hold the paper with your left hand at H, and . . .

12 Tuck D and C behind. Fold down G. Carefully pleat the wings.

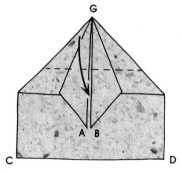

7 Fold G down to AB. Crease firmly.

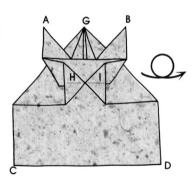

10 ... pull B and A away from G (see the next drawing to check the new position). Flatten and crease. Turn over.

13 The Angel complete.

STREAMER

DESIGNED BY ED SULLIVAN, USA

Here is a model which can be as long as you like! Learn the technique on one strip, fold another, and then join them together by gluing the last pleat of one to the first pleat of another. Repeat as many times as you wish, being careful to fold all sections from identical strips. The result is spectacular.

STAR RATING ★★★★

PAPERS
Use a long, narrow strip of lightweight paper or foil, about 3 in (8 cm) wide. As you get more confident, you can experiment by altering the paper width.

OTHER EQUIPMENT
Glue.

1 With the right side of the paper facing you, mountain fold edge AB on a diagonal, so that AB lies under the bottom edge of the strip.

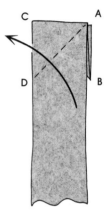

3 Now fold the strip to the left along diagonal crease DA. Be careful to keep all the layers lined up at the edges.

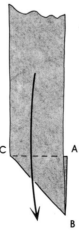

2 Fold the length of the strip down along horizontal crease CA.

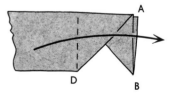

4 Fold the strip to the right, making a vertical crease.

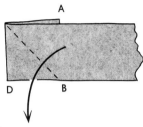

5 Fold the strip down along a diagonal crease. Keep the layers lined up.

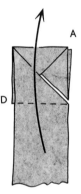

6 Fold the strip back up, making a horizontal crease . . .

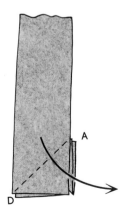

7 . . . and then fold to the right along a diagonal crease.

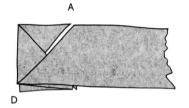

8 Continue the sequence established above until the whole strip is folded up. Be extremely careful to keep all the layers lined up exactly.

9 Unfold the strip to see this crease pattern along the strip.

10 Now mountain fold the other diagonals on each square, all along the strip. Keep it neat, and be careful to make the creases the same way up as the existing diagonals.

11 Fold valley creases through the exact point where the diagonals intersect. Note that both diagonals are mountain creases, and all horizontals are valleys.

12 The creases made in Step 11 form squares along the strip. Mountain fold diagonals on these squares just formed, connecting the top left- to the bottom right-hand corners of each square . . .

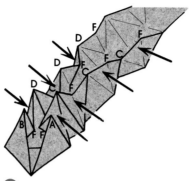

13 . . . and then the top right to the bottom left corners. Keep it neat!

15 Hold the edges of the strip at the first DC pair along from BA. Push them together gently and E should collapse downward. Push a few more DC pairs together, moving along the strip. F should tuck in and down on top. Continue like this, pushing BA up, to squeeze together all the Es and to reinforce the creases. Note that all creases form – nothing is wasted.

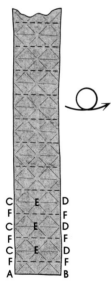

14 Make valley folds midway between the existing valley creases. These new creases each pass through two mountain diagonal "crosses." This is the completed crease pattern. Check that when you look at the paper all the diagonal creases are mountains, all the horizontals are valleys, and all the creases join, connect or intersect with accuracy. Identify AB, Cs, Ds, Es and Fs. Turn over.

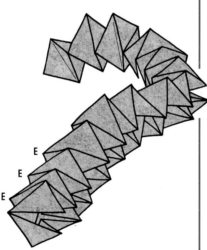

16 When squeezed together, the strip will look something like this. Repeat with as many strips of identical width as you wish to fold. Glue them into one enormously long strip. Alternatively, bend one end of the streamer around to meet the other and glue to form a circular decoration. If the creases need to be redefined, push the ends toward each other, squeezing the folds flat together. The streamer can be stored easily in this position from one Christmas to the next.

BELL

DESIGNED BY PAUL JACKSON, UK

Inflatable origami – blow-ups – are always fun to make, but there are very few such models; the Waterbomb is perhaps the best known.

When folding, leave a small hole at the bottom corner to blow into. Do not close it completely by folding *too* neatly! If the hole *is* too small, snip it open with scissors.

STAR RATING ★★★

PAPERS
Use a 6–8 in (15–20 cm) square of light- or mediumweight paper or foil.

OTHER EQUIPMENT
To suspend the bell you will need a needle and thread.

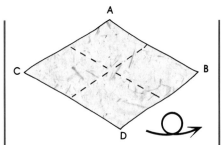

1 Fold horizontal and vertical valley folds across the paper. Turn over, so that the creases rise toward you.

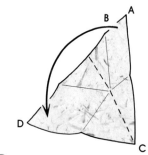

2 Fold A over to D as shown. Unfold. Repeat this move, folding B over to C.

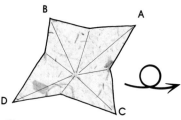

3 The crease pattern should look like this. The paper is three-dimensional. Turn over so that the middle rises up. Push the horizontal and vertical mountain folds toward each other so that the central peak rises up, as shown. Four triangles are formed, meeting at E.

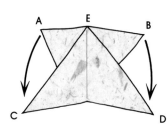

4 Flatten the paper so that two triangles lie either side of the center.

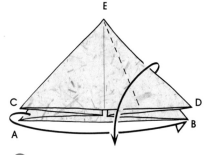

5 Fold D inward so that edge ED lies along the center crease. (It may help to mark ABCD in pencil.) Swing A on the left around the back to the right so that it lies behind B.

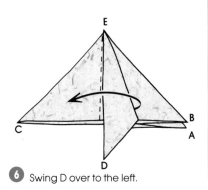

6 Swing D over to the left.

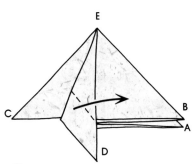

7 Fold up D as shown so that it lies along edge CB.

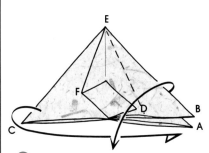

8 The paper now looks like this. The folds in Steps 5–7 are now repeated with B, then A and then C. As in Step 5, fold B inward so that edge EB lies along the center crease, covering D. Swing C on the left around the back to lie behind A on the right.

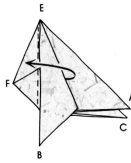

9 Swing B over to the left to lie on top of F. Fold up B like D in Step 7.

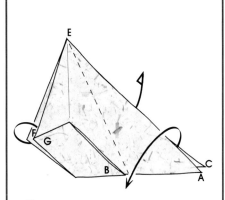

10 As in Step 5, fold A inward so that edge EA lies along the center crease, covering B. Swing F on the left around the back to lie hidden behind C on the right. Swing A over to the left to lie on top of G. Fold up A like D in Step 7.

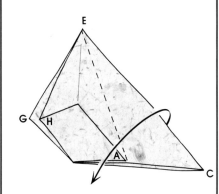

11 As in Step 5, fold C inward so that edge EC lies along the center crease, covering A.

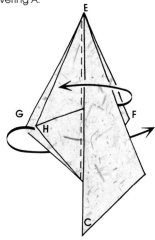

12 Swing G on the left around the back and to the right to lie behind F. Swing C over to the left, to lie on top of H.

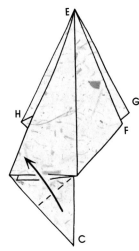

13 Fold up corner C, as shown. Crease flat.

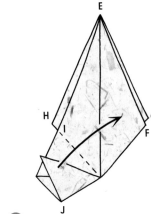

14 Fold the flap up as shown . . .

15 . . . and slide J under the edge that runs down the center of the paper, pushing it deep into the pocket.

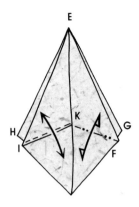

16 The paper is now symmetrical. Carefully form valley creases between I and K, and H and K on the left and mountain creases between F and K, and G and K on the right. Do not crease beyond the center.

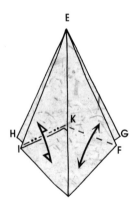

17 Now make mountain creases on the left and valleys on the right, placing these creases on top of the previous ones. This will form creases that can bend backward and forward. Bend them to and fro several times so that they are very flexible.

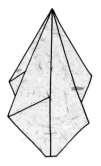

18 At the bottom end, there should be a small hole. Blow into it and the bell should inflate! Inflating it is easier if the four flaps are spread apart and if the hole is clearly visible. The flexible creases just made will form a definite rim to the bell.

19 The Bell complete. To suspend, attach a loop to the top of the bell with needle and thread.

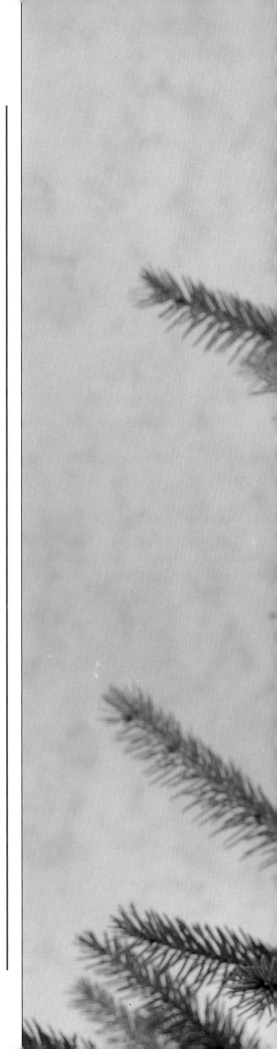

STAR

DESIGNED BY PAUL JACKSON, UK

A good way to form geometric shapes is to fold a number of simple shapes which can interlock. This is commonly known as "modular origami." The Star is a simple example of this kind of folding, and to experiment try folding six, eight or more modules to make stars with more than four points.

STAR RATING ★★

PAPERS

You will need four sheets of lightweight paper or foil about 4 in (10 cm) square in two colors or textures which work well together. Choosing complementary papers with care always adds to the finished piece.

OTHER EQUIPMENT

To suspend the star you will need a needle and thread.

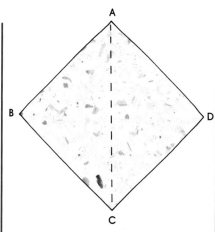

1 Fold B over to D. Crease and unfold.

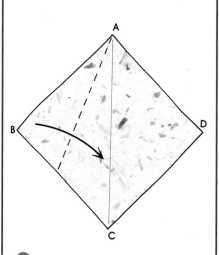

2 Fold in edge AB to lie along crease AC.

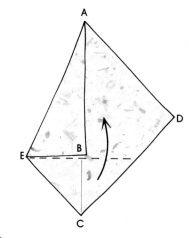

3 Fold up C along a crease which follows edge EB, covering B.

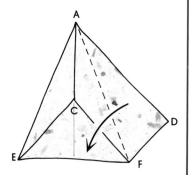

4 Fold in edge AD to the center so that it half covers C.

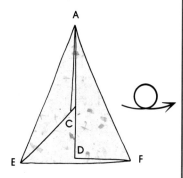

5 The paper looks like this. Turn over.

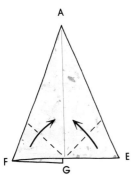

6 Fold in F and E to lie along crease AG.

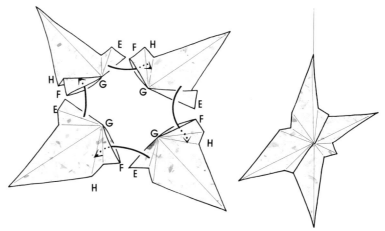

9 Tuck corner E of one section in between the layers of another at F and continue to push it farther in until E touches H and the two Gs touch. The mountain and valley creases should line up where they overlap. In the same way, tuck in the third and fourth sections, alternating the types of paper, and finally locking the first section into the fourth. Strengthen and sharpen all the creases.

10 The Star complete. To suspend, attach a loop to one point of the star with needle and thread.

7 Fold F and E back out to the sloping edges just formed which meet at G. E is shown already folded. Keep the folds neat at G.

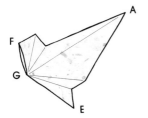

8 Unfold the last two steps so it looks like this. This is one point of the star. Make three more sections just the same as the first, but make two of them in another (maybe patterned) paper.

2

CHILDREN'S PARTIES

★ ★ ★ ★ ★

BOW TIE

DESIGNED BY PAUL JACKSON, UK

Simple to make and fun to wear, the Bow Tie is an ideal way of breaking the ice at parties for all age groups!
Decorate the Bow Tie with some self-adhesive colored shapes – dots or squares, for example – for a truly individual effect.

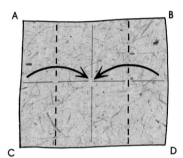

1 Fold the napkin in half horizontally and vertically. Unfold. Fold AC and BD to the central vertical crease.

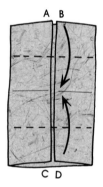

2 Fold AB and CD to the central horizontal crease.

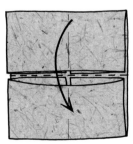

3 Fold in half across the middle.

4 The folding is now complete.

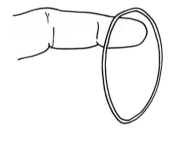

5 Take the elastic band . . .

6 . . . and wrap it around a finger three times.

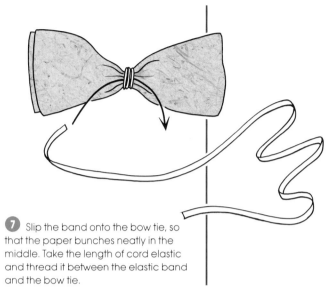 

7 Slip the band onto the bow tie, so that the paper bunches neatly in the middle. Take the length of cord elastic and thread it between the elastic band and the bow tie.

8 Tie the ends of the cord elastic together, decorate the front of the bow with self-adhesive colored shapes, if wished, and the Bow Tie is ready to wear.

BUFFET SERVER

TRADITIONAL

This is a practical and quick-to-make design that is ideal for buffets – to pre-wrap sets of cutlery – or for children's parties.

STAR RATING ★

PAPERS
Use paper napkins; 4-ply is the best, but 3- or 2-ply are adequate. Starched linen napkins may also be used.

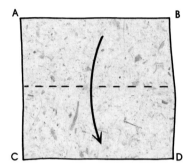

1 If the napkin is already folded into quarters (as most are), skip forward to Step 3. Otherwise, fold AB down to CD.

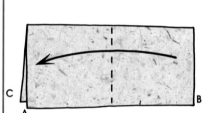

2 Then fold BD across to AC.

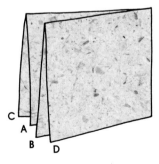

3 Note CABD. Rotate to the Step 4 position.

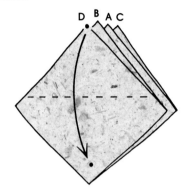

4 Fold down D almost to the bottom corner.

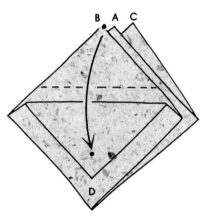

5 Fold B almost to D.

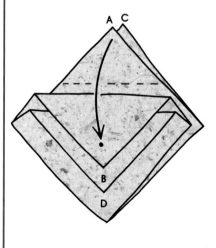

6 Fold A almost to B

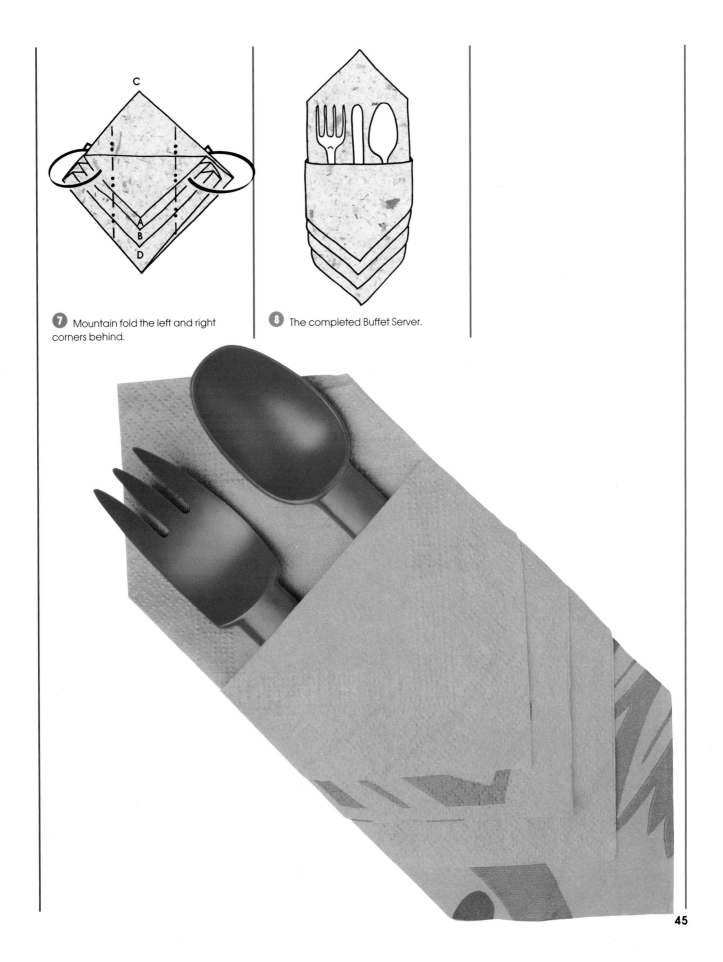

7 Mountain fold the left and right corners behind.

8 The completed Buffet Server.

TOOT-FLUTE

TRADITIONAL

Of the few musical instruments that can be made from paper, this is perhaps the simplest and you will be amazed by the sound it produces. A must for any children's party, get your young guests to make their own and mount a competition for the loudest "toot"!

STAR RATING ★

PAPERS

Use a lightweight sheet of 8½ × 11 in (21.5 × 27.9 cm) paper. For deeper musical tones, use larger sheets; for higher tones, use smaller ones. The Toot-Flute can also be made from a paper drinking straw, cut to a point at one end rather like the nib of a fountain pen, and then snipped in the appropriate place to give it an arrowhead shape.

OTHER EQUIPMENT

Pencil; adhesive tape; scissors (safety scissors if children are making their own toot-flutes).

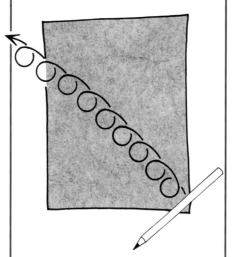

1 Wrap a corner of the paper around a pencil and roll it across the sheet at 45° to the edge.

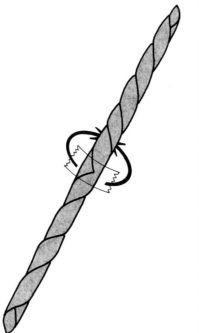

2 Drop the pencil out and secure the loose corner with a piece of adhesive tape.

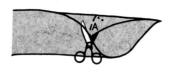

3 Starting from the notch at one end, make a cut to free A . . .

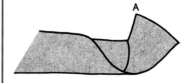

4 . . . like this.

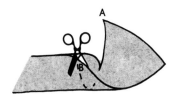

5 Repeat at the other side of the notch, to free B.

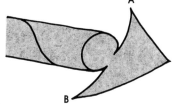

6 Note that the triangle is joined to the tube by only a small edge. The smaller the edge, the easier the triangle will vibrate and so the louder the flute will sound.

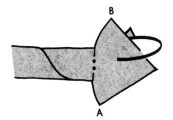

7 Fold the triangle against the tube.

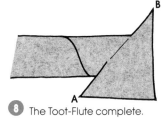

8 The Toot-Flute complete.

BELOW With the triangle at the bottom of the flute, *suck* gently and the flute will buzz! Alternatively, put the triangle into your mouth (be careful not to wet it) and *blow* gently to produce a buzz, too.

PIRATE'S HAT AND SHIRT

TRADITIONAL

Many readers will be familiar with the basic triangular hat shown in Step 5, but few will know that it can be developed into the stronger Pirate's Hat at Step 10 and later torn to create the fun Shirt. Step 13 could even be a pirate ship!

Provide a Step 10 pirate hat for each child (or adult, if it's that sort of party!), and then choose an appropriate moment to show how the hat can become a shirt. Stand back, and watch the chaos as everyone makes their own!

STAR RATING ★★

PAPERS
Use a complete double-page leaf from a broadsheet (large format) newspaper.

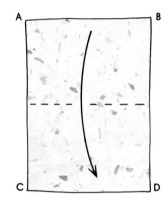

1 Fold in half from top to bottom.

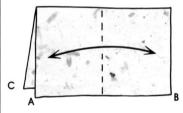

2 Fold in half, left to right. Unfold.

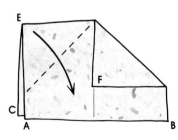

3 Fold corners E and F to the center crease. F is shown already folded.

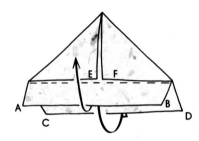

4 Fold up edge AB along a crease which runs along the bottom of triangles E and F and, similarly, fold up CD behind.

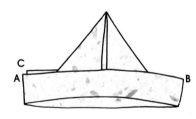

5 This makes a simple, though rather large and floppy, hat.

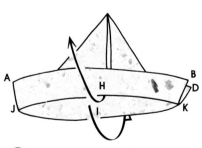

6 Hold as shown at H and I. Pull H and I apart, so that J and K come toward each other.

OPPOSITE To complete the Pirate's Hat and Shirt, turn the page for the remaining instructions.

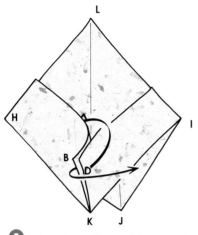

7 This makes a diamond shape. Tuck D behind B to flatten the front. Repeat behind, tucking A under C.

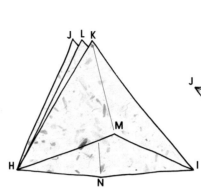

10 As you did in Step 6, open up the bottom to form the Pirate's Hat. To make the Pirate's Shirt, bring H and I together by pulling M and N apart, as in Steps 6–7.

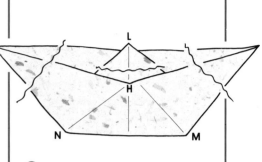

13 Could this be a pirate ship? Tear off J, K and L as shown. Carefully, completely unfold the remainder of the ship.

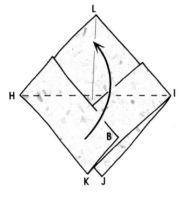

8 Fold K up to L, and behind fold J to L.

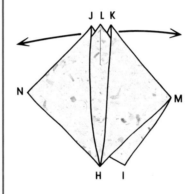

11 Hold K and J and pull them away from L . . .

14 And here is the Pirate's Shirt!

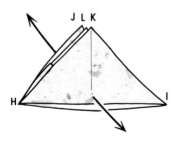

9 It should look like this.

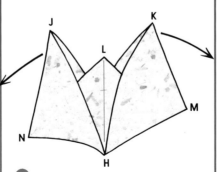

12 . . . like this. Continue to pull until Step 13 is made.

SUN HAT

DESIGNED BY PAUL JACKSON, UK

No party is complete without a party hat, but on this model the visor gives good protection from the sun, so it can be worn both in and out of doors.

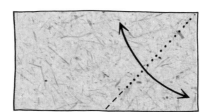

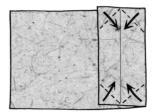

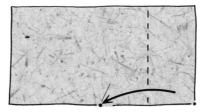

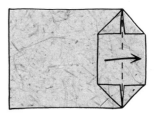

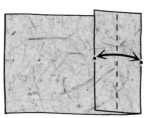

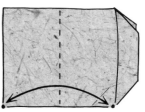

STAR RATING ★★

PAPERS

Use a sheet of mediumweight paper, proportioned 5:8. For a child's head, use a sheet 10 x 16 in (25 x 40 cm).

1 Bring the bottom right-hand corner up to the top edge, in such a way that if a crease was made it would start at the top right corner. However, do not make a crease, but instead make a short pinch at the bottom edge.

2 Fold the bottom corner to the pinch.

3 Fold the flap in half. Unfold.

4 Turn in the corners to the center crease in the flap.

5 Fold the flap in half, left to right, creating a pocket.

6 Fold the bottom left corner to the edge of the pocket. Unfold.

51

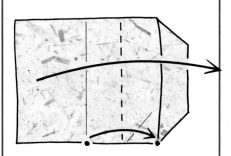

7 Fold the Step 6 crease to the edge of the pocket.

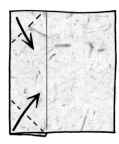

8 Turn in the corners to the Step 6 crease.

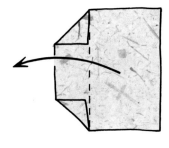

9 Fold the loose flap back to the left.

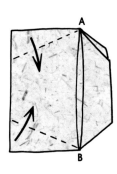

10 Turn in the corners a little. Note the gash between A and B.

11 Fold the loose flap across to the right.

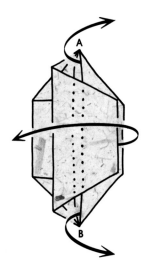

12 Lift up the top flap and open out the gash between A and B, creating a box form . . .

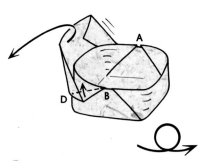

13 . . . like this. Swivel the visor out and to the left, and crease DB (repeat at back) to hold the visor in place. If the angle of the visor is too high or too low, re-crease Step 11 in another position. Turn over.

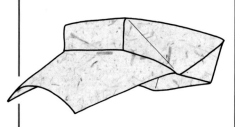

14 The Sun Hat complete.

DOGGY BAG

DESIGNED BY PAUL JACKSON, UK

Here is a cheap and fun way to make a sturdy bag for your party guests to take away their gifts and goodies.

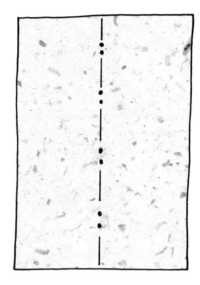

1 Make a mountain fold down the middle. Unfold.

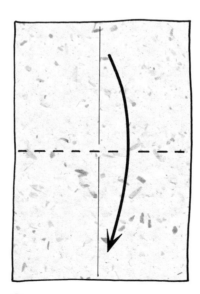

2 Fold the top edge down to the bottom.

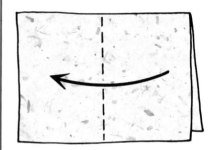

3 Fold the right edge across to the left.

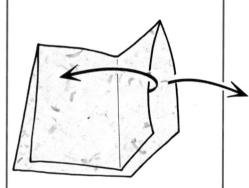

4 Let the right-hand side stand upright. Pull open the layers . . .

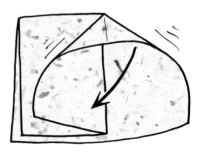

5 . . . and squash flat . . .

6 . . . like this. Turn over.

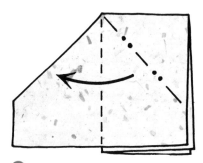

7 Repeat Steps 3–6 on this side.

8 Swivel the front edge at the right across to the left, and swivel the rear edge at the left across to the right.

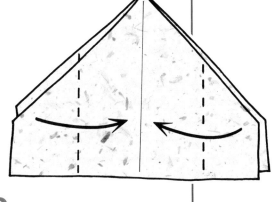

9 Fold the sides to the middle. Repeat behind.

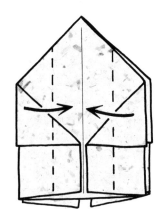

10 Again, fold the sides to the middle. Repeat behind.

11 Turn the paper upside-down.

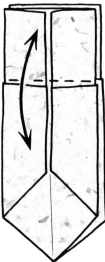

12 Fold and unfold as shown. Repeat behind.

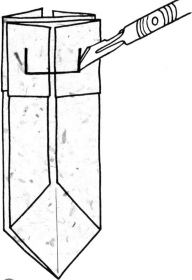

13 With a craft knife, using a metal ruler as a guide, cut through all the layers as shown.

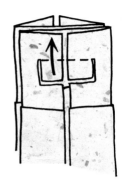

14 Fold up all the layers as shown . . .

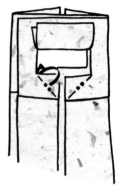

15 . . . to create a handle for the bag. Tuck in the loose corners. Repeat behind.

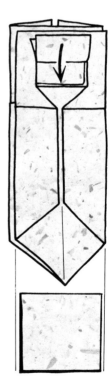

16 Unfold the handle. For added strength, cut out a square of card a little smaller than the width of the bag.

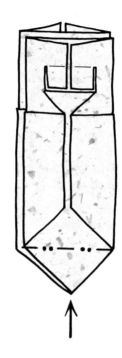

17 Push up the bottom to open the bag.

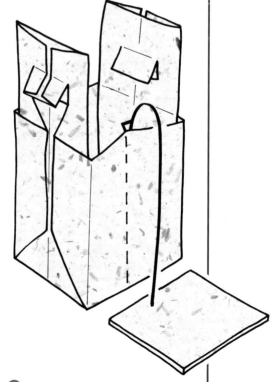

18 Put the card into the bag and close up the handles.

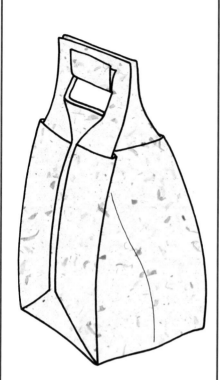

19 The completed Doggy Bag.

3

FESTIVE MEALS

★ ★ ★ ★ ★

COCKADE NAPKIN

TRADITIONAL

This is one of the most decorative and spectacular napkin folds, impressive enough to use on the most important occasions.

STAR RATING ★★

PAPERS

Use a 4-ply paper napkin for the best results, although 3- and 2-ply are adequate.

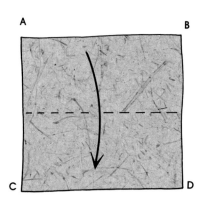

1 If the napkin is already folded into quarters (as most are), skip forward to Step 3; otherwise, fold AB down to CD.

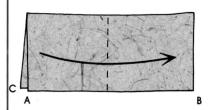

2 Fold AC across to BD.

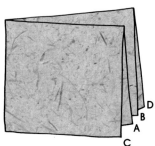

3 Note CABD. Rotate to Step 4 position.

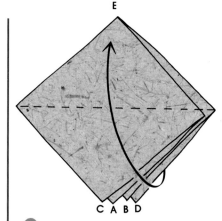

4 Fold CABD up to E.

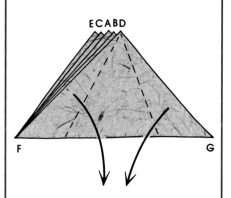

5 Fold the sloping edges of the triangle inward so that FE and GE meet in the middle.

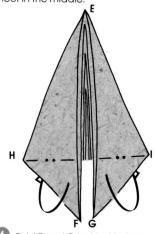

6 Fold F and G behind to form a straight edge between H and I.

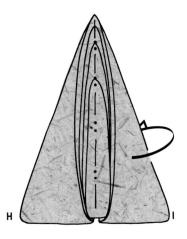

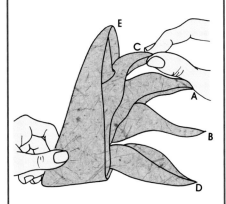

7 Fold I behind, folding the shape in half down the middle.

8 Grip H and I firmly with one hand. With the other hand pull D out as far as possible from the nest of layers. Repeat with B (not pulling it as far as D) and likewise pull out A, and finally C.

9 The Cockade Napkin complete.

PLACE CARD

DESIGNED BY PAUL JACKSON, UK

A finishing touch to a place setting is to make a card which carries the name of the guest who is to sit there. This same design can also hold photographs, artwork, or give exhibition information.

STAR RATING ★

PAPERS

Use a mediumweight paper 8½ × 11 in (21.5 × 27.9 cm) for the frame, and thin card for the insert.

OTHER EQUIPMENT

Scissors or craft knife and metal ruler; writing pen.

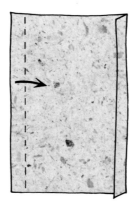

1 Fold in about ½ in (1 cm) along the longer edges. The right-hand side is shown already folded.

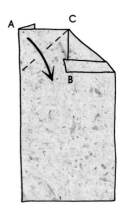

3 Fold A and B into the middle, using the pinch at C to find the point on the top edge where the creases meet. B is shown already folded.

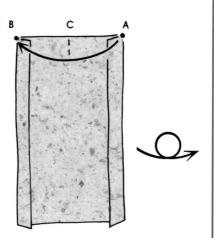

2 Bring top corners A and B together and pinch to locate the middle of the top edge (C). Do not make a long crease. Unfold and turn over.

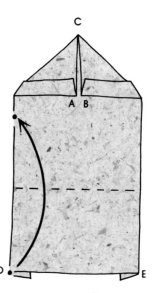

4 Fold up D and E to lie just below the base of the triangle. The exact placement is unimportant.

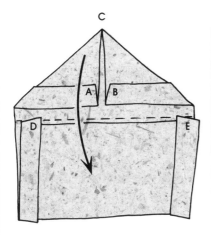

5 Fold down C and crease along a line just above DE.

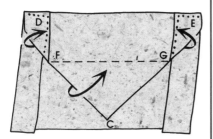

6 Flip loose corners D and E to the front, trapping the corners of the large C triangle behind them. Make a valley crease between F and G, lifting corner C.

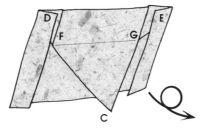

7 This is the back of the place-card holder, with C forming a stand. Turn over.

8 Measure the proportions of the holder. Cut a piece of paper or card which is fractionally smaller. Write the person's name on it and tuck the short edges into the pockets at the sides of the place-card holder.

9 The Place Card complete.

NAPKIN RING

DESIGNED BY PAUL JACKSON, UK

Instead of folding paper napkins, roll up linen napkins and present them at the side of each place setting inside the napkin ring described here. The effect is less flamboyant, but just as impressive.
To personalize each napkin ring, stencil a monogram, initial or image, such as a flower, onto the central shield.

STAR RATING ★★★

PAPERS
Use a 2:1 rectangle of light- or mediumweight paper, approximately 8 × 4 in (20 x 10 cm).

OTHER EQUIPMENT
To decorate the napkin ring you will need a purchased or homemade stencil; brush and paints, or coloring pencils, felt-tip pens, etc.

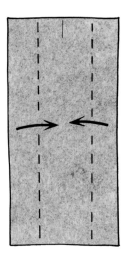

1 As you did in Step 2 of the Place Card, fold the top edge in half and pinch to locate the center of the edge. Then fold the long edges into the middle, using the pinch as a location point.

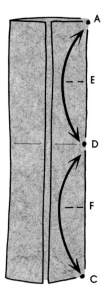

3 Fold A to D making only a short crease at the right-hand edge (E), and unfold. Repeat, folding C to D, to make F.

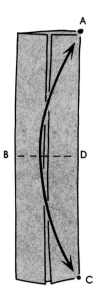

2 Fold A down to C to make crease BD. Unfold.

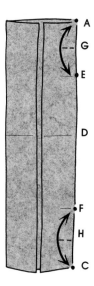

4 Fold A to E, making a short crease at the right-hand edge (G). Repeat, folding C to F, to make H.

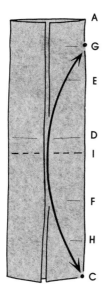

5 Fold C up to G. Crease right across to make I and unfold.

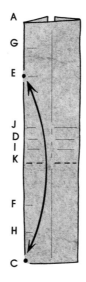

7 This is the crease pattern at present. Fold C up to E. Crease right across to make K and unfold.

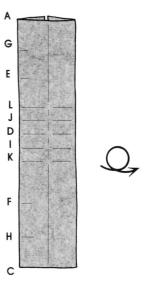

9 This is now the crease pattern. Turn over.

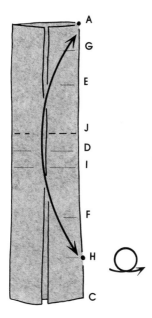

6 Fold A down to H. Crease right across to make J and unfold. Turn over.

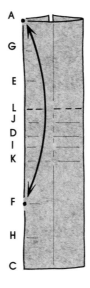

8 Fold A down to F. Crease right across to make L and unfold.

10 Fold the long edges into the middle. Unfold.

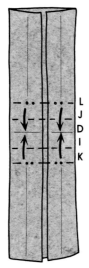

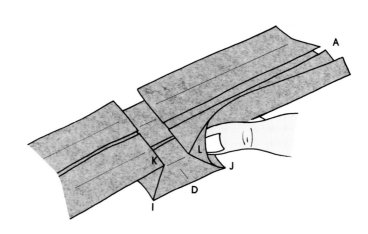

11 Pleat along the existing creases, bringing K and L to D.

14 Dig your thumb into the pocket between L and J, forming a curved arc. Squash it flat into a triangle . . .

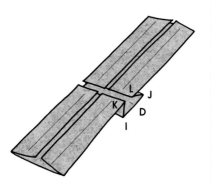

12 It should now look like this.

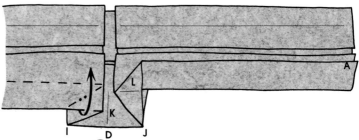

15 . . . like this. Repeat with K, folding it across, pulling it into an arc, digging a thumb in the pocket under K, and squashing it to make a triangle. The points of the triangles should meet.

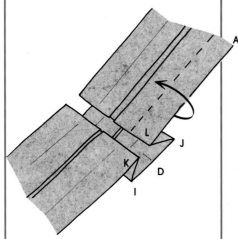

13 Fold the long edge AL in toward the middle along the crease made in Step 10.

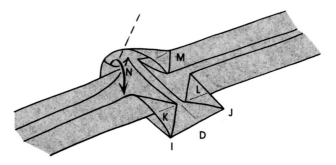

16 Now fold in the long edges on the opposite side of the strip, but instead of digging your thumb in the pockets as you did under K and L, swing M and N right across, opening up another pocket. Squash this flat, forming a triangle. The points of the triangles point away from each other, the long sides meeting.

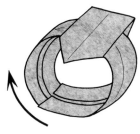

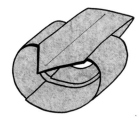

18 Feed one end of the strap into the other to fasten the ring.

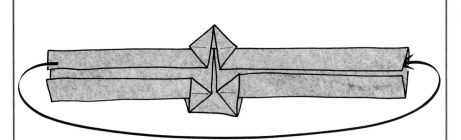

17 It should look like this. When turned over there should be a simple shield shape on the reverse.

19 The Napkin Ring complete.

CORNUCOPIA NAPKIN

TRADITIONAL

Ideal for Thanksgiving or Harvest Festival meals, this is a simple but elegant folded napkin. Use a piece of fruit to hold it open.

STAR RATING ★

PAPERS
Use 4-ply napkins for the best results.

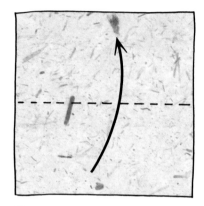

1 Fold the bottom edge of an open napkin up to the top.

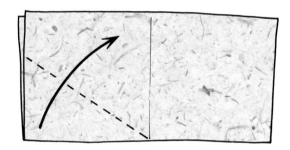

2 Fold in the bottom left-hand corner, as shown.

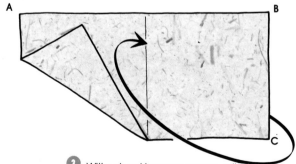

3 Without making any creases, roll BC across to the left, so that C comes to rest against the middle of the top edge . . .

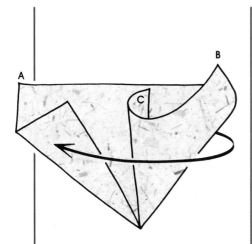

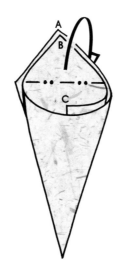

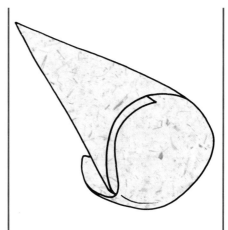

4 . . . like this. Continue to roll, so that B comes to rest in front of A.

5 To lock, fold A and B behind.

6 The Cornucopia Napkin complete.

FLORAL CENTERPIECE

IRIS: TRADITIONAL JAPANESE
LEAVES AND VASE:
DESIGNED BY PAUL JACKSON, UK

Of all the projects in the book, this is the one that will require the most time, the most equipment and will take the most artistry to design and arrange. That said, it is also the project that will be the most admired. It makes a stunning centerpiece to any room or dining table for any occasion. Choose your papers with great care, coordinating the colors, tones and textures.

STAR RATING ★★★★

PAPERS

For the **iris**, use light- or mediumweight paper approximately 6–8 in (15–20 cm) square.

For the **leaves**, use mediumweight paper 8–10 in (20–25 cm) square – the paper should be a little larger than that used for the iris.

For the **vase**, use heavyweight paper 10–14 in (25–35 cm) square – the paper should be 1½ times the size of that used for the iris. For a particularly sturdy vase, use thick artists' paper – Ingres or watercolor paper – and employ the "wet folding" process explained in the section on Papers (see Introduction).

OTHER EQUIPMENT

Pencil; scissors; florists' wires (3 or 4 for each stem); florists' tape (green binding tape, available from florist shops); adhesive tape; glue; and tapioca balls or rice grains.

IRIS

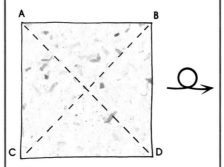

1 Crease the two diagonals, both valleys. Turn over.

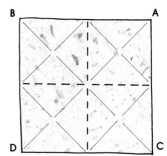

3 Valley fold in half vertically and unfold. Valley fold in half horizontally.

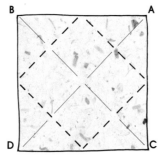

2 The creases now rise toward you. Fold the four corners into the middle. Unfold.

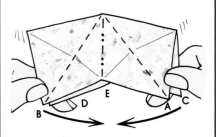

4 Push the four corners together into the middle so that the valley folds on the diagonals collapse inward . . .

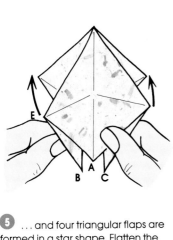

5 ... and four triangular flaps are formed in a star shape. Flatten the paper so that there are two flaps either side of the center ...

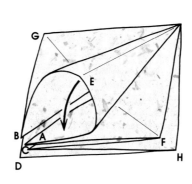

8 Continue to press on E, until it squashes flat. Crease it firmly.

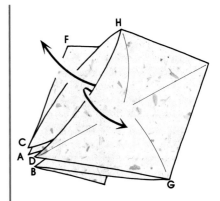

11 ... and press down on the fold to open its pocket, as in Step 8, to squash H flat. Keep the points ABCD together.

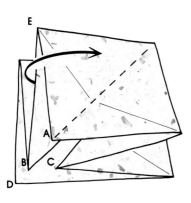

6 ... like this. Lift E so that it stands vertically.

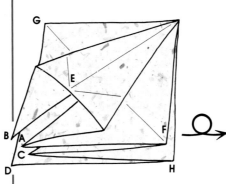

9 Turn over.

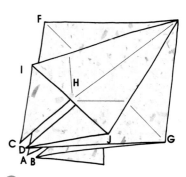

12 It should now look like this. Fold I over to touch J. Then lift F so that it stands upright. Press down on the fold to squash it flat. Turn over and repeat with G.

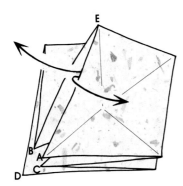

7 Press the folded edge to open the pocket inside E. Hold ABCD neatly together.

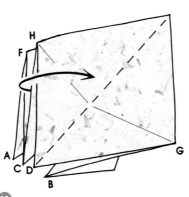

10 Lift up H ...

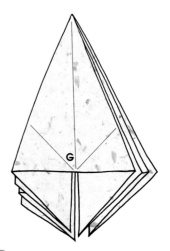

13 All four flaps are now squashed and the paper is symmetrical.

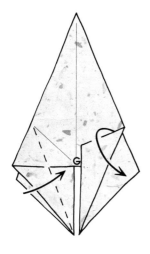

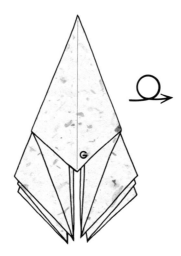

14 Fold in the side points of the top layer at the lower, broader end to lie along the central crease, covering G. The right-hand side is shown already folded. Unfold.

16 Turn over.

18 The paper is now completely symmetrical, with four layers on each side. Fold one layer from the right over to the left.

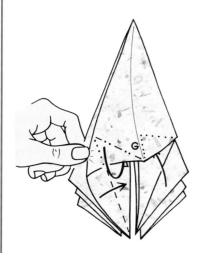

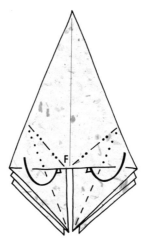

15 With one hand, lift up G. With the other, re-form the creases made in the last step. Push these folds under G, using the old mountain creases made in Step 2, until the paper lies flat, as shown on the right of the diagram.

17 Repeat Steps 14–16 on either side of F. There should now be four layers to either side of the center. Fold two layers on the right over to the left and turn over, so there are two layers on the left and six on the right. Fold two on the right over to the left . . . so that there are four layers on either side with H on top. Repeat Steps 14–16 with H. Turn over and repeat with E.

19 This will expose a blank face. Fold in the top edges of the upper layer so they lie along the middle. Keep it neat!

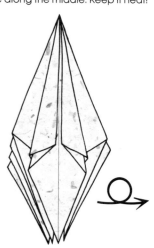

20 This is the result. Turn over.

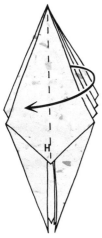

21 Fold one layer over from right to left.

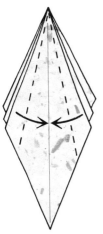

22 Fold as in Step 19. Repeat the process on the other two blank faces. The paper will crease easier and neater if the layers are symmetrical.

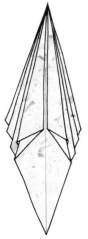

23 It should now look like this. Move the layers around so that there are four to either side of the center, but so that the top layer is the one you have just folded. Turn upside-down.

24 The iris now has a narrow stem. Fold down the petal facing you . . .

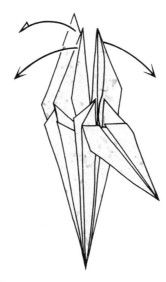

25 . . . like this. Turn over, and fold down the petal. Repeat with the other two petals . . .

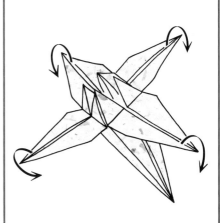

26 . . . like this. Now loosely roll each of the petals in turn around a pencil. This will give them a soft, curled shape.

27 The Iris complete.

LEAVES AND STEM

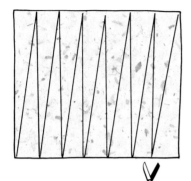

1 Cut the square into long, tapering strips, as shown. One square will make 12 or more leaves.

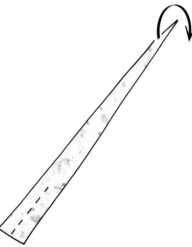

2 Fold the paper in half at the square end by about 1 in (2½ cm).

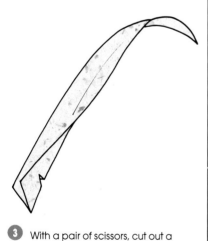

3 With a pair of scissors, cut out a small "V" shape in the middle of the crease, not too near the end.

WIRING UP

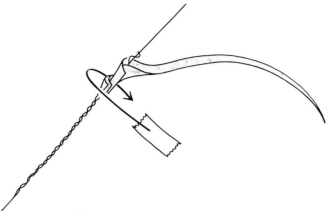

1 Overlap two florists' wires and twist together. Overlap another wire and join it by twisting. For longer stems, simply twist in more wires. Poke one end of the wire through the cut in the leaf, position the leaf a little way down the wire, and then twist the square end of the leaf tight around the wire, at such an angle that the leaf points upward, not horizontally. Secure the end of the twisted leaf with a piece of adhesive tape.

2 Now push the end of the wire through the bottom of the iris. This can be tricky, but rather than cut the paper to make a hole, moisten it with your tongue. This should weaken the paper enough to push the wire through. Once through, bend over the top of the wire (as shown), and then drop the end of the wire back into the flower until it catches tight near the base of the stem. Wind green florists' tape onto the wire, starting at the bottom. At the top, carefully wind the tape around the base of the iris, pulling it very tight as you go to secure the iris to the wire. Wind the tape to the bottom of the stem.

VASE

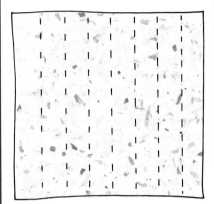

1 Divide the square into eighths, making sure that all creases are valleys.

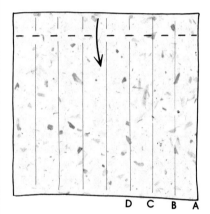

2 Fold down the top edge by about 1 in (2½ cm). Turn over.

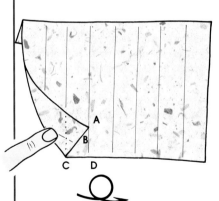

3 Fold A across to touch the third crease (D) and make a sloping crease between the first and second creases (B and C) that will exactly touch C. Make sure this crease does not extend beyond the first and second creases.

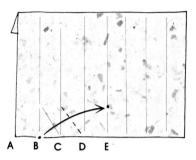

4 Unfold, moving A back to its original position. The crease should be like this, to the left of C. Repeat Step 3, but this time folding B over to the fourth crease (E), and make a crease between C and D.

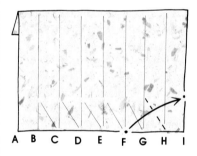

5 Keep repeating this move by folding C to crease 5 (F), then D to crease 6 (G), E to crease 7 (H), and F to the right-hand edge (I). The creases should look like this.

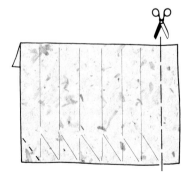

6 Fold a crease which runs into B, from the left-hand edge, parallel to the crease which runs into C. Cut off the right-hand ⅛th of paper. Turn over.

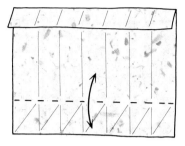

7 Make a horizontal valley crease which connects the tops of all the sloping creases. Unfold.

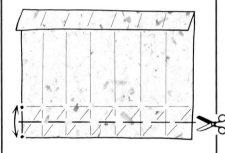

8 Fold the bottom edge up to the horizontal crease just made. Then cut along this crease, discarding the bottom piece.

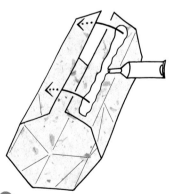

9 Reinforce the vertical creases to form a tube. Glue the right-hand panel, then bring over the left-hand edge and tuck the right-hand panel under the flap at the top to help lock it in place. The vase now has six sides.

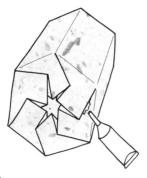

10 Push the end of the vase in so the sloping creases all overlap each other, collapsing into the center.

11 Glue beneath the triangles to lock them in place.

12 The completed Vase. Before arranging the flowers, weight the vase with tapioca balls or rice. This also helps the iris stems to stand straight, instead of falling to the vase's edge.

4

EASTER

★ ★ ★ ★ ★

EGG WARMER

DESIGNED BY PAUL JACKSON, UK

Paper is an excellent insulator, so this design really will help to keep boiled eggs warm as well as adding a festive touch to the breakfast table.

STAR RATING ★

PAPERS
Use an oblong of lightweight paper about 8 × 6 in (20 x 15 cm).

SPECIAL NOTE
To begin this design complete Steps 1–7 of the Doggy Bag (see page 54) and then continue with the steps on this page.
Reverse folds are explained in detail in the section on Folding Techniques (see Introduction).

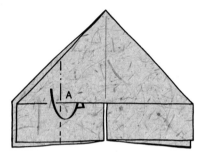

1   See Special Note. Reverse fold the front left layer into the middle. Note A. Repeat with the rear left layer.

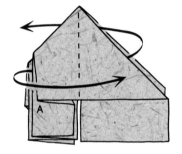

2   Swivel the front left layer across to the right and swivel the rear right layer across to the left.

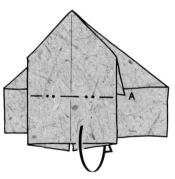

3   Fold the bottom edge into the pocket at A.

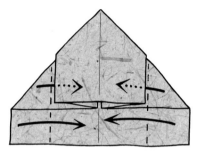

4   Tuck the sides into the middle.

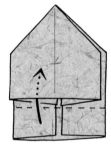

5   Tuck the bottom edge into the pocket.

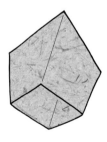

6   The completed Egg Warmer.

CHICK

DESIGNED BY PAUL JACKSON, UK

Having completed this design, you will see how, in origami terms, a chick could be said to be a blob with a beak. Once this is understood, it becomes an easy challenge for a paper folder to design a chick. Have a go yourself.

Make a clutch of chicks and some Easter Bunnies (see next project) to make a centerpiece for the dining table, or use one or two to decorate the top of an Easter cake.

STAR RATING ★★

PAPERS
You will need a lightweight yellow paper, 4 in (10 cm) square for each chick.

OTHER EQUIPMENT
Pencil.

SPECIAL NOTE
The reverse folds featured in Steps 10 and 11 are explained in detail in the section on Folding Techniques (see Introduction).

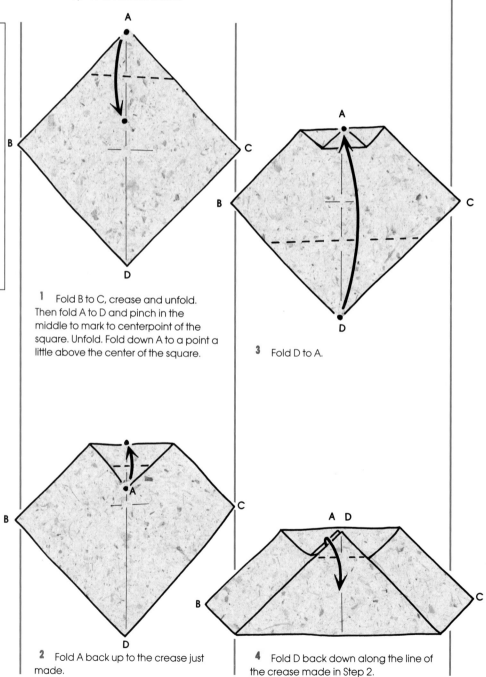

1 Fold B to C, crease and unfold. Then fold A to D and pinch in the middle to mark to centerpoint of the square. Unfold. Fold down A to a point a little above the center of the square.

3 Fold D to A.

2 Fold A back up to the crease just made.

4 Fold D back down along the line of the crease made in Step 2.

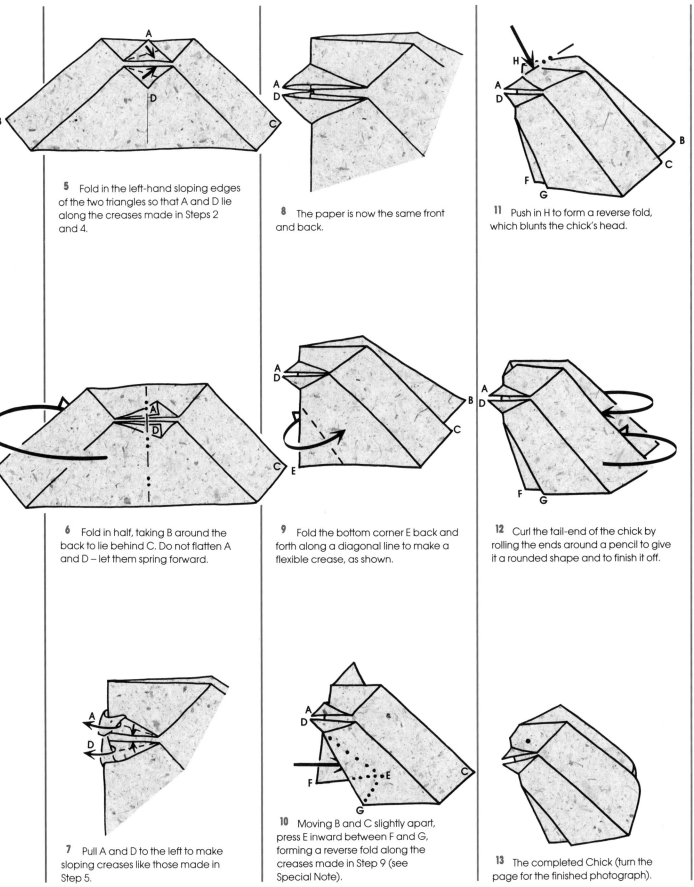

5 Fold in the left-hand sloping edges of the two triangles so that A and D lie along the creases made in Steps 2 and 4.

8 The paper is now the same front and back.

11 Push in H to form a reverse fold, which blunts the chick's head.

6 Fold in half, taking B around the back to lie behind C. Do not flatten A and D – let them spring forward.

9 Fold the bottom corner E back and forth along a diagonal line to make a flexible crease, as shown.

12 Curl the tail-end of the chick by rolling the ends around a pencil to give it a rounded shape and to finish it off.

7 Pull A and D to the left to make sloping creases like those made in Step 5.

10 Moving B and C slightly apart, press E inward between F and G, forming a reverse fold along the creases made in Step 9 (see Special Note).

13 The completed Chick (turn the page for the finished photograph).

EASTER BUNNY

*DESIGNED BY AN UNKNOWN CREATOR
AND PAUL JACKSON*

There are many origami bunnies, but here is one with a difference: it is one of the few made from two pieces, and the only one in which both sections are blow-ups.

STAR RATING ★★

PAPERS
Use two squares of lightweight paper, the head square about two-thirds the size of the body square, for each bunny.

OTHER EQUIPMENT
Glue.

SPECIAL NOTE
To begin both the Body and Head sections of this design, complete Steps 1–4 of the Bell (see page 34) and then continue with the instructions given here.

BODY

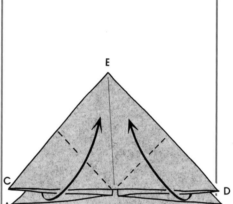

1 See Special Note. Fold C and D up to E.

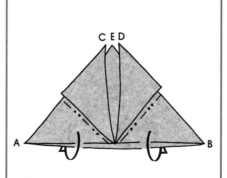

2 Fold A and B behind to E.

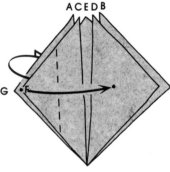

3 Fold F across to the right so that it goes a little beyond the center crease. Repeat behind with G.

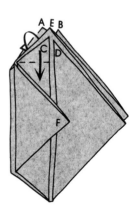

4 Fold down corner C. Repeat behind with A.

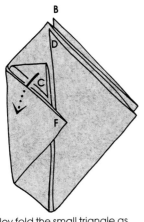

5 Valley fold the small triangle as shown, and tuck it *between* the two layers of paper which run down to F. Repeat behind with A.

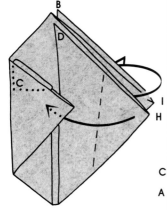

6 Fold H across to the left, tucking it underneath F. Repeat behind with I.

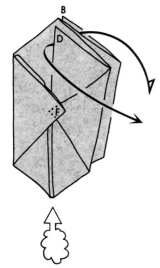

7 Fold down D along the edge which runs down to H. Repeat with B behind. Carefully blow into the hole at the bottom to inflate the body (if necessary, you can enlarge the hole with the point of a pencil).

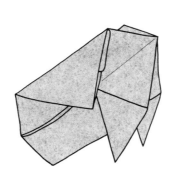

8 The completed body.

HEAD

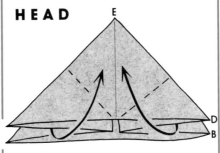

1 See Special Note. Fold C and D up to E.

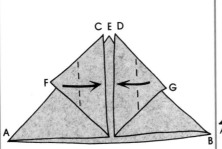

2 Fold F and G into the middle.

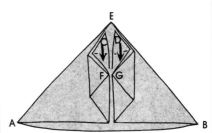

3 Fold down C and D.

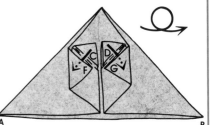

4 As in Step 5 of the body, valley fold the small triangles just formed where shown, and tuck them *between* the two layers of paper which run to F and G. Turn over.

87

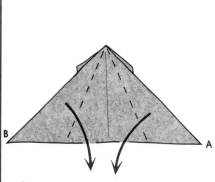

5 Fold down B and A as shown.

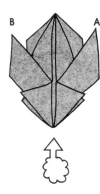

8 It should look like this. As with the body, carefully blow into the hole at the bottom to inflate the head.

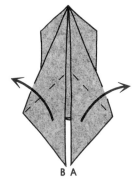

6 Fold B and A back out at such an angle that BA forms a long horizontal edge. See Step 7 to check.

9 The completed head. If needed, use a little glue to attach the head to the top of the body.

7 Fold up B and A as shown, so that the bottom edge lies along the middle crease. These are the bunny's ears.

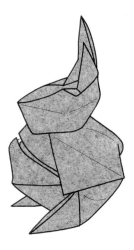

10 The Easter Bunny fully assembled.

EGG BASKET

DESIGNED BY PAUL JACKSON, UK

This basket has clean lines and is very strongly locked together. It is ideal for displaying eggs at Eastertime, but can be used all year round as a presentation or storage bowl. Made with strong paper, it lasts a surprisingly long time.

STAR RATING ★★

PAPERS

Use heavyweight paper, 10–15 in (25–38 cm) square. For a very sturdy basket, use thick artists' paper – Ingres or watercolor paper – and employ the "wet folding" process explained in the section on Papers (see Introduction).

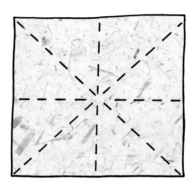

1 Crease horizontally, vertically and diagonally as shown, making sure that all creases are valleys.

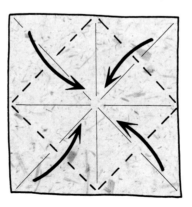

2 Fold the corners into the middle.

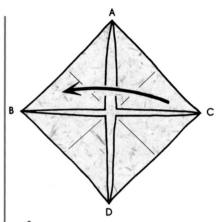

3 Fold C across to B.

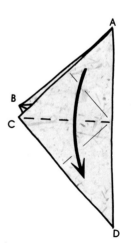

4 Fold A down to D.

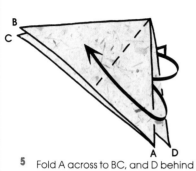

5 Fold A across to BC, and D behind to BC.

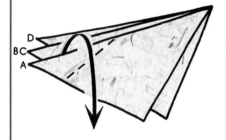

6 Fold down A as shown.

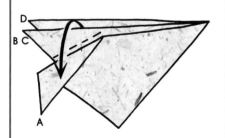

7 Fold down BC on top of A.

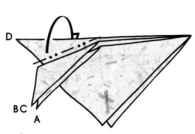

8 Fold D behind. Unfold back to Step 3 position.

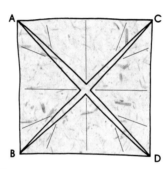

9 This is the crease pattern.

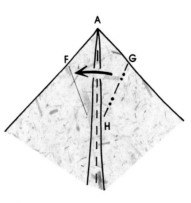

10 The crease that runs to corner A should be a valley and the short crease from G to H, a mountain. If not, crease them . . .

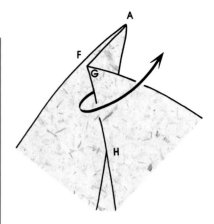

11 . . . folding G across to F. Unfold.

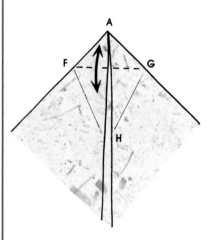

12 Crease and unfold a valley fold between F and G.

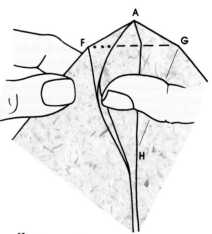

13 Open up the paper on the left as shown, along the valley crease between F and H. Corner A will lift toward you.

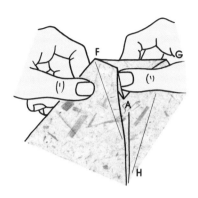

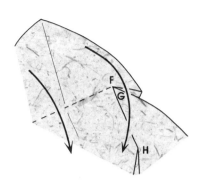

14 Continue to open up the paper, letting A rise until it collapses down between the layers on the left, in an asymmetric way.

17 Lower the single layer on the left back to its position in Step 15 but folding it down in front of G, trapping G between the layers.

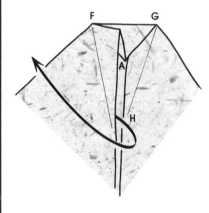

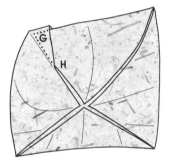

15 Lift up the whole of the single layer of paper left of center, but letting A remain collapsed down.

18 This neatly locks the paper into a tight, slightly rounded corner. Repeat Steps 10–18 on the other three corners.

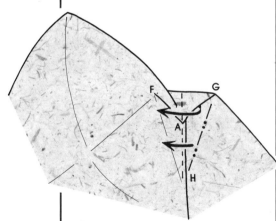

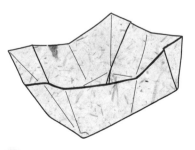

16 As in Step 10, re-crease along AH and GH, bringing G across to F, on top of A.

19 The completed Egg Basket.

HALLOWEEN

★ ★ ★ ★ ★

FANGS

DESIGNED BY ERIC KENNEWAY, UK

This delightfully simple fold is great fun, and easily within the abilities of older children. Advanced folders could develop fangs which are longer and sharper – try experimenting.

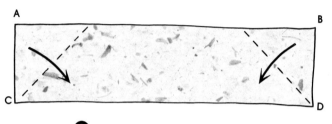

❶ Turn in corners A and B.

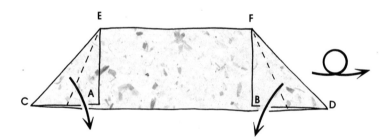

❷ Fold edge EC to lie along EA, and edge FD to lie along FB. Turn over.

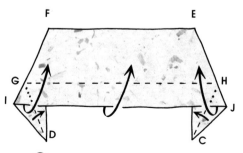

❸ Make crease GH, so that ID lies along DF and JC lies along CE . . .

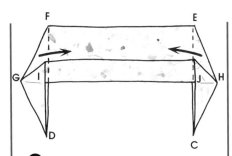

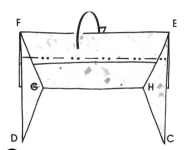

4 . . . like this. Fold G and H toward the middle.

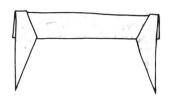

5 Mountain fold FE behind to lie along GH.

6 The completed Fangs.

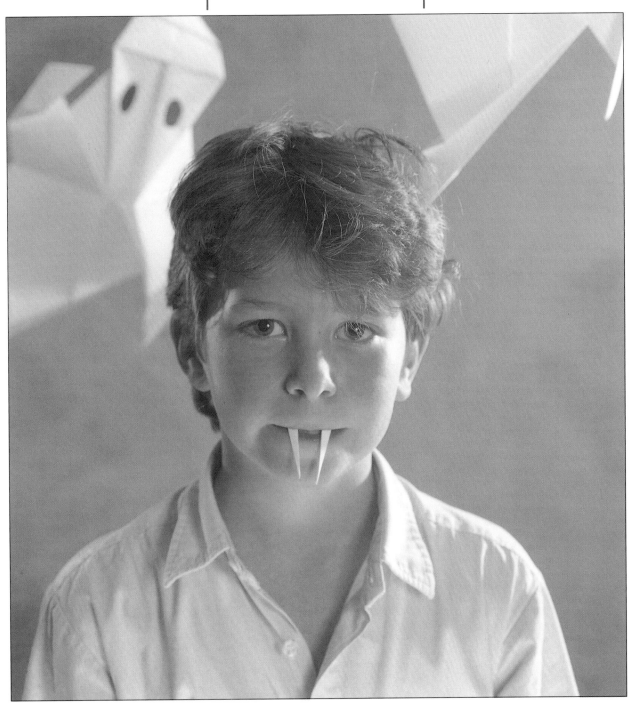

MAN IN THE MOON

DESIGNED BY JOHN NORDQUIST, USA

This design looks very attractive on a greetings card or as a hanging decoration, suspended on a length of thread. Watch out, though – you must make the reverse folds very carefully or the proportions of the face will distort.

STAR RATING ★★★

PAPERS
Use a 6–10 in (15–25 cm) square of light- or mediumweight paper.

OTHER EQUIPMENT
To suspend the model you will need a needle and thread.

SPECIAL NOTE
Reverse folds (see Steps 6, 7 and 11) are explained in detail in the section on Folding Techniques (see Introduction).

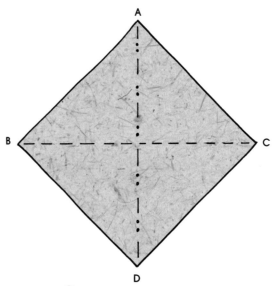

❶ Crease BC as a valley and AD as a mountain. Unfold both.

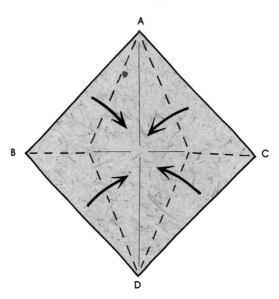

❷ Fold edges AB and AC to crease AD, creasing down from A only as far as crease BC. Repeat on the bottom half, folding DB and DC to crease AD and creasing from D up as far as BC. Crease from this intersection to B and C, collapsing the paper . . .

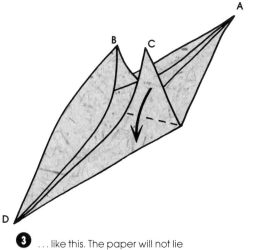

3 . . . like this. The paper will not lie flat. Flatten C towards D.

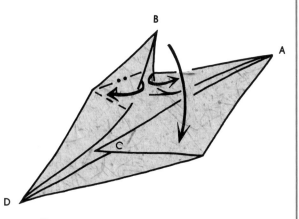

4 Pull B open and squash flat . . .

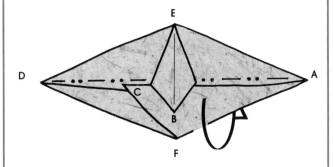

5 . . . like this. Fold F behind to E. Rotate the paper to look like Step 6.

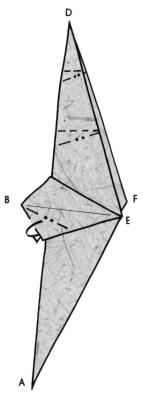

6 Narrow B by folding behind as shown. Make two sets of crimp folds on the upper triangle as shown. The exact placement is important. Make the larger pair first, reverse folding along the mountain crease, then back along the valley. Repeat on the smaller pair.

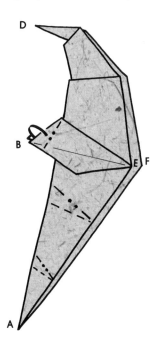

7 Fold B behind as shown. Make two more sets of crimp folds on the lower triangle as described above, the larger set first.

99

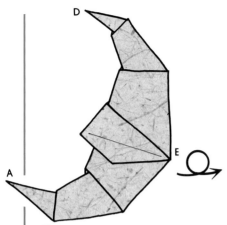

8 The crimps complete. Turn over.

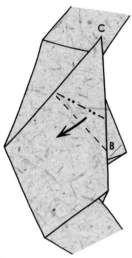

9 Pleat C as shown, so that it creates . . .

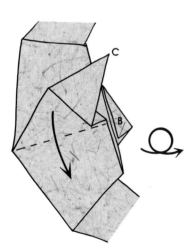

10 . . . this shape. Fold C downward. Turn over.

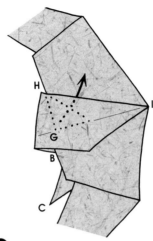

11 Pull out corner G with a reverse fold, so that G becomes visible above edge HI.

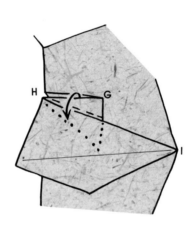

12 Pull down the top layer of edge HG, partly squashing G open to form an eye . . .

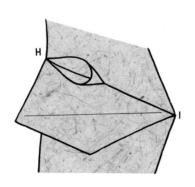

13 . . . like this.

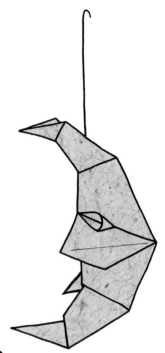

14 The Man in the Moon complete. To suspend the model, attach a loop to the top with needle and thread.

GHOST

DESIGNED BY PAUL JACKSON, UK

Several Ghosts, of varying sizes, could be suspended on a thread to decorate the home for Halloween, or smaller ones can be used to decorate invitation cards to a "Trick or Treat" party. The drawn eyes are a cheat, perhaps, but they do add a suitably ghoulish effect.

STAR RATING ★★★

PAPERS

Use a square of lightweight white paper; start with a sheet 6–8 in (15–20 cm) square.

OTHER EQUIPMENT

Marker pen; to suspend the ghost, you will need a needle and thread.

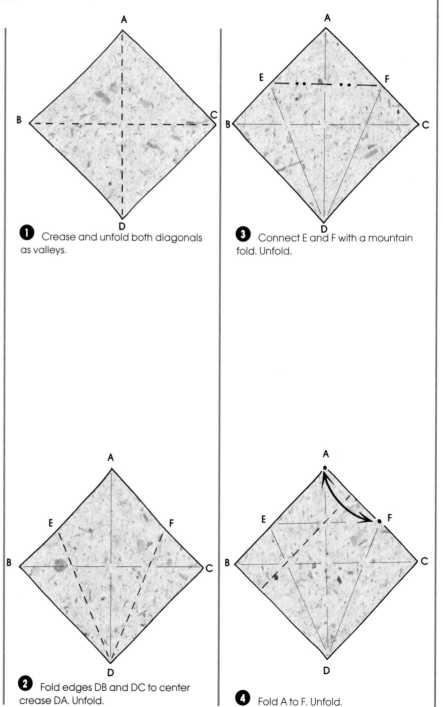

❶ Crease and unfold both diagonals as valleys.

❸ Connect E and F with a mountain fold. Unfold.

❷ Fold edges DB and DC to center crease DA. Unfold.

❹ Fold A to F. Unfold.

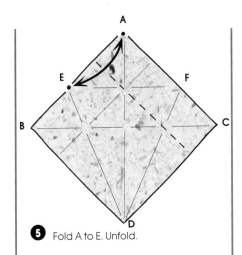

5 Fold A to E. Unfold.

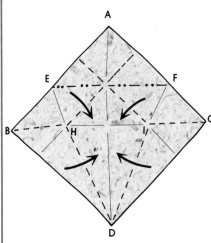

6 Carefully collapse along the marked creases. Bring E and F into the center. Let A swing down to touch EF. Pull B and C downward. Look at Step 7.

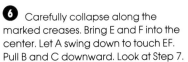

7 Fold in the diagonal edges above EF to the center crease, then fold down the top corner G on top.

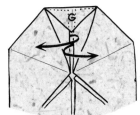

8 Unfold the side triangles, leaving the top corner folded down.

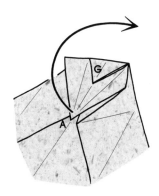

9 Pick up the single layer corner A, and swivel it up and over the top edge of the paper . . .

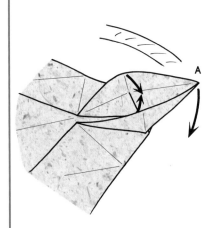

10 . . . like this. The paper becomes 3-dimensional. Flatten corner A, allowing the sides to collapse inward toward the center crease.

11 The maneuver complete. Technically, the process shown in Steps 7–10 is known in origami as a petal fold.

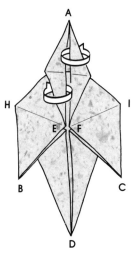

12 Unfold AEF almost to a flat sheet, swinging edges AE and AF behind to touch G . . .

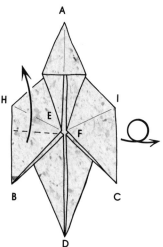

13 . . . like this. Note the large triangle now below A. Fold up corner B. Turn over.

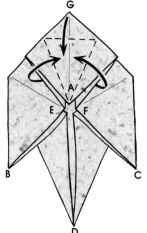

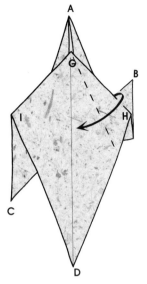

14 Fold in edge GH, not quite as far as crease GD.

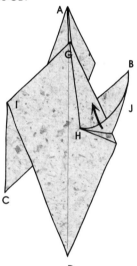

15 Collapse flat the triangle between H and J . . .

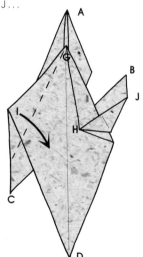

16 . . . like this. Fold in edge GI, as shown.

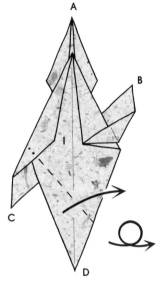

17 Fold out D to the right. Turn over.

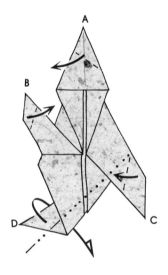

18 Fold A out to the left. Fold in B and C. Pleat D downward.

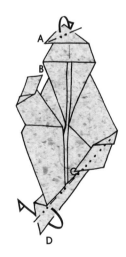

19 Narrow A. Pleat D back upward.

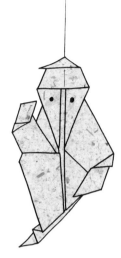

20 The completed Ghost. Draw in the eyes as shown with a marker pen, and suspend using a needle and thread to attach a loop to the ghost's head.

WITCH ON A BROOMSTICK

DESIGNED BY PAUL JACKSON, UK

Although simple in its final appearance, this model is tricky to fold. The secret is to make the early folds very accurately so that it collapses into shape without difficulty.

The Witch on a Broomstick is ideal for suspending from the ceiling. Make a whole coven to accompany a Man in the Moon (see page 98) and a haunting of Ghosts (see page 102) for a suitably eerie Halloween celebration.

STAR RATING ★★★★

PAPERS
Use a 6–8 in (15–20 cm) square of lightweight paper which is white or colored on one side and black on the reverse.

OTHER EQUIPMENT
To suspend the model you will need a needle and thread.

SPECIAL NOTE
Reverse folds (see Steps 7 and 8) are explained in detail in the section on Folding Techniques (see Introduction).

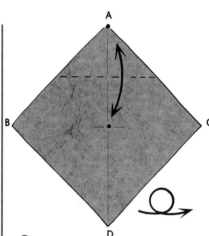

1 Black side up, fold B to C, crease and unfold. Then fold A to D and pinch in the middle to find the center point of the square – unfold. Fold A to the center mark. Unfold. Turn over.

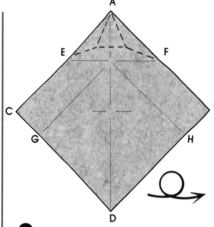

3 Make five short, separate creases on triangle AFE. Turn over.

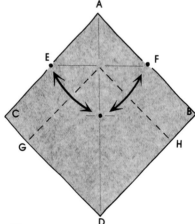

2 White or colored side up, fold E to the center mark, creasing only from G to crease EF. Unfold. Repeat with F, creasing from H to crease EF. Unfold.

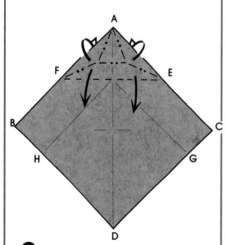

4 Fold down crease FE, neatly collapsing all of the Step 5 creases . .

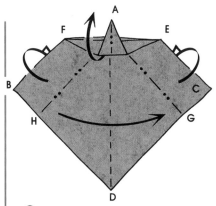

5 . . . like this. Collapse the paper in half by lifting the triangle below A, folding edges BF and CE behind and swinging H across to G. Look at Step 6.

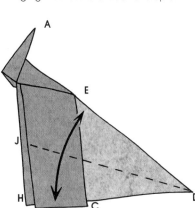

6 Fold edge GD to edge ED. Unfold. Repeat behind.

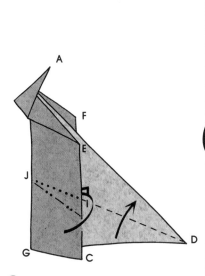

7 Refold the Step 6 crease, but reversing the short crease JI to a mountain, pushing G up behind E. This is a reverse fold. Repeat behind.

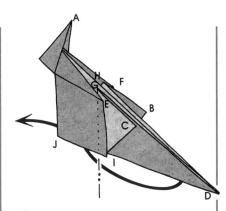

8 Reverse fold D, so that the crease begins at G and is hidden behind the C flap. Edge GD reverses to touch corner J . . .

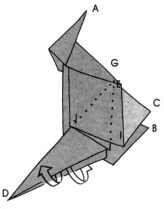

9 . . . like this. Turn the layers on triangle D completely inside out, so that the triangle (the broomstick) turns from black to white (or colored). To do this open out the paper back to Step 5 . . .

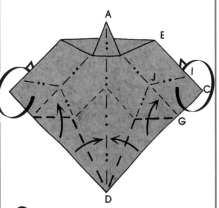

10 . . . like this. This diagram shows the pattern of creases. Refold the creases shown by a heavy dash from mountain to valley creases – all other creases remain the same. Collapse back to result in Step 11.

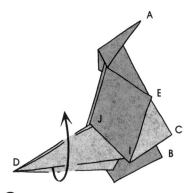

11 Open out triangle D and view from below.

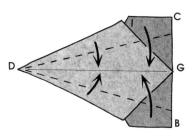

12 Narrow triangle D, folding into the crease DG, taking B and C in with the white edge.

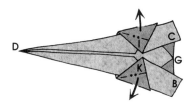

13 Squash I and K . . .

107

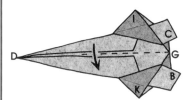

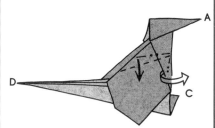

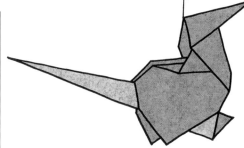

14 . . . like this. Fold in half to resemble Step 10.

15 Crimp across the body to form the arms, allowing the extra layer at the witch's spine to swivel backward to create a hunched back.

16 The completed Witch on a Broomstick. To suspend, attach a loop to the witch's hat (experiment to find the best position to balance the model) with a needle and thread.

MASK

DESIGNED BY PAUL JACKSON, UK

The problem when designing an origami mask is in creating holes for the eyes without resorting to scissors. One solution is to use a strip of paper for folding, as in this case. Using this strip-folding technique, many other mask designs can be created. Try some of your own and decorate to suit the occasion.

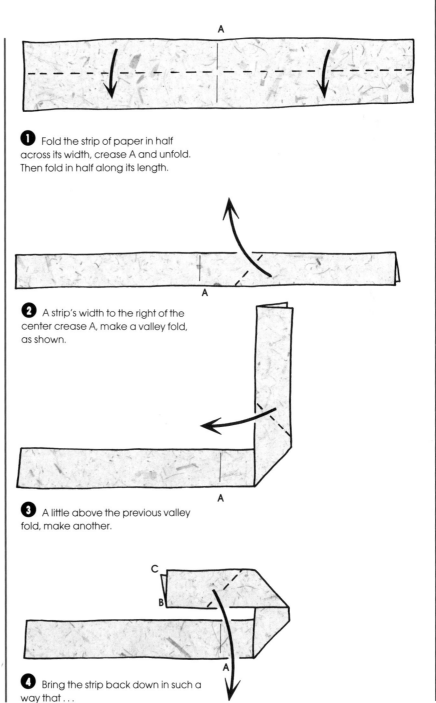

STAR RATING ★★

PAPERS

Use a strip of lightweight paper, proportioned 6:1; 24 × 4 in (60 x 10 cm) for adults and 18 × 3 in (42 x 7 cm) for children, are good average sizes.

OTHER EQUIPMENT

Adhesive tape; length of cord elastic.

A

❶ Fold the strip of paper in half across its width, crease A and unfold. Then fold in half along its length.

A

❷ A strip's width to the right of the center crease A, make a valley fold, as shown.

A

❸ A little above the previous valley fold, make another.

C
B
A

❹ Bring the strip back down in such a way that . . .

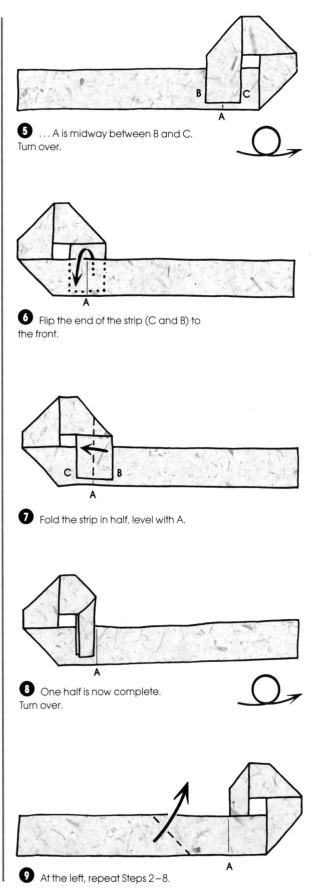

5 . . . A is midway between B and C. Turn over.

6 Flip the end of the strip (C and B) to the front.

7 Fold the strip in half, level with A.

8 One half is now complete. Turn over.

9 At the left, repeat Steps 2–8.

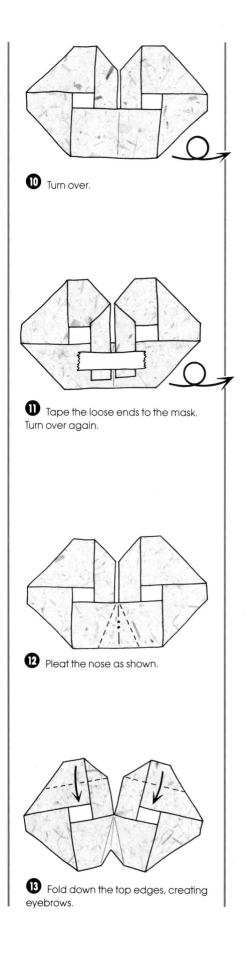

10 Turn over.

11 Tape the loose ends to the mask. Turn over again.

12 Pleat the nose as shown.

13 Fold down the top edges, creating eyebrows.

MASK

DESIGNED BY PAUL JACKSON, UK

The problem when designing an origami mask is in creating holes for the eyes without resorting to scissors. One solution is to use a strip of paper for folding, as in this case. Using this strip-folding technique, many other mask designs can be created. Try some of your own and decorate to suit the occasion.

STAR RATING ★★

PAPERS

Use a strip of lightweight paper, proportioned 6:1; 24 × 4 in (60 x 10 cm) for adults and 18 × 3 in (42 x 7 cm) for children, are good average sizes.

OTHER EQUIPMENT

Adhesive tape; length of cord elastic.

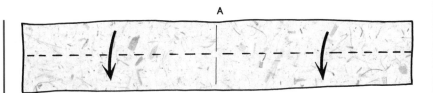

1 Fold the strip of paper in half across its width, crease A and unfold. Then fold in half along its length.

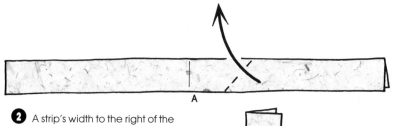

2 A strip's width to the right of the center crease A, make a valley fold, as shown.

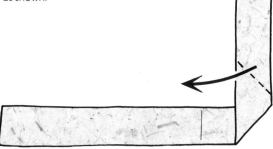

3 A little above the previous valley fold, make another.

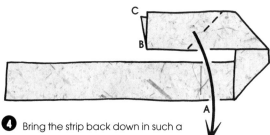

4 Bring the strip back down in such a way that . . .

109

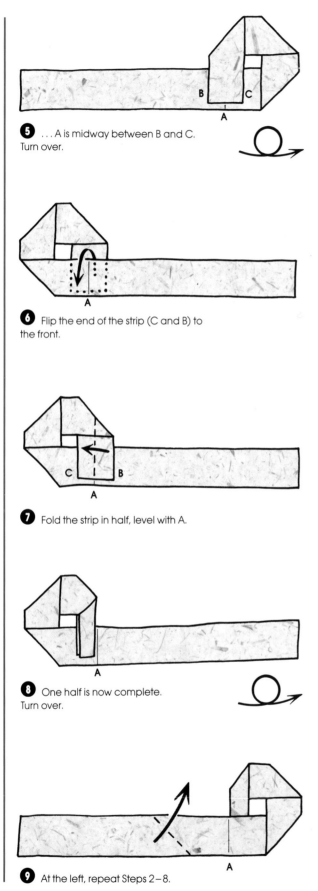

5 . . . A is midway between B and C. Turn over.

6 Flip the end of the strip (C and B) to the front.

7 Fold the strip in half, level with A.

8 One half is now complete. Turn over.

9 At the left, repeat Steps 2 – 8.

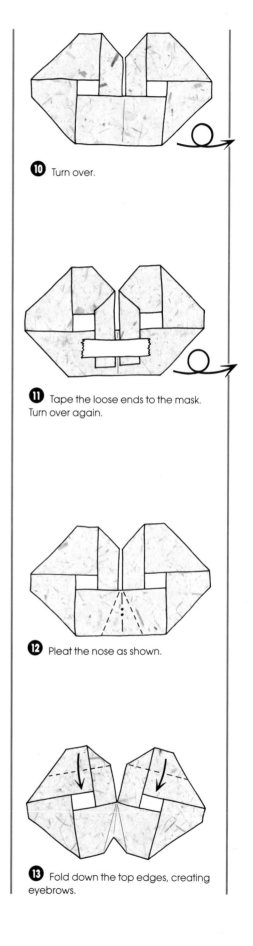

10 Turn over.

11 Tape the loose ends to the mask. Turn over again.

12 Pleat the nose as shown.

13 Fold down the top edges, creating eyebrows.

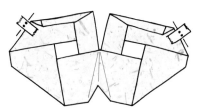

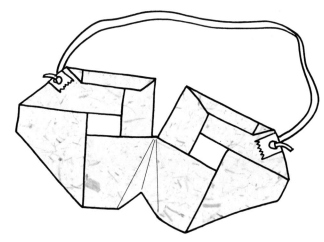

14 Add adhesive tape as shown. To create enough strength to hold the elastic without tearing, tape a few layers over each other. Pierce the tape and feed the elastic through. Tie the ends to the mask, leaving enough elastic between the knots to hold the mask to your head.

15 The completed Mask.

6

GIFTS

★ ★ ★ ★ ★

STANDING HEART

DESIGNED BY PAUL JACKSON, UK

A Valentine's Day design for the practical romantics among us, this free-standing heart is durable enough to last for months displayed on a table or shelf – maybe even until the Buttonhole (see page 123) arrives the following year . . .

STAR RATING ★★★

PAPERS
You will need a 6–8 in (15–20 cm) square of light- or mediumweight paper which is white on one side and red on the other.

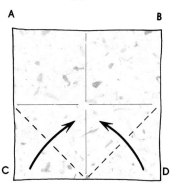

1 White side up, fold the square in half, horizontally and vertically. Unfold. Fold C and D to the center.

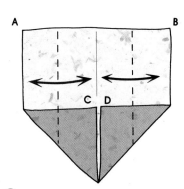

2 Fold A and B to the center crease. Unfold.

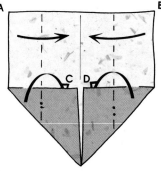

3 Refold along the Step 2 creases, but reverse folding the colored triangles behind C and D . . .

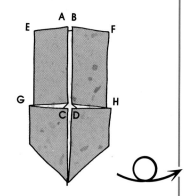

4 . . . like this. Turn over.

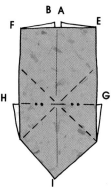

5 Pre-crease as shown. Note that GH is a mountain crease.

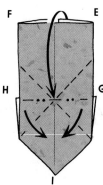

6 Collapse so that edge FE drops to be level with corner I.

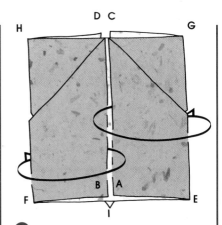

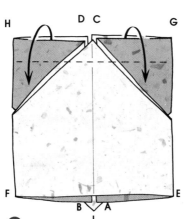

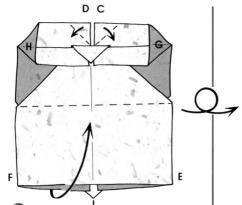

7 Open the central slit and fold B and then A behind edge FE, so that the new top layer becomes white. To do this, unfold the paper almost back to Step 1, then re-crease and collapse back to Step 8.

8 Pull down edge HG as shown and squash flat the triangles at H and G . . .

9 . . . like this. Turn in D and C. Lift edge FE along a horizontal crease midway up the paper, separating FE from I and providing a back edge to support the heart when it is stood up. Turn over.

10 The completed Standing Heart.

GIFT ENVELOPE

——

T R A D I T I O N A L

This envelope should not be mailed, but it is an attractive and creative way to present a card delivered by hand.

STAR RATING ★★

PAPERS
Use lightweight paper, preferably textured, patterned or hand-decorated.

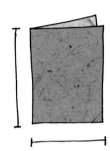

1 Measure the greeting card.

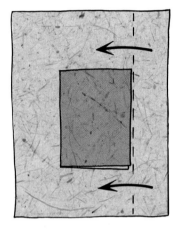

3 Place the card approximately in the center of the paper, square to the edges. Fold in the right-hand edge.

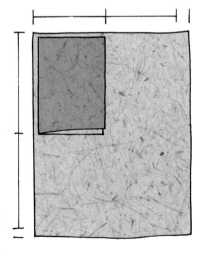

2 Put the card into a corner of the envelope paper. Measure twice the height and twice the width of the card on the paper, then add a little extra. Trim the paper to these dimensions.

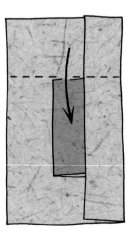

4 Fold down the top edge.

OPPOSITE Gift envelopes in an array of sizes, shapes and colors add a special touch to hand-delivered greeting cards for all occasions. Turn the page for the continuing instructions for this project.

VARIATION

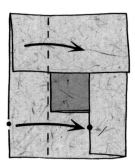

5 Fold in the left edge, as shown.

6 Fold and unfold the bottom edge, as shown.

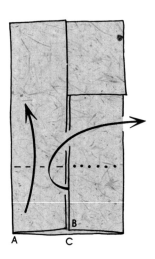

7 Valley fold A up the left-hand edge. Open B . . .

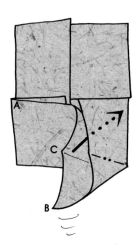

8 . . . and push C deep inside, making a mountain fold across the bottom.

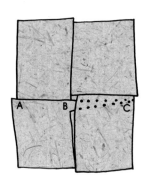

9 The completed Gift Envelope.

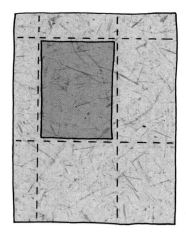

1 The card can be placed anywhere on the paper at Step 3, even right up into a corner, as shown.

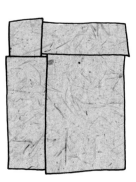

2 Follow the steps as before to achieve this off-center look.

GIFT BOXES

DESIGNED BY PAUL JACKSON, UK

All the lids in these examples are locked using the same twist technique, but a change in the angle of twist can create surprisingly diverse results. Both lids and boxes must be constructed with great accuracy so that all the edges are parallel, the angles are equal and the creases are placed with care. Take your time if you want a really professional result.

STAR RATING ★★★

PAPERS

Use heavyweight paper or thin card for the boxes and their lids. If you wish to use the "wet-folding" process explained in the section on Papers (see Introduction), select heavyweight Ingres or watercolor paper.

OTHER EQUIPMENT

Paper glue; protractor; ruler; pencil.

LID

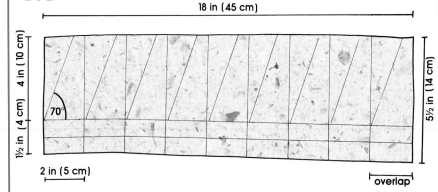

1 Carefully measure the outside dimensions of the lid (18 × 5½ in/45 × 14 cm) and cut out the lid as shown. Draw in the positions of the nine panels and pleats and the bottom lip using the measurements shown. The critical angle of 70° should be accurately made for each pleat.

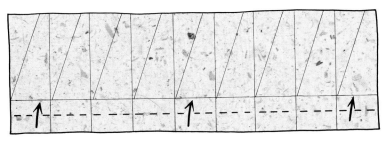

2 Fold up along the bottom crease.

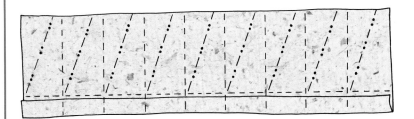

3 Crease mountains and valleys as shown.

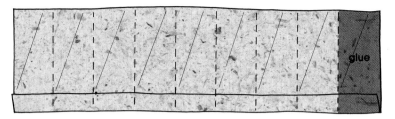

4 Reinforce the vertical creases. Apply glue to the right end panel, and then join it to the back of the left end panel. This will create an eight-sided sleeve.

BOX

15½ in (39 cm)

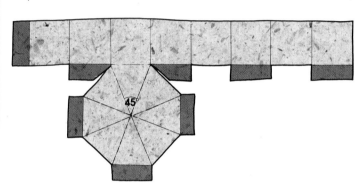

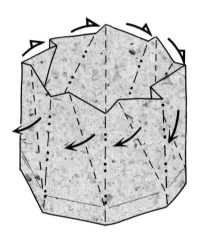

5 Carefully pleat mountains and valleys as shown. For Step 6 to form, *all* ceases must form at the same time and interlock equally around the middle. It may take a little time to wriggle all the pleats into place, but it will help if the bottom edge is kept as close to a perfect octagon as possible. If it goes out of shape, the locking will become more difficult.

1 Measure out the box paper as shown, so that the panels are fractionally narrower than the lid panels. In this way, the lid will fit snugly over the box. Construct the octagonal using a protractor to measure the angles (see Tip – Making Boxes). Apply glue to the tabs and fold the box into shape.

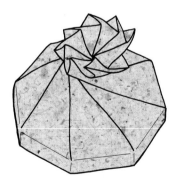

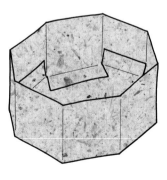

OPPOSITE The completed eight-sided gift box (right). To make six-sided and five-sided boxes (left and center) with flat lids, turn the page for the instructions.

6 The lid complete.

2 The completed box. The lid will fit on top.

FLAT LIDS

EIGHT-SIDED

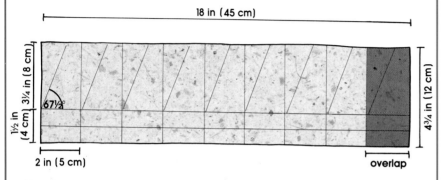

18 in (45 cm)

3¾ in (8 cm)

1½ in (4 cm)

67½°

4¾ in (12 cm)

2 in (5 cm)

overlap

1 The lid on the first drawing had a 70° angle. This caused the locking point to rise above the level of the lid, creating a pyramid effect. If you reduce the angle to 67½°, the lock will be level with the top of the lid and so the lid will be flat. In all other respects, make the lid as before.

SIX-SIDED

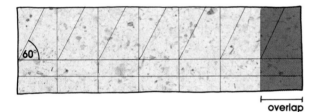

60°

overlap

2 A 60° angle with seven panels (one to overlap) will create a flat six-sided lid. The box piece must also, of course, be six-sided, with an hexagonal base (see Tip – Making Boxes).

FIVE-SIDED

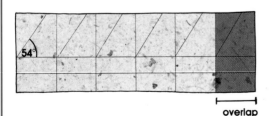

54°

overlap

3 Similarly, a 54° angle with six panels will create a flat five-sided lid.

TIP – MAKING BOXES

To accurately construct the regular-sided base of a box with the required number of sides, follow this method. Divide the number of sides into 360°. Draw a dot on the paper or card used to make the box and, with a protractor, measure off around it the equal angles found in the previous sentence. Connect these points to the center dot with ruled lines, to create a "spoke" effect. With the point of a pair of compasses on the center dot, draw a circle of the required size (slightly smaller than the circumference of the matching lid). Draw lines between the points where the circle crosses the spokes to complete an accurate, regular-sided shape.

BUTTONHOLE

LEAF: DESIGNED BY ALICE GRAY, USA
FLOWER: TRADITIONAL JAPANESE

This is a beautiful design that will make a much-admired gift, particularly if the papers are chosen with care. The flower is the Iris from the Floral Centerpiece (see page 70).

STAR RATING ★★★

PAPERS
The **leaf** and the **flower** are each made from a 4 in (10 cm) square of lightweight paper (such as origami paper). These dimensions will make quite a small buttonhole, so fold with care.
The **stem** is made from a square of lightweight paper, half the size of that used for the flower or leaf, and trimmed to a 3:1 rectangle.

LEAF

1 Form a center crease between two points and unfold. Fold the top edges to the center crease.

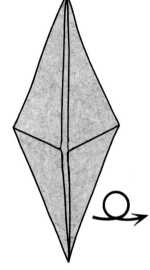

3 Turn over.

2 Fold the bottom edges to the center crease.

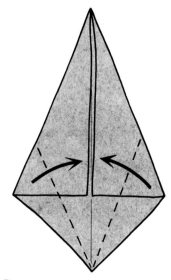

4 Fold the bottom edges to the center crease.

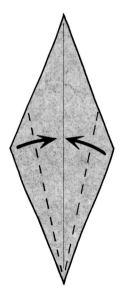

FLOWER

See Floral Centerpiece (page 70) and follow the instructions for the Iris to complete the flower.

5 Mountain fold the right half behind the left half.

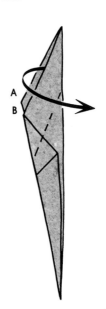

6 Fold the front layer B across to the right. A and B will separate.

STEM

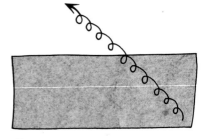

1 Roll up the paper for the stem as tightly as possible.

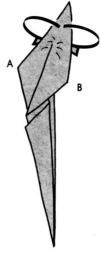

7 Invert the leaf from a concave shape to a convex one.

8 The completed leaf.

2 At the loose end, roll over the tip to lock the tube.

3 The stem complete.

ASSEMBLY

1 With your tongue, wet the bottom of the flower to soften the paper. Push the stem through the wet paper, so that the rolled end catches deep inside the bloom, preventing the stem from falling right through.

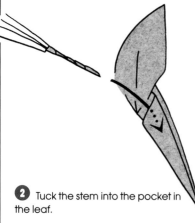

2 Tuck the stem into the pocket in the leaf.

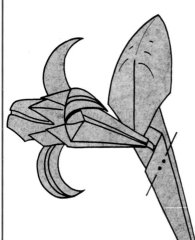

3 The completed Buttonhole. A better shape may be achieved if a mountain fold is made where shown.

124

INDEX

INDEX

ACKNOWLEDGMENTS

The author would like to thank the following for permission to publish their designs: Dave Brill, Alice Gray, John N. Nordquist and Ed Sullivan.

The *Fangs* and *Man in the Moon* were first published in the monthly origami magazine *The Flapping Bird*, edited by Sam Randlett and published by Jay Marshall, Chicago, USA, between 1968 and 1976. The *Bauble* is by an unknown author, possibly in the USA: further information would be gratefully received. The head section of the *Easter Bunny* was first published in *Paper Magic* by Robert Harbin, published by Oldbourne, UK, 1956.

ORIGAMI SOCIETIES

If you have enjoyed folding the designs in *Festive Folding*, you may like to join an organized club of paper folders. The three listed here cater well for the beginner and have many overseas members. The first two listed also publish a magazine and sell origami books and papers:

British Origami Society
253 Park Lane
Poynton
Stockport
Cheshire SK12 1RH
England

The Friends of the Origami Center of America
15 West 77th Street
New York NY 10024

New Zealand Origami Society
79 Dunbar Road
Christchurch 3
New Zealand

Inquiring and Problem-Solving in the Physical Sciences

A Sourcebook

Vincent N. Lunetta
The University of Iowa
Iowa City, Iowa

Shimshon Novick
The Hebrew University
Jerusalem

KENDALL/HUNT PUBLISHING COMPANY
Dubuque, Iowa

Reviewers

H. James Funk	*Indiana University—South Bend*
Roy Unruh	*University of Northern Iowa*
Jerry Doyle	*Science and Mathematics AEA. Fort Madison, Ia.*
Ronald D. Simpson	*North Carolina University*
Leon J. Zalewski	*Governors State University*

Copyright © 1982 by Kendall/Hunt Publishing Company

Library of Congress Catalog Card Number: 81–85618

ISBN 0–8403–2631–9

Printed in the United States of America

C   402631 01

Contents

Preface

Most science teachers want to help their students improve inquiring and problem-solving skills in the course of studying science. To reach this goal teachers need a large array of appropriate resources, experiments, and projects in the sciences. They also require efficient methods for organizing and supporting the problem-solving activities. This sourcebook has been designed to respond to those needs.

Teachers of physics, chemistry, and physical science will find in this book a collection of activities designed to help students acquire a variety of skills necessary for understanding science and for solving meaningful problems in their environment. The activities are grouped by topics and concepts normally included in introductory courses in physics, chemistry, and physical science. A science topic index assists in identifying the activities that pertain to a specific science concept. Resource materials and references for the teacher are included for each activity.

The activities in Part I may be used at junior high, senior high, and introductory college levels with students who have a variety of intellectual skills. Each activity bears symbols showing the approximate range of student abilities for which it seems most appropriate. Some of the activities are especially suited for gifted and talented science students whereas others are ideal for those who are less science oriented.

The activities have been selected from many sources, including the authors' experiences, using the following criteria:

materials and equipment needed are generally available in secondary school laboratories or in the community;

the experimental procedures are relatively simple to perform;

the activities can be used by students of different levels of ability, experience and intellectual development; and

the striking or unexpected phenomena are likely to stimulate students to raise questions and to seek explanations.

The last criterion is at the heart of the authors' intent. Wherever possible, the activities include questions that tie the phenomena to experiences in the students' lives. Students then become involved in:

a. observing a wide range of phenomena in the physical sciences, especially physics and chemistry;
b. asking questions leading to the discovery of relationships and to the invention of explanations;
c. seeking support for explanations and relationships from previously accepted theory or from new experimental evidence;
d. discovering how the phenomena and concepts apply to other problems, to technology and to everyday living;
e. searching for new information and developing new experiments and research studies to increase their understanding.

In Part II teachers will find numerous practical suggestions for conducting and evaluating the activities. They may decide to use an activity to begin the study of a new topic or to extend investigation of a topic introduced earlier. Teachers may use the activities with large groups, small groups or individual students by making minor modifications. Some of the activities involve potentially dangerous chemicals or procedures. These are specifically identified in the safety precautions section of each activity. Teachers who wish to use such activities in their classes should follow the safety precautions carefully and completely. Part II concludes with a discussion of ideas from the philosophy of science and from learning theory that provide a basis for inquiring and problem-solving. The teacher will find some answers to questions regarding the relevance of inquiring and problem-solving to goals for science teaching, to the nature of science, and to the ways people learn.

In spite of the many sound reasons for developing problem-solving skills as an important component of science teaching, there has been some movement away from this goal in recent years. One of the factors contributing to this movement in the physical sciences has been the lack of appropriate curriculum resources enabling concerned teachers to organize and conduct problem-solving activities. This sourcebook has been designed to respond to that need. The authors believe that use of the sourcebook will encourage and aid students and teachers in the processes of inquiring and problem-solving in the physical sciences. They anticipate that through careful use of the activities students will find science more interesting, increase their understanding of physical science concepts, and develop inquiring and problem-solving skills.

Acknowledgments

Creating this sourcebook has helped us see more clearly how dependent we are upon others for scientific information and understanding. Our ideas have been shaped in large measure through direct and indirect contact with the ideas of many other people. In preparing activities we have referenced published sources both to provide further resources for teachers and to acknowledge what often has been the source of an idea.

We are grateful for the helpful and stimulating resources within our universities and professional communities. The interest and help of students and secondary school and university colleagues have been invaluable. We wish it were possible to acknowledge each person's contributions individually, but the list would be very lengthy.

We especially thank Dr. Euwe van den Berg who has contributed activities and ideas included in the manuscript in several places. We are also indebted to Lois Lunetta for editorial contributions, Jenean Arnold for the preparation of figures, and Marci Donovan who typed the manuscript and performed many essential chores. Last, but not least we acknowledge the support of our families throughout the entire effort.

Vincent Lunetta and Shimshon Novick

Use of the Sourcebook Activities

The activities in Part I have been selected because they provide special opportunities for students to develop inquiry and problem-solving skills at a variety of levels of sophistication. Many activities in the collection are based on discrepant events designed to arouse interest and create "cognitive dissonance". Wherever possible, relevant applications in the student's world have been included to enhance interest. The inquiry/problem-solving activities are grouped by topics normally taught in chemistry, physics and physical science courses. Activities especially relevant to specific topics in physics and chemistry can be identified by searching the table of contents and the topical index.

We have rated the general level of complexity of each activity on four different dimensions. These ratings are shown at the beginning of each activity to assist teachers in choosing and adapting activities to their own local needs. Each of the four dimensions are rated on a scale of 1 to 4 according to the following plan:

Dimension		Level			
		1	2	3	4
C	Science concepts	elementary ◄————————► advanced			
E	Equipment and techniques	simple ◄————————► complex			
D	Data processing skills (computation, making tables, graphing)	elementary ◄————————► advanced			
L	Logical skills (intellectual development)	concrete/ ◄————————► abstract/ few variables many variables			

Most of the activities potentially can illustrate more than one science concept and develop more than one skill. Teachers should consider in advance goals or outcomes they wish to emphasize. Pre-lab and post-lab discussions provide particularly appropriate opportunities to address such concerns.

The *materials* section of each activity outlines materials needed to conduct the activity. The quantity shown is the amount needed for one student, for one small group, or for a demonstration. Basic requirements are listed as well as some of the materials needed for important optional activities. Generally, the basic materials are simple and readily available in school science laboratories. Optional equipment is occasionally more complex but still generally available in secondary school.

The *suggested activities* section forms the bulk of each investigation presented in Part A; the activities have been selected to be interesting and instructive to students at a variety of levels of development and skill. At times the activities may be used to initiate the study of a new topic; at other times they may be used to extend the study of topics introduced earlier. While lengthy cookbook instructions have been avoided, the authors have included a large array of questions for each inquiry, and it is not reasonable to expect a class or an individual student to explore all the questions that are raised. The questions are included, however, to point out the rich possibilities for inquiry related to the phenomena being investigated; thus, teachers can encourage students to inquire about questions that are of special interest to them. The section is written, generally in second person form, to facilitate classroom adaption by busy teachers. They should bear in mind that the questions are not generally worded as they would be in a laboratory manual. The narrative is intended to provide *opening* questions that will be further elaborated whenever necessary. Teachers may want to build more highly structured inquiry activities for some aspects of their teaching; in that case they may well draw upon questions and ideas written in these activities to prepare written instructions for students. At other times, teachers may wish simply to refer to the sourcebook to enrich their own thinking about a problem prior to discussing related topics with their class.

The suggested activities section is followed by a paragraph outlining special *safety precautions* if any are warranted. These are also written in a form that can be directly transferred to student instructions. Generally, the activities are not dangerous, but proper safety precautions should always be practiced. This concern is especially important when students are working independently on different projects, sometimes outside the classroom, and are not constantly under direct teacher observation.

The *comments* section of each activity is designed to provide teachers with background information that will aid in helping students use the activities. More extensive information is available in the references cited at the end of each activity. The references also cite, wherever possible, an original source for the inquiry activity. While these references are provided primarily for teacher use, it may be appropriate at times to share them with students who are pursuing an inquiry thoroughly.

A more general list of references is included in Part I, Section *X4*. These books, journals, and magazines can serve as resources for new ideas upon which meaningful and relevant student inquiry can continue to develop. Many of these references served as sources for the inquiry activities outlined in this sourcebook. Regular contact with some of the periodicals will help teachers keep in touch with contemporary thinking in science and in science education and will stimulate ideas that will go well beyond teaching and learning through inquiry.

A collection of activities like those gathered in this sourcebook will never be complete. New activities and improved versions of old ones are constantly being developed by creative science teachers. Thus, this collection should be viewed as a starting point for teachers seeking to increase the frequency and depth of inquiry activity by their students. By adopting the strategies exemplified in these activities, teachers will be able to extend them to a broader range of curriculum materials, and will more effectively accomplish some of the important goals of learning through inquiry.

Part I

A Collection
of Activities

A Environmental and Consumer Issues

1. Searching for "Soft" Energy

Science Topic   Energy production; Environmental impact of energy production.

Level   C:2–3   E:2–4   D:2–3   L:2–4

Overview

Students are introduced to the "soft path" thesis for energy production. Through reading and discussion they examine "hard path/soft path" alternatives for energy production and the impact of these alternatives on the economy, on resources, and on society. The activity proceeds with small groups of students or individuals searching for appropriate sources of soft energy in their own community and region. They grapple with the problems of bringing such soft energy production "on the line", with the quantity of energy that can be produced on a regular basis in this manner, and with the probable costs of doing so.

Materials   Reading materials on "soft energy"

Suggested Activities

In 1976, *Foreign Affairs* published a report by Amory Lovins on America's energy future that resulted in intensive conversation and debate in scientific and governmental circles. This debate can be followed in publications of the Center for the Study of Democratic Institutions, the American Association for the Advancement of Science magazine, *Science,* and numerous other publications. Lovins labels the present energy production system in the United States as "the hard energy path" for it generates energy in very large scale production and distribution systems that exhaust non-replenishible fuel supplies and have severe environmental and economic impact. The "soft path" of energy production that he advocates involves multitudes of relatively small components operating on renewable resources including the sun, water, bio-mass residue, and wind. He claims that the soft path is considerably less expensive on the long term and far less subject to the danger of massive technical failure since risks are spread across a large array of relatively simple systems rather than being concentrated in a few high technology plants operating on coal, gas, or nuclear fuels. Start up time is shorter, the technology is relatively simple, systems are more reliable with less down time, and far less money has to be invested in providing massive back-up systems in the event of failure of one part of the massive energy production network. Lovins points out that large conventional power stations are "off the line" from about ten to thirty-five percent of the time for good technical reasons. "If one of these thousand megawatt stations dies on you, it is like having an elephant die in the drawing room, you simply have to have another elephant standing nearby to haul the carcass away. You need a thousand megawatt reserve margin to back you up. That costs a lot of money." Depending upon several stations of a few hundred megawatts each instead, would "let you do the same job for about a third less new capacity. If you went to, say, ten megawatt units at the substation, you could do the same job with something like 60 or 70% less new capacity." There is little doubt that moving from a hard energy to a soft energy orientation will not be easy, but it may be necessary for survival.

Look around your community. What are the major sources of energy that are in use today? What are the major sources of energy that were used 50–100 years earlier? What are the sources of soft energy that are potentially available in your region? Think about possibilities involving solar heating, water power, wind power, conversion of farm and forestry residues to liquid fuels, . . . Shop around and be creative! In many places in the United States, one does not have to be especially creative for there are rivers that formerly were used for the generation of electrical or mechanical power that are no longer being used for that purpose. To some people a decade or two ago, continued development of relatively small sources of energy was not considered to be economical and efficient. However, in the light of current energy costs and new understanding of non-renewable resources and world development problems, it is appropriate to take a new look at some of the abandoned energy sources of the past and possibly apply creative modern technology to their development.

What industrial or agricultural products or byproducts available in your community have the capacity to serve as a source of energy? Can sewage be used for this purpose? Is there a lot a sunlight or wind in your region?

Identify one potential source of soft energy in your community or region. Do a very thorough analysis of the availability of that source for energy production. For example, if a river is to be used, approximately how many gallons of water will flow per minute at peak periods and in periods of drought? What is the approximate vertical drop in the river as it passes through your region? Determine the amount of energy available from this source under ideal and under realistic circumstances. Can a dam be built? If so, what kind of environmental impact would be probable? Examine the problems of bringing this energy source "on the line". (These kinds of problems may be very great from a contemporary point of view. However, if one looks at the need for energy self-sufficiency, the probability of a cut off of external supplies, and the serious and unresolved problems of disposal of nuclear waste, the magnitude of the problem may well look different.)

Do a thorough study on the energy source you choose to investigate, but be creative. Survival and certainly quality of life may depend on your ingenuity and understanding.

Our posterity have as much right to "inherit the earth" as we have. Or do they? Should we/can we insure that there is earth for them to inherit. . . .

References

References with varying orientation and bias are available from many local sources. Many states now have an energy policy council that examines energy options and that makes information available to the public. Electric utilities normally distribute an array of literature, some of it technical, that may be a worthwhile resource.

Lovins, A. B., "Energy Strategy: The Road not Taken", *Foreign Affairs,* 1976, pp. 65–96.

Lovins, A. B.: *Soft Energy Paths: Toward a Durable Peace,* 1977. Ballinger Publishing Co, Cambridge, MA.

Stobaugh, R. and Yergin, D.: *Energy Future: Report of the Energy Project at the Harvard Business School,* 1979. Random House, New York.

2. Help! Our Soil Is Leaving Us

Science Topics   Erosion, geology, earth science

Level   C:2   E:1–3   D:1   L:1–3

Overview

This activity provides students with an exercise in recognizing erosion marks in their environment and in designing and testing methods of erosion prevention.

Materials

Landscape models made out of sand, mud, or different soils.
(An alternative is to use student-constructed landscapes outside.)
Field trip(s) or the use or pictures and maps can supplement the study.

Suggested Activities

The teacher provides a simple definition of erosion and then shows several landscape models or takes the students on a field trip along several erosion sites. Students are asked (individually or in small groups) to identify erosion marks and subsequently to work in small groups to generate ideas for anti-erosion measures for the models or for the sites.

What evidence of erosion can you find in this environment: weathered or carved out rocks, evidence of floods, sedimentation in the river, stream/drainage patterns in the rain, places with heavy soil loss?

What are the effects of: vegetation patterns, snow/ice, winds/storms, location of dams, drainage ditches?

(Make list of possible erosion marks in group discussion *after* students have tried to identify them using their own conceptions of how erosion results might be seen.)

What is the soil content of river water at various places?

What are the effects of farming on erosion?

What is the role of the river in the erosion process?

How may the landscape have looked thousands of years ago; how may it look some thousand years from now?

How can we prevent various kinds of erosion in this particular landscape model or on this site?

Design some experiments to test your predictions and to examine the effects of:

dams on water flow;
contour plowing, terracing, or plowing in straight rows across hills;
planting trees at crucial places;
rain and sand storms;
different kinds of soils;
building a road through the landscape model;
plants and animals.

What are the effects of erosion on plants and animals that live in the environment?

Comments

Model landscapes can be used made out of sand or mud with some kind of water supply (faucet/shower) to simulate water-flow and rain. A fan might be added to simulate wind. Models are easy to make (see references) and one could even take students outside to make their own models in mud or sand.

Complementary activities include taking students outside to a location with clear erosion marks or presenting them with pictures and maps of such places. (Do the latter only with older students.) Students can identify erosion marks in the environment and design erosion prevention measures using the maps.

Students involved in this activity may examine effects of soils, drainage and riverflow, vegetation, "shape" of the landscape, and altitude differences. They may also study the effects of anti-erosion measures such as: contour plowing, wind screens (artificial or natural vegetation), dams, dikes, crop selection, etc. Students may also consider the formation and shaping of mountain landscapes and the effects of ice and snow in erosion processes.

References

Joseph, A., et al.: *A Sourcebook for the Physical Sciences,* 1961. Harcourt, Brace, and World, New York, p. 62–63.

New Unesco Source Book of Science Teaching, 1973. Unesco, Paris, p. 192–193.

3. Energy for Washing

Science Topics   Heat, energy, environmental ethics

Level   C:2   E:1–2   D:2–3   L:2–3

Overview

The activity involves measurement of water volume and temperature differences to help make decisions relating to energy consumption.

Materials   As suggested by students

Suggested Activities

In the age of energy crisis, every citizen must consider alternative sources of energy and efficient ways to utilize them. This inquiry focuses upon finding the most efficient mode of energy utilization for washing up. (Similar kinds of activities are involved in choosing fuel sources, e.g., solar versus fossil fuels for home heating.) From an energy conservation standpoint, is it more desirable to shower or to bathe?

What factors determine the amount of heat energy used for showering or for bathing?

Are any of these factors constant in both activities? How can they be measured? What are the "norms" for people?

How can the heat energy consumed be calculated?

Suggest an experimental procedure and the measurements that must be made.

Tabulate data and calculate heat energy consumption and cost.

Based on combined class results, what appears to be the least wasteful method—showering or bathing? What is "preferred" by people today? How could people conserve more in bathing and showering?

Compare results obtained by different groups and suggest possible reasons for variations.

Water is also becoming a scarce commodity. How can water be conserved in these activities?

You may want to continue this kind of inquiry investigating issues like: Should we heat water for coffee with an electric immersion heater or on a gas burner?

Comments

Simple experimental procedures and heat transfer calculations can help solve this practical problem that is relevant to the conservation of energy and personal practice.

The primary factors affecting heat energy consumption that will have to be determined are: volume of water and temperature difference between hot and cold water.

Heat $= mc\triangle t$ where specific heat of water $(c) = 1$ calorie/gram/degree

Reference

Foote, J., "To Shower or to Bathe", *The Science Teacher* 43, 7; October, 1976, p. 47.

4. Chemicals and Plants

Science Topics Pollution

Level C:2–3 E:2–3 D:1–2 L:2–4

Overview

This activity involves simple controlled experiments designed to find out some effects of common industry-related gases and liquids on seeds and plants.

Materials

Wide-mouth jars   Planting pots
Matches
Wide-mouth plastic containers
Selected chemicals such as lead nitrate, zinc sulfate, ethanol, acetic acid, bleach
Seeds such as corn, lima beans, radish, lettuce, carrot
Plants such as corn, dwarf bean, radish, weeds

Suggested Activities

Near industrial areas many chemicals find their way into the air, as well as into water supplies. Design and carry out some controlled experiments to find out the effects of some pollutant gases on seeds. (Seeds in a bottle or jar can be exposed to automobile exhaust fumes which contain carbon monoxide. Dropping a few lighted matches in a bottle containing seeds will trap sulfur dioxide.) Immediately close the bottles after exposing to the gases and let them stand (with the seeds) for two days. It is best to repeat the procedure for a total of four days exposure. Try to determine the least amount of gas exposure which will still allow the seeds to sprout.

Design and carry out some controlled experiments to test the effects of the same gases on plants. (A minute or two exposure of the plants to the gases is enough to show a marked effect.) Weeds are more resistant to many gases than cultured plants. Find two small nearly identical weeds in a lawn or field and place a jar full of gas over one of the weeds and a jar full of air over the other with the jar's rim about ¼ inch below the surface of the soil to prevent the gas from escaping. Let the jars sit over the weeds for a day and then remove the jars. Carefully observe and report your findings.

Design and carry out some controlled experiments to test the effect of some dissolved industrial chemicals on plants. The choice of chemicals should, if possible, reflect their use in nearby industries. Place the plants (using one species will make your work easier) in identical pots and place these in wide-mouthed plastic containers in which a 1 cm depth of water is maintained throughout the experiment. Fifty ml of aqueous solution containing an industrial chemical are added to the appropriate pot. Make careful observations and report on your findings. Use data tables wherever possible. Test the effect of concentration to determine critical levels at which detrimental effects occur. Examine effects on growth rates. Test other chemicals. Is the effect of one acid specific or general to other acids? Test the effect of pollutants at various stages of plant growth.

Comments

The following solutions were used in the project described in the Sanderson reference.

Substance	Source	Amount contained in a liter of aqueous solution
zinc sulfhate	(zinc refining)	200 grams
lead nitrate	(automobile exhaust)	200 grams
chlorine-bleach	(a widely used industrial chemical)	200 ml
ethanol	(a major industrial product)	500 ml
glacial ethanoic acid	(acetic acid—a petrochemical)	200 ml

References

Latta, R., "Polluted Plants", *Science Activities,* 14, 6; November/December, 1977, p. 28.

Sanderson, P. L., "What Can Industrial Chemicals Do To Plants? A Pollution Study for a Secondary School General Science Course", *School Science Review,* 61, 217; June, 1980, pp. 756–759.

5. Saltiness

Science Topics   Electrical conductivity, density, precipitation, titration

Level   C:2–3   E:2–3   D:2–3   L:2–4

Overview

There are many ways to detect "saltiness", the most obvious being taste. In this activity students consider various approaches to measuring salinity and use one or more of these techniques to determine the salinity of sea water or brackish water in their environment.

Materials

Sodium chloride   Distilled water
Beakers
Sea water (or other saline water samples)
12 volt power source (dry cells or power supply)
Electrical wire and alligator clips
Rubber stopper through which metal pin electrodes are inserted one inch apart.

Suggested Activities

Is all water fit to drink? Is all water fit for irrigation? The amount of salt present is one of the factors that makes a big difference. Salinity is defined as grams of solid material per kilogram of solution. How could you find out how much salt there is in a sample of sea water? [Evaporate a weighed amount of water and weigh the residue, measure the conductivity of the water and compare it to a standard table of conductivities (conductivity apparatus), measure the density of the water and compare it to a standard table of densities (hydrometer), determine the concentration of chloride ion by titration with silver ion.]

What are some factors you would need to take into account in using these methods? [Time and energy involved, accuracy and reliability of measurements, temperature dependence, relationship between ion concentration and salinity, relationship between conductivity and salinity, depth of electrodes, distance between electrodes. . . .]

Design an experiment which will enable you to predict the salinity of sea water samples based upon conductivity. What assumptions are made in these predictions? [Conductivity depends only on the concentration and not on the nature of the dissolved salts.] Construct a standard conductivity table for a series of sodium chloride solutions of known concentration.

Measure the conductivity of a sea water sample. Based on your result, predict the salinity of the sample. (The average salinity of ocean water is 35 grams per kilogram of water.) Check the accuracy of your prediction by determining the salinity directly by evaporation and weighing. Measure the density and compare it to a standard density-salinity table. What is the percent error in the various methods? Explain.

- -

Where does the salt in ocean waters come from?

What factors cause changes in the salt content of sea water over time?

What is the importance of water salinity in agriculture, industry, and the world's food supply?

What methods are used for water desalination? How are they related to energy and pollution problems?

Determine salinity by the Mohr titration method.

Comments

This activity provides opportunities to follow pre-lab discussion with different class members responsible for pursuing different measurement methods. These methods of measuring salinity can be compared in post-lab discussion.

References

Gymer, R. G.: *Chemistry: An Ecological Approach,* 1973. Harper and Row, New York, pp. 341–350, 404–422.

*Raemist, R. J., "Salinity Measurement", *Science Activities,* May, 1971, pp. 20–23.

6. Compare Before You Buy

Science Topics   Consumer chemistry

Level   C:1–3   E:1–3   D:1–3   L:2–4

Overview

Students discuss the kinds of information given on labels of consumer items and their significance in making purchasing decisions. After working out a plan, small groups collect information about one or more classes of items. This information is then used to make value judgements about the best buy.

Materials   Labels from assorted consumer goods

Suggested Activities

Suggest a plan for canvassing and evaluating the "best buy" among different classes of products (e.g., meats and cereals, candy and dairy products, soft drinks, canned soups, fruits and vegetables, laundry soaps and detergents, coffee and tea, floor waxes and bleaches) in a nearby market using the information on container labels. To facilitate pooling of information after gathering the data it will probably be helpful for your class to develop a common form for recording information. It may also be helpful to specify which product groups will be examined and who will do what tasks.

How can labels help us choose which brand of a particular item to buy? [ingredients (contents), form of the package, amount in the package, weight, volume, . . .]

What factors should determine a buying choice among different brands or forms of a product? Unit price (e.g., cents per ounce), intended use, nature of ingredients, ease of use . . . ?

What additional information should you have to evaluate the relative value of your products? Should manufacturers be required to print this information on their labels?

After the information is collected, use the data to recommend how you would spend $5.00 in your product area. Present your case for class discussion and debate.

Comments

This activity can be centered entirely upon the information available on labels. Questions can then be raised and the information processed in large group discussion and in small group teams. Consumer preferences may be gathered through interviews as an extension to the inquiry. Another extension involves questioning and testing the accuracy of the information on the label.

Reference

Zipko, S. J., "Consumer Science and Comparison Shopping, A Short Interdisciplinary Course", *Science Activities,* 15, 2; Summer, 1978, p. 36.

7. Testing Claims

Science Topics   Chemical and physical tests, consumer judgements

Level   C:2–3   E:2–4   D:1–3   L:2–4

Overview

Using references such as *Consumer Reports* and appropriate science literature, students design and perform a controlled experiment to compare consumer products and check out advertising claims.

Materials

Consumer Reports   Chemistry and physics texts
Manuals and reference books
Available laboratory equipment and materials as needed

Suggested Activities

We have all seen advertisements claiming to show "scientifically" why a particular brand of product is best for you. Select one advertisement whose claim you would enjoy examining. Design a controlled experiment to test the claim about the product.

Collect as many other brands of the same product as you can;
Select and justify a criterion for comparing different brands;
Develop a procedure for making the tests;
    Is the experiment valid (will it answer your question)?
    Is it reliable (will it give the same results when repeated on the same brand)?
    Are all important variables controlled?
Based on the results of your test(s), rank the brands investigated.
Is the advertising claim justified? Defend your position.

Comments

This kind of inquiry provides excellent opportunities for discussing the design of experiments and for developing student ability to define questions and to design tests and procedures. Guided inquiry and/or class discussions can be very important in facilitating the development of these skills, and of course, it is important to raise questions and to suggest activities that are appropriate for the student's own level of development.

Some of the many consumer products for which advertising claims can be investigated are:

Shampoos   Paper towels
Pain relievers   Moisture creams
Laundry detergents   Mouthwashes
Soaps   Toothpastes
Cigarettes   Spray paint
Cosmetics

References

Barrett, M. S., "Science in a Packet of Cornflakes", *The School Science Review*, 60, 210; September, 1978, pp. 132–133.

Barrett, M. S., "Science in a Saucebottle", *The School Science Review* 57, 200; March, 1976, pp. 585–586.

Carter, E., "Who Tells the Truth?", *Science Activities*, 14, 5; September/October, 1977, pp. 18–21.

Hudson, A. G., "Experiments to Determine the Water Content of Foods", *The School Science Review*, 61, 214; September, 1979, p. 132.

Ridley, E. R., "Testing Household Detergents", *The School Science Review*, 61, 217; June, 1980, p. 754.

Zipko, S. J., "Consumer Science and Comparison Shopping, A Short Interdisciplinary Course", *Science Activities*, 15, 2; Summer, 1978, p. 34.

8. What's Best for Heartburn?

Science Topics   Neutralization, acid-base reactions, consumer chemistry

Level   C:2   E:2   D:2   L:3

Overview

In this activity students investigate the neutralizing power of commercial antacid tablets and consider other factors relevant to making choices regarding competing remedies for heartburn.

Materials

A variety of unbuffered antacid tablets (e.g., Tums, Rolaids)
Erlenmeyer flasks (250 ml)
2M HCl
0.25M NaOH
Phenolphthalein or other indicator
Burette

Suggested Activities

Locate and examine advertising claims for antacid tablets. Which brand is preferable? When does one need to take an antacid tablet? How does it give relief? How could we measure its effectiveness?

When comparing commercial products, should we compare tablets or recommended doses of each? Explain.

Suggest a procedure for determining the neutralizing power of an antacid tablet.

Determine the neutralizing power of several kinds of antacid tablets by titrating a measured amount of acid with 0.25M NaOH both before [blank] and after adding an antacid tablet. The "neutralizing power" expressed as cc of 0.25M NaOH, is:

$$\begin{bmatrix} \underline{\quad} \text{ ml of NaOH needed} \\ \text{to titrate the acid} \\ \text{blank} \end{bmatrix} \text{ minus } \begin{bmatrix} \underline{\quad} \text{ ml of NaOH needed} \\ \text{to titrate the acid after} \\ \text{tablet was added} \end{bmatrix}$$

Prepare a bar graph showing the effectiveness of each product expressed as neutralizing power (the volume difference between the two titrations).

What gas is evolved when HCl is added to an antacid tablet? Can you notice any relationship between the rate of evolution of gas during neutralization and the effectiveness of the tablet? Is neutralizing power the only factor to be considered in selecting an antacid? Consult your physician or relevant literature. Which product would you recommend?

- -

Design and (if possible) carry out a survey of consumers who regularly use antacid tablets.

What kinds of questions should be asked?

What are the limitations of such a survey?

Comments

This activity provides a good opportunity to apply chemical principles and techniques to a biological problem (digestion), and it has clear implications for the consumer.

The strength of the acid is an important factor in the amount of 0.25M NaOH needed for neutralization. Five ml of 2M HCl diluted to about 50 ml with distilled water is recommended.

For rapid determination of the neutralizing power of an antacid tablet: add one tablet to 5 ml 2M HCl in a 250 ml Erlenmeyer flask. After the reaction has subsided dilute to about 50 ml with distilled water, and titrate residual acid with 0.25M NaOH using phenolphthalein indicator.

A variation of this activity is described in Armitage and McKendrick using bromthymol blue indicator to determine the number of drops of vinegar necessary to neutralize a commercial antacid tablet.

The activity is designed to give students an opportunity to use scientific inquiry processes in seeking answers posed by enlightened consumers. Similar activities can be designed for a wide variety of consumer products, e.g. vitamin C in foods, cleaning action and pH of detergents, drying properties of paints, combustibility of plastics. This kind of activity is appropriate and relevant for science students at many levels of development.

References

Armitage, G. M. and McKendrick, J., "Antacids as an Extension to Neutralization", *The School Science Review,* 60, 210; September, 1978, pp. 100–101.

Beisenherz, P. C., "Modifying Laboratory Activities", *Science Activities,* 13, 5; September/October, 1976, pp. 13–15.

Graham, B., "Excess Stomach Acid Treatment", *The Science Teacher,* 40, 9; December, 1973, p. 48.

Horwood, B., "More on Stomachs", *The Science Teacher,* 41, 2; February, 1974, p. 49.

9. Truth in Advertising—Soaps and Detergents

Science Topics   Detergents, properties of materials, solutions, consumer chemistry

Level   C:2   E:1–3   D:1–2   L:2–3

Overview

In this activity students compare the effectiveness of soaps and detergents. Control of variables is an important part of the inquiry, and comparison of findings with the misinformation presented in commercial advertising can be of interest.

Materials

Pieces of various natural and synthetic fabrics such as cotton, wool, polyesters, etc.
Several well known detergents or soaps or stain removers
Dirty oil   scissors
Thermometers
Beakers

Suggested Activities

Most of us have been exposed to soap and detergent commercials on TV claiming better and less expensive cleaning, skin protection, brightness of colors, cleaning in "hard" water, and over-all happiness for the entire family. Are we being told the truth in these commercials? What criteria are truly important in the soaps and detergents we purchase? How do they really compare? What should the commercials really be telling us if they are to make sense? Answering these kinds of questions is very important for consumers in making decisions regarding the use and purchase of a wide variety of items.

In this kind of inquiry there are many variables that will make a difference on the effectiveness of cleaning agents and we must identify them and control them if our results are to be useful. What are the variables with which we ought to be concerned when making comparisons between detergents? Test some commercial soaps or detergents or stain removers and compare their effectiveness. [Variables will include: size of the piece of cloth, the quantity of dirty oil, the concentration and temperature of the detergent solution, washing time, amount of agitation or rubbing. . . .]

What kinds of criteria can we define to measure outcome variables such as cleanliness, color brightness, removal of all dirt, textile damage? Select an experimental variable to study (such as the brand of detergent or the water temperature or washing time) and design an experiment making certain that all other variables are kept constant.

What do you observe in your inquiry? (Try to make these observations as quantitative as possible.) How can your observations be explained? What new questions does your inquiry raise? What possible flaws exist in your experimental procedure? What new experiments need to be conducted? What variables have not been examined or controlled?

What is the "best" brand available to meet the needs and desires of consumers? What do consumers desire in a detergent?

Which brand is most cost-effective?

Can you observe through a series of experiments any interaction effects between various detergents and water temperature, water hardness, etc.?

Contrast your results with advertising claims of various detergents. Perhaps you could set up a special investigation to test certain claims. Are the advertising claims valid? What recommendations would you make to governmental regulatory agencies to improve the accuracy of detergent advertising?

Environmentalists have expressed real concerns about the damaging effects of detergents upon rivers and the environment generally. What are their special concerns? How do "biodegradable" detergents perform in the tests you have conducted? What are the effects of "phosphate-content"?

How do soaps and detergents "work"?

Safety Precautions

Wear old clothes or lab coats or aprons to protect clothing from clumsiness with dirty oil.

Comments

Activities of this kind can easily be confusing for there are many variables. It is important to discuss relevant variables and the importance of controlling them. Specific ways to control variables should be discussed, and with less sophisticated students, controls should be specified in order to examine the effects of one variable. This kind of inquiry can enable students to improve understanding and skill in controlling variables.

In this activity it may very well be appropriate to have groups of students in the class examine the effects of different variables. Then the small groups can come together and pool their information. The pooled information can be the basis for a discussion of broader results of the inquiry in which several variables have been manipulated and can serve as a basis for discussion of what new experiments still need to be conducted.

This activity has some very interesting consumer dimensions and some students may spend some time examining "truth in advertising", ethical implications, cost-effectiveness, etc.

References

H. Misselbrook (ed.), *Nuffield Secondary Science,* vol. 7, Longman; London, 1971.

Dowler, F.: *The Science of Laundering.* American Gas Association, Inc., Arlington, VA.

10. Where's the Bargain Bleach?

Science Topics   Halogen oxidation-reduction processes, consumer chemistry

Level   C:2–3   E:2–3   D:1–4   L:2–4

Overview

Combining chemical analysis data with cost information provides a basis for consumer decision making. Commercial bleach preparations are analyzed by reducing active chlorine with iodide ions; the released iodine is reduced by thiosulfate in the presence of starch indicator.

Materials

Part I—assorted pieces of cloth and oil

Part II—1.5 M H_2SO_4 Starch indicator
10% KI   Graduate (100 ml)
Burette   Pipettes (10 ml, 20 ml)
Erlenmeyer flask (250 ml)
0.025 M $Na_2S_2O_3 \cdot 5H_2O$ (6.2 grams/liter boiled water)

Suggested Activities

In a market there may be many brands of the same material and as consumers we must decide which will give us best value for our money. Take bleach for instance—which brand gives greatest value?

I. What information do we need to decide which bleach gives best value? Obtain some bottles of recently purchased bleach; get the following information: price, volume, contents, etc. Then test some sample dirty pieces of cloth with different brands of bleach and compare their effects. (In this inquiry there are many variables that will effect the "whitening power" and the usefulness of bleach. What are the important variables and how can we control them in our experiment?)

What are the effects of temperature, hardness of water, dilution, age of bleach, kind of fabric, kind of stain, amount of rubbing, etc.? Do the bleaches damage the fabrics in different ways?

What new questions does your inquiry raise? What new experiments need to be conducted?

What is the "best" brand?

What's in bleach that whitens our clothes? Try to find out by searching the literature.

II. Compare the strength of the chlorine present in a fixed volume of different brands of bleach. (Different students may examine different brands.) Also you may want to check to see if the "age" of the bleach makes a difference in C1 strength. Titrate the mixture with 0.025 M $Na_2S_2O_3$ in the presence of starch indicator.

Determine the mass of active C1 per liter. Also note the volume of the contents of a full bottle and the price per bottle. Then determine the price per liter, and the cost per 100 grams active Cl.

What data should be used to decide which brand gives best value, cost per liter or cost per 100 grams active Cl? Why?

How does the mass of active Cl per liter relate to "whitening power" examined in Part I?

Which brand would you recommend?

Safety Precautions

Wear lab coats or aprons to protect clothing. Wear goggles to protect eyes.

Comments

The analysis for active chlorine is based on the following reactions:

$$Cl_{2(aq)} + 2I^-_{(aq)} \longrightarrow I_{2(aq)} + 2Cl^-_{(aq)}$$

$$2S_2O^{2-}_{3(aq)} + I_{2(aq)} \longrightarrow S_4O^{2-}_{6(aq)} + 2I^-_{(aq)}$$

To determine the cost per 100 grams of active Cl:

$$2(\underline{\hspace{1cm}} cc\ Na_2S_2O_3 \times \frac{0.025\ moles}{1000\ cc}) = moles\ I_2 = moles\ Cl_2$$

$$\underline{\hspace{1cm}} moles\ Cl_2 \times \frac{71\ grams}{mole} = \underline{\hspace{1cm}} grams\ active\ Cl\ (in\ 20\ cc\ of\ diluted\ sample)$$

$$\frac{\underline{\hspace{1cm}}\ grams\ active\ Cl}{20\ cc} \times \frac{1000\ cc}{liter} = \underline{\hspace{1cm}} grams\ active\ Cl/liter\ (diluted\ bleach)$$

$$\frac{\underline{\hspace{1cm}}\ cents/bottle}{\underline{\hspace{1cm}}\ cc/bottle} \times \frac{1000\ cc}{liter} = \underline{\hspace{1cm}} cents/liter$$

$$\frac{\underline{\hspace{1cm}}\ cents/liter}{\underline{\hspace{1cm}}\ grams\ active\ Cl/liter} \times 100 = \underline{\hspace{1cm}} cents/100\ grams\ active\ Cl\ in\ commercial\ bleach$$

Combining:

$$\underline{\hspace{1cm}}\ cents/100\ grams\ active\ Cl\ in\ commercial\ bleach = \frac{\underline{\hspace{1cm}}\ cents/bottle \times 10^6}{\underline{\hspace{1cm}}\ cc/bottle \times cc\ Na_2S_2O_3 \times 71}$$

Preparation of starch indicator: prepare a paste of 1 gram soluble starch in 10 cc cold water. Add the paste to 90 cc boiling water, stir and allow to cool. The indicator can be stabilized by adding a few crystals of HgI_2.

References

Dowler, F.: *The Science of Laundering.* American Gas Association, Inc., Arlington, VA.

*Ormerod, M. B., "A 'Which' Investigation of Bleaching Fluid", *The School Science Review,* 45, 157; June, 1964. p. 672.

11. Animal, Plant or Synthetic?

Science Topics   Decomposition, combustion, macromolecules

Level   C:2–3   E:2–3   D:1   L:2–4

Overview

The destructive distillation of clothing fibers by heating in a test-tube yields products which can be characterized by simple observations (odor, change in color of indicator paper, etc.). By careful observation of heated clothing fibers and their decomposition products, students can propose tests to distinguish between animal and plant fibers and between natural and synthetic fibers.

Materials

Red and blue litmus paper
Lead acetate paper
Test-tubes
Test-tube holder
Burner
A large variety of natural and synthetic fibers:
Wool, silk (animal)
Cotton, linen (plant)
Rayon, polyesters, etc. (synthetic)

Suggested Activities

We've collected many kinds of fibers, used mainly in clothing. Learn as much as you can about their origin (animal, plant, synthetic) and their properties. Try burning a few fibers, holding them with tweezers and igniting with a match. Observe carefully, smell. . . .

Place a small piece of each material in a test tube and heat with a burner. Test the vapors with moist red and blue litmus paper [plant fibers produce acid fumes, animal fibers containing protein produce basic fumes] and with moist lead acetate paper [only fumes from wool, which contains sulfur, will cause the paper to turn black or dark brown due to formation of lead sulfide].

Record your observations. How do you explain your observations?

What are the effects of burning and of heating on the different fibers? What characteristics distinguish some of the fibers you have investigated? What generalizations can you make, if any?

Based on your results, suggest, if you can, a possible way to find out if a fiber is of plant or animal origin? Explain. Can you suggest a good way to find out if a fiber is natural or synthetic? Explain. What are the limitations of your methods?

- -

Investigate other chemical tests for fibers to improve your ability to distinguish between fiber sources. (Refer to technical handbooks.)

Comments

This activity requires making careful observations and recording them systematically.

Prepare lead acetate paper by dipping strips of filter paper in a solution of lead acetate and drying them in an oven or over a flame.

References

Dowler, F.: *The Science of Laundering.* American Gas Association, Inc., Arlington, VA.

*Joseph, A., et al.: *A Sourcebook for the Physical Sciences,* 1961. Harcourt, Brace, and World, Inc., New York, pp. 301–304.

12. Iron in the Garbage

Science Topics   Corrosion, oxidation, biodegradability, environmental chemistry

Level   C:2   E:2   D:1   L:2–3

Overview

In this activity students investigate the effect of two plant products, tannic acid and salicylic acid, on iron.

Materials

Glasses or beakers   Iron nails (uncoated)
Steel wool
Powdered tannic acid (available
     from local pharmacy)
Aspirin

Suggested Activities

While more and more metals (aluminum beverage cans, "tin" cans—really iron thinly coated with tin, copper wire, solder, brass and bronze fittings) in garbage are being recycled, small pieces remain in decomposing garbage. These metals rust and corrode by oxidation, but they also react with certain compounds in leaf, fruit, and vegetable refuse.

What is the role of metals, particularly iron, in decomposing garbage destined for fertilizer? What is the effect of the garbage on the iron? To begin, let's investigate how two substances found in plant material, tannic acid and salicylic acid, affect iron. Design an experiment to investigate the effects of salicylic acid and tannic acid on iron. What variables are involved in your experiment? [Kind of plant product, concentration of plant product, surface area of metal, temperature. . . .] How can the variables be controlled? (To vary concentration of tannic acid, use ¼, ½, 1 tablespoon tannic acid powder in a glass ⅔ filled with water; for salicylic acid start with three aspirin tablets stirred into a glass of water; to vary surface area use a nail and use steel wool. . . .)

What do you observe? Explain.

Design an experiment to find out if rust reacts with tannic acid. What do you conclude?

Do similar experiments with other metals found in garbage and discuss similarities and differences.

Investigate the waste management literature and prepare a short report on the role of metals in garbage decomposition. Prepare a short report on recycling metals from garbage.

Reference

Schatz, A. and Schatz, V.: *Teaching Science With Garbage,* 1971. Rodel Press, Emmaus, PA, pp. 32–34.

B Mechanics

1. A Sky Hook

Science Topics   Center of gravity or mass, torque, stability

Level   C:2   E:1   D:1   L:2–3

Overview

The sky hook appears, at first glance, to defy gravity and can be an interesting way to introduce the study of center of gravity and stability.

Materials

One sky hook—constructed locally from a dowel or small block of plastic or wood
One leather belt (of at least moderately stiff texture)
Assorted objects of different shapes for center of gravity study

One form of sky hook can be cut from a block of low-density wood or plastic using the full-size pattern shown in Figure 1.
Thickness should be sufficient for rigidity.

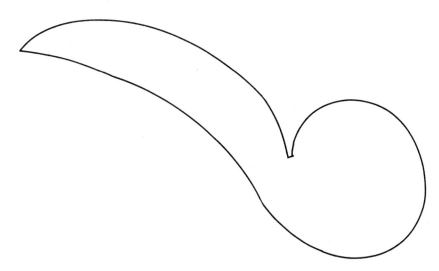

Figure 1

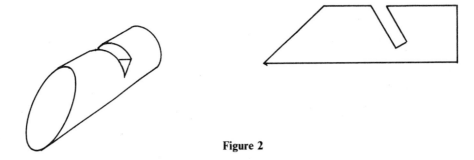

Figure 2

Another form of sky hook can be made by cutting a ½″ diameter wood dowel to approximately 6cm in length. The dowel may be cut as shown in Figure 2.

Suggested Activities

Hang a belt from the slot on the sky hook and arrange the system so it balances on the tip of your finger or on some other object.

Describe your observations.

Explain why the system doesn't fall to the floor.

Test your tentative explanations (hypotheses) by experimenting with other objects to see under what conditions they are stable and under what conditions they tip.

Can you come up with a rule that will enable someone to know whether or not an object will be stable? If so, state that rule as precisely as you can. Use diagrams to help.

Does your rule explain the stability of the sky hook?

Use your rule to show how to arrange unstable systems into stable ones.

A young magician wants to be able to balance a whole potato on the rim of a glass. He says it will be OK to use eating utensils if necessary. Can you use your rule to help him?

Comments

An object will be stable if a vertical line drawn through its "center of gravity" passes within its base of support.

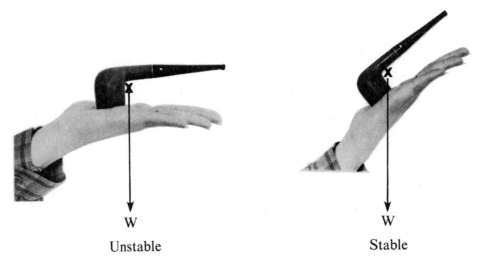

Unstable   Stable

Figure 3

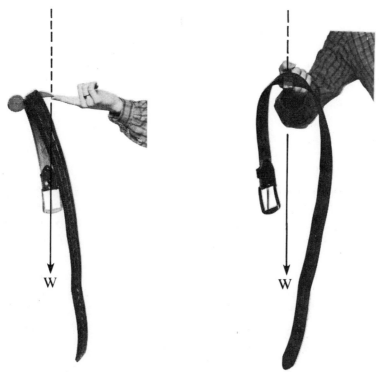

Figure 4

The center of gravity of the belt-sky hook system is beneath the point of support when the system is properly arranged and in equilibrium.

Reference

Williams, J. E., et al.: *Modern Physics,* 1980. Holt, Rinehart, and Winston, New York, pp. 83–86.

2. Friction

Science Topic   Friction

Level   C:1–4   E:2   D:2   L:2–4

Overview

In this activity students gather information about frictional forces between two surfaces and about the variables that affect them. It is designed to introduce the study of friction *before* it is pursued in depth. The activity can be used with students to assist in the development of their ability to control variables, to graph data, and to propose an alternative hypotheses and explanations.

Materials

Spring Balance
Surfaces of different texture (wood, metal, plastic, . . .)
Identical blocks/bricks

Suggested Activities

Frictional forces are ever-present throughout the world in which we live. Often we use them to advantage such as in braking an automobile; at other times they get in the way and we seek to reduce them such as in lubricating an engine. For many centuries frictional forces were a source of confusion as people tried to understand relationships between forces and motion. Thus there are many reasons why we should try to improve our understanding of friction.

What factors do you think would affect the frictional forces between two surfaces? Design an experiment in which you control these variables (vary one while holding all others constant . . .), and observe their effects on friction.

- -

In one such experiment you might pull a brick across a surface at a constant slow speed and record the force necessary to do so. You might then record the forces necessary to pull a stack of two bricks, three bricks, four bricks, etc. What does a graph of frictional force versus the number of bricks look like? What kind of mathematical relationship is there? Can you write a mathematical formula that describes the relationships and that predicts frictional forces you did not measure?

What is the effect of changing the amount of surface area in contact? Pull the brick and piles of bricks on their sides to find out. What does a graph of the data look like?

What is the effect of the surface? What does the graph look like when the bricks are pulled across a different surface?

Is the amount of friction constant throughout the sliding or does it vary? Is "starting friction" different from "sliding friction"? If so, in what way?

In general terms, what can be done to reduce the amount of friction between sliding objects? Make some practical suggestions for the bricks you have been pulling and propose some hypotheses to explain your suggestions. Test your suggestions and gather more data.

What happens to the frictional forces when the bricks are piled on roller skates and pulled across the surface? Explain.

Propose some possible hypotheses that will explain frictional forces. Are they the result of forces of attraction between molecules of the different sliding materials? Are they electrical or magnetic? Are they due to irregularities in the surfaces that bump into one another? Are they some kind of "stickiness"? Discuss how you would design tests of your hypotheses if you had the time, equipment, and information.

What are the best hypotheses that you and other members of your class have proposed? How do you know?

What is the current thinking of scientists on this question . . . ?

- -

Conduct a study examining towels sliding off a towel rack. What variables affect sliding time? Examine the effects of different shoe soles on the walking/running process. . . .

References
Rabinowicz, E., "Resource Letter F-1 on Friction", *American Journal of Physics, 31,* 897, 1963.
Rabinowicz, E., "Direction of the Friction Force," *Nature 179,* 1073, 1957.
Rabinowicz, E., "Stick and Slip," *Scientific American, 194,* 109, May 1956.

3. Moving Spools

Science Topics   Newton's Laws, friction, torque, center of gravity or mass.

Level C:2   E:1   D:1   L:1–2

Overview

In this activity, students make predictions about the motion that will result when force is applied to a wound spool through the attached string. The probability of incorrect predictions is very high and experimenting with the system makes the discrepancies between prediction and reality evident. Hypotheses can then be developed (and tested) to explain what is observed.

Materials   Spool wound with string or thread

Suggested Activities

Predict in what direction the spool will roll if the string is directed over the top of the spool and pulled.

Predict what way will the spool roll, when the string is directed from the bottom of the spool and pulled horizontally.

Pull on the string in various ways and study the effects on moving the spool. Describe what you observe.

Will spools of different diameter, texture, or weight behave differently?

Are your observations consistent with your predictions? How can your observations be explained? Are you certain of your latest explanations? Test them with new predictions and tests.

Comments

This little activity normally results in inaccurate predictions and provides an excellent example of the importance of experimental tests of intuition and hypotheses in the development of scientific theory.

Reference

Williams, J. E., et al.: *Modern Physics,* 1980. Holt, Rinehart, and Winston, New York, pp. 83–86.

4. Paper Helicopters*

Science Topic   Aerodynamics, air resistance

Level   C:1–2   E:1–2   D:1   L:1–3

Overview

Studying the flight characteristics of paper helicopters can be a very interesting activity that can result in successive analysis of the effects of a number of variables. This activity can help students develop skills in controlling variables and increase understanding of the effects of air friction and of stability.

Materials

Paper
Scissors
Stapler
Meter stick
Timing device

Suggested Activities

Have you ever watched seed pods from maple trees 'float' to the earth? They spin as they fall, like little helicopters. What causes them to spin? Do they always spin in the same direction? Is the same end always pointing down? What can we learn from the seed pods that might help us design better helicopters?

---

*Paper helicopter figures and construction details reprinted with permission from A. Ward, "Exploring air resistance with paper helicopters" and "Researching and developing paper helicopters", *School Science Review, 57*:198, September 1975, 140–141 and *61*:215, December 1979, 325.

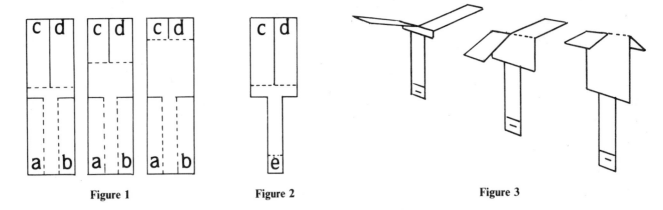

Figure 1   Figure 2   Figure 3

One way to begin the inquiry is to construct paper helicopters (simulated seed pods or helicopters) and study the effects of various design characteristics such as weight, wing area, etc. (To do so, we should select one characteristic like wing area and vary it in successive trials while holding all other characteristics constant). Figure 1 shows three patterns that will result in paper helicopters with three different wing areas, but identical weight.

Three scissors cuts are made in each strip, but notice that the vertical cut to the sides of which 'wings' c and d will be formed, are progressively less such as 9, 6 and 3 cm. Fold parts a and b inward, to resemble Figure 2. Then bend up the bottoms (e). These bent up parts can be stapled flat. Finally bend out the wings (Figure 3). The weight of the helicopters can be varied by changing the number of staples used.

Before dropping your paper helicopters, predict which one will fall fastest, . . . slowest.

How do you describe the falling of the paper helicopters?

Are the paper helicopters a good simulation of the seed pods?

Are they a good simulation of real helicopters?

How are they similar to helicopters and seed pods? How are they different?

What other variables do you think affect falling time? You may want to study these variables carefully too.

Does a paper helicopter fall at approximately constant speed or does its speed change during flight? Explain your observation.

Predict how a helicopter will fall if its wings are vertical (not folded out) when you release it. Then, drop it this way to test your prediction. What do you observe? Experiment with the helicopter to better understand what is happening. How can one explain these observations? [Explanations might include reference to gyroscopic motion, centrifugal reaction "force", dynamic inertia, air resistance. . . .]

If helicopters are dropped upside down will they right themselves?

What are the effects on flight if the wings are not identical? What if there is only one wing?

What variables affect the rate of spinning? What can be done to a particular helicopter to make it spin faster as it falls?

What kind of helicopter is least affected by winds and breezes?

Do all helicopters spin in the same direction? What can you do to change the direction of spin?

Predict how these helicopters would fly on the moon.

Compete with your classmates to see who can design the helicopter (using similar quantities of materials) that will remain in the air for the longest time when dropped from the same height—and that will come closest to a marked target. . . .

Comments

This kind of inquiry can also be conducted with other kinds of flying objects such as "Frisbees", flying discs, paper airplanes. . . .

Reference

Alan Ward. "Exploring air resistance with paper helicopters" and "Researching and developing paper helicopters", *School Science Review, 57:*198, September 1975, 140–141 and *61:*215, December 1979, 325.

5. Parachutes

Science Topics   Aerodynamics, air friction, terminal velocity

Level   C:1–3   E:1–4   D:1–2   L:2–3

Overview

The fall of a parachute is dependent on many factors, some of which can be manipulated. Students design and construct parachutes, launch them from some high place and measure the time needed for fall and other variables. Since there are so many factors, this activity is an excellent one to help develop skills in controlling variables.

Materials

Squares of 30 × 30 cm or other sizes of different kinds of paper, cloth, and plastic
Weights (anything will do, but uniform washers are handy)
Timing device (watch, stopwatch or other device)
Use of a multi-story building or another high launching site
Scissors
String

Suggested Activities

To begin, the teacher or a student may demonstrate the fall of a parachute (from a multi-story building or some other high point). The class may briefly discuss what a "good fall" of a parachute could be but should not dwell on this question prematurely. Students form groups of three or four. They are asked to make a parachute, to improve on its fall characteristics and to study the effect of using different materials in the construction of the parachute. While working, students should also define "good fall characteristics" and to summarize these near the end of the activity.

Make one or more parachutes and observe how they fall. What characteristics can you observe? vertical and horizontal velocity, rotation, swinging, sensitivity to air currents and drafts, damage upon landing. . . ?

Can you make the parachute fall faster or more slowly?
Can you prevent dangerous swinging?
Can you prevent dangerous rotating?
Can you decrease or increase parachute sensitivity to drafts and air currents?
What happens when the load of the parachute increases or decreases?
What happens when the distance from the top of the parachute to the load increases or decreases?
What happens when you make a hole in the top of the parachute? More holes?
What happens when you increase or decrease the surface area of the top sheet?
What is the influence of the top sheet material?
Can you use the parachute to measure wind direction and velocity? How would you design it?
How does the travel time of the parachute depend on the surface area of the parachute top?

Can you fairly accurately predict where the parachute will land? What design changes can be made to increase the predictability of the landing place? Can you steer the parachute by design? How would you define a "good fall"?

Would you use different parachutes for dropping freight than you would for dropping people? How would they be different? How is good fall dependent on the purpose of the parachute user?

You may wish to extend your study to examine other floating objects such as birds or model planes. You may also wish to study aerodynamics in a wind tunnel you might set up using a vacuum cleaner to simulate air currents. What are the effects of air currents on parachute design? What are the effects of air currents on various wing surfaces? . . .

Safety Precautions

The teacher should remain on the roof with most of the class. A few students should take turns recovering parachutes, observing, and timing from below, etc.

Comments

The activity depends upon the availability of a good launching point and the possibility of working outside the classroom. Teachers need to be especially sensitive to whether or not individual students have developed the ability to control variables.

Good fall may be described in terms of "steadiness", horizontal and vertical velocity, predictability of the landing place and perhaps some other criteria. Among the parachute characteristics students may discover and change are: material, shape, and size of the sheet, a hole or holes in the top, mass of the load carried, distance of the load from the top.

6. Accelerometers

Science Topic   Motion/Kinematics, Acceleration, Inertia, Properties of Matter

Level   C:2–3   E:2–3   D:1–3   L:2–4

Overview

In this activity students examine the characteristics of one or two liquid accelerometers that provide visual representation of the direction and magnitude of the acceleration vector of an object. Initial contact with an accelerometer generally results in erroneous predictions about what will happen when the device is moved, and it generates much interest as students try to figure out why it behaves the way it does. Students of a broad spectrum of ages can use accelerometers to study certain properties of matter and inertia, while older more advanced students can use them for quantitative empirical analysis of acceleration.

Materials

I. Water and cork accelerometer

Acquire a large water-tight clear glass or plastic bottle with a cap. Select a cork that will fit easily into the uncapped bottle. Attach the cork to the bottle cap using a thread or light string that will enable the cork to hang approximately two-thirds of the way into the bottle when the cap is on. Fill the bottle with water, insert the cap and string, and tighten the cap; then invert the bottle.

II. Liquid-Surface Accelerometer

These can be found in high school physics laboratories or can be constructed using a rectangular plastic container approximately half filled with a colored liquid.

Figure 1

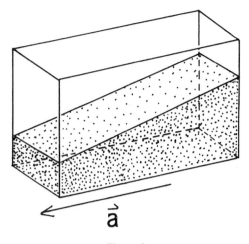

Figure 2

Suggested Activities

Acquire or construct an accelerometer. (An accelerometer is used to show the presence of acceleration or to measure acceleration.)

Before moving your accelerometer predict how it will behave when you move it in various ways: straight line at constant speeds; at increasing or decreasing speeds; in a circular path. . . .

Move the accelerometer and check out your predictions.
Describe your observations.
Were your predictions accurate? Explain.
How can your observations be explained?
Test your new explanations in the laboratory.

Make accelerometers using other materials. (The *Project Physics Handbook* outlines four interesting designs.) Compare the characteristics of accelerometers of different design. What kinds of accelerometers are best for specific uses?

- -

What do you observe in the liquid surface accelerometer when it is moving under the influence of a constant force over as long a distance as possible?

(To do this, you might put the accelerometer on a cart and then pull the cart by attaching a string with weight attached over a pulley as shown in Figure 3.)

What happens to the acceleration if the cart changes direction while the constant force is applied? (Push the cart so that initially it travels away from the force applied through the string.)

How can the accelerometer be used to measure the magnitude of acceleration?

Using the liquid surface accelerometer a simple formula can be derived that enables an observer to determine the magnitude of acceleration by measuring the height of the liquid at the end of the cell above or below its rest position. Derive the formula yourself or find it in a reference (Harris and Ahlgren, for example). Then validate/check the formula experimentally by measuring acceleration in other ways (such as with stroboscopic photographs or with ticker tape or spark timers).

Calibrate your accelerometer so it can be used directly to measure acceleration in convenient metric units.

Use your accelerometer to study factors affecting acceleration in a variety of vehicles and situations.

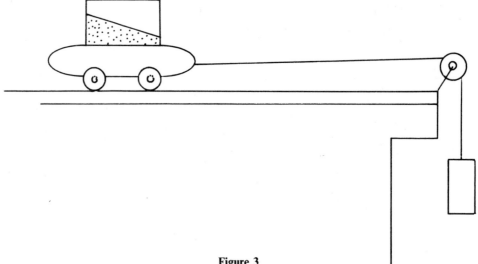

Figure 3

Comments

Water and Cork Accelerometer.

Since the cork has less inertial mass than the volume of water it displaces, when the bottle is accelerated, the water in the bottle will tend to resist the acceleration and will tend to remain stationary or in constant velocity motion relative to the accelerating jar thus pushing the less massive cork in the direction of acceleration. . . .

Liquid-Surface Accelerometer.

Constant linear horizontal acceleration will result in a constant liquid slope. Greater acceleration will result in greater slope:

$$\tan \theta = \frac{\text{acceleration}}{g}$$

$$\tan \theta = \frac{h}{l}$$

$$\frac{h}{l} = \frac{\text{acceleration}}{g}$$

$$\text{acceleration} = \frac{h}{l} \times g$$

The theoretical derivation is discussed in detail in Harris and Ahlgren.

References

Haden, H., "A Demonstration of Newtonian and Archimedean Forces", *The Physics Teacher,* 2, 4; April, 1964, p. 176.

Harris, J. and Ahlgren, A., "Some Simple Experiments and Demonstrations, *The Physics Teacher,* 4, 7; October, 1966, pp. 314–315.

Rutherford, F. J., et al.: *Project Physics Handbook,* 1970. Holt, Rinehart, and Winston, New York, pp. 46–49.

7. Low Friction Motion

Science Topic Newton's laws, Inertia

Level C:2   E:1–3   D:1–3   L:2–3

Overview

This activity gives students opportunity to gain first-hand experience with low-friction motion that will enhance understanding of Newtonian physics. The inquiry can be extended in many directions and, if continued, can lead inductively to the development of Newton's laws.

Materials

"Frictionless" pucks using plastic beads, air, or balloons
Puck Table surrounded by rubber band
Air Table or air track—optional
Low-friction carts

Suggested Activities

Aristotle thought that all moving matter ultimately comes to rest. Newton, on the other hand, argued that moving matter will continue to move in a straight line, unless an unbalanced force is applied to change its motion.

Play with these low-friction objects, push them around and observe how they move under various conditions.

What evidence can you cite to support Aristotle's thinking? Newton's? Use examples from experiences elsewhere if they may help develop the case. What happens to the motion of an object when frictional forces approach 0? Are there any places or situations where there is no friction?

- -

Apply a constant force to a low-friction object and describe the motion that results.
Is the velocity constant? Changing?
Is the acceleration constant?
What factors affect the acceleration of an object if we can reduce the effects of friction?
Study the effects of these factors experimentally. For example, vary the force applied to a cart in successive trials while holding all other variables constant and carefully measure the acceleration that results using a stroboscope or a ticker tape timer. . . . What does a graph of force versus acceleration look like? Is the slope constant or changing? What does this mean? Does the curve pass through the origin? Explain your data if you can. Develop an algebraic equation that relates force and acceleration.

Change other variables in your inquiry to discover their effects on motion.

References
Physical Science Study Committee: *Physics Laboratory Guide,* 1971. D.C. Heath, Lexington, MA., pp. 34–37.
Rutherford, F. J., et al.: *Project Physics,* 1975. Holt, Rinehart, and Winston, New York, Chapter 3, pp. 90–92.
Rutherford, F. J., et al.: *Project Physics Handbook,* 1970. Holt, Rinehart, and Winston, New York, pp. 21–24.

8. Falling Objects

Science Topic   Acceleration of gravity, Free fall, Newton's laws

Level   C:2–3   E:2–4   D:2–3   L:2–4

Overview

All too often, students are passive observers in demonstrations or lectures in which they hear "The acceleration of gravity is independent of mass. . . ." The words are not easily understood, but first-hand experience with this phenomenon will enhance understanding and increase the likelihood that explanations will begin to make sense.

Materials

Objects of various weights, materials, and shapes

Suggested Activities

Aristotle wrote that the speed of a falling object is constant and proportional to its weight. Thus, a heavy rock would fall faster and reach the ground sooner than would a lighter object released at the same time. Galileo, on the other hand, argued that all objects in free fall would have generally the same acceleration; thus two objects of different weight dropped at the same time and place would reach the ground at the same time.

Drop many pairs of objects from the same height and compare their falling times. What do you observe? Does the Aristotelian or the Galilean explanation fit your data best? If there are differences between your observations and the "theory" you think best, how can these be explained?

Can your inquiry and explanation be extended to objects of different weight sliding down an incline?

In free fall, the force causing acceleration is an object's weight. Thus a 100 lb. object in free fall would have an accelerating force that is 10 times larger than a freely falling object weighing 10 lbs. With this information would it not be reasonable to expect that the 100 lb. object would have an acceleration 10 times greater than the 10 lb object? Explain your answer. Can you perform tests to check your explanation?

- -

Since the time of Galileo, the acceleration of gravity (g) near the surface of the earth has been measured in many different ways. In addition to measurements of an object in free fall using stroboscopic photographs and measurement of the time to fall a measured distance ($d = \frac{1}{2}gt^2$), the formula for the period of pendulum is commonly used ($T = 2\pi\sqrt{\frac{1}{g}}$).

The Project Physics Handbook describes six of these experimental methods. With your classmates measure g in a variety of ways. Which method is likely to result in the "best" results? Explain. How do your empirical measurements of g compare with official values for your location? What percent error is present in your measurement? What factors most probably account for this error?

Reference

Rutherford, F. J., et al.: *Project Physics Handbook,* 1970. Holt, Rinehart, and Winston, New York, pp. 34–38.

9. Losing Weight in an Elevator

Science Topic Newton's Laws, Inertia, Acceleration

Level C:3 E:1–2 D:2–3 L:2–4

Overview

This activity provides first-hand experience with force and acceleration and with the concept of inertia. The use of an elevator will provide built-in interest for some students. It is intended for use *after* students have been introduced to Newton's laws and the property of inertia. It can be the basis for an excellent group discussion, and predictions can be tested by a small group in an elevator. A report can be made to the large group followed by more extended discussion.

Materials

Bathroom Scale

- - - - - - - - - - - - - - - - - - -

Spring Balance }
Weight set   } optional

Suggested Activities

Should a person who wants to weigh less weigh himself or herself on an elevator that is descending? Make a prediction and explain your rationale.

If you were to stand on a scale and weigh yourself while riding on an elevator, predict your approximate weight (as measured by the scale) at different points in the ride. Explain your rationale.

Go to an elevator and test your predictions. While in the elevator, gather as much precise data as possible for analysis later. Record data throughout all parts of the elevator ride. Over what time interval does acceleration occur? If time permits, get data on the weights of different people and/or other objects. Record relevant information inscribed on the elevator certificate or specification plate.

Were your predictions validated by empirical evidence? How can the evidence be explained? How does the data relate to Newton's explanations and laws of motion?

Use the data to calculate the maximum acceleration of the elevator. Does the starting and stopping acceleration have the same magnitude? direction? Are these the same when the elevator moves up and when it moves down?

In what kind of elevator motion would a person truly weigh less relative to the floor over an extended period of time? Explain.

Can your comments be extended to explain the "weightlessness" experienced by astronauts in earth orbit? If so, how?

Comments

When a person stands on a scale in an elevator the scale will read the person's actual weight except for brief periods at the beginning and end of the ride while the elevator is accelerating in bringing the elevator up to a constant velocity for the trip or in stopping it. Throughout most of the trip the elevator travels at approximately constant speed and thus during that interval no unusual forces exist between the elevator floor and the person's feet. Once accelerated (positively or negatively) the person's inertia causes him or her to move along at constant speed (Newton's first law). The unusual forces present during acceleration are described by Newton's 2nd law (F = ma).

Thus during acceleration (up or down)

$$W_{\text{eight on scale}} = W_{\text{eight Actual}} + F_{\text{accel. max.}}$$

Using an example—if a 100 lb person "weighs" 110 lb during maximum upward acceleration, then 10 lb is the force applied to cause the acceleration.

$$F = ma$$

$$F = \frac{W}{g}a$$

$$10 = \frac{100}{32} \times a \qquad\qquad (g = 32 \text{ ft/sec}^2)$$

$$a = 3.2 \text{ ft/sec}^2$$

The maximum acceleration is 3.2 ft/sec².

If the maximum acceleration in stopping were −3.2 ft/sec², then the same person would "weigh" 90 pounds when the elevator was at maximum negative acceleration.

Reference

Williams, J. E., et al.: *Modern Physics,* 1980. Holt, Rinehart, and Winston, New York, pp. 57–59.

10. A Water Rocket

Science Topic   Newton's Third Law, Impulse and Momentum, Pressure

Level   C:2–3   E:2–4   D:2–3   L:2–4

Overview

Children's toy water rockets have inherent interest, are a very appropriate resource for the practice of inquiry skills, and can provide experience with a number of scientific principles. They provide an interesting way to make predictions from scientific principles that ought to have an effect on flight and then to test those predictions and discuss discrepancies. . . .

Materials

Water rocket
Timer

Suggested Activities

What factors affect the flight of a water rocket?

Will it go higher if we fill it with water or if we just fill it with air before pumping it and releasing it?

Test your prediction. What do you observe?

How can these observations be explained? Test your explanations with further tests on the water rocket or on other devices.

What is a good way to measure the height reached by the rocket? Can you design or find a measuring device that can be used?

Is there a best water-air mixture that will result in the water rocket reaching the highest altitude when it is shot straight up?

How can your findings be explained?

Using a fixed amount of water, how does the number of pump strokes affect the flight time and the height the rocket reaches? Study these relationships as precisely as possible and graph the mathematical data. What relationships do you observe?

Calculate the average upward and downward speed of the rocket in each of these trials. Are they the same?

How does the weight of the rocket affect the height it attains and its average speed? (You might vary the weight of the rocket by attaching weights to it incrementally—in a way that does not change other variables like shape).

How does the temperature of the water affect the height the rocket reaches?

Does the temperature or humidity of the air affect the height it reaches?

- -

What variables affect the stability of the rocket? Would a spinning rocket be more stable?

If the rocket is not launched vertically how will the distance it travels vary with the angle of launch? Make some predictions about this relationship and then test them.

Holding other variables constant vary the angle of launch and measure the distance the rocket travels along the ground (range), its maximum height, and the length of time it is in the air in each trial. What relationships do you observe? Explain in terms of physical principles if you can. For each trial calculate the average horizontal speed (distance traveled across the ground ÷ time).

How does the average horizontal speed compare with the total distance travelled? How do you explain this? What are the effects of air friction? If you could reduce the effects of air friction, how would you expect your results to change . . . ?

What is the angle of launch that results in maximum distance travelled across the ground?

Explain your findings in terms of physical principles, if you can. Can you predict the range if given the angle of launch of the water rocket? Can you predict the range for different quantities of charge?

- -

Conduct a contest with your classmates to see which person or team can come closest to hitting a distant target with a water rocket.

- -

A toy water rocket is not designed for precision flying or for perfect stability and control in flight.

Prepare some design recommendations for a manufacturer of projectiles that would result in a better product.

Is momentum conserved during all or part of the flight of the rocket? Is energy conserved? Explain. . . .

- -

Extensions

This kind of inquiry can be run on different kinds of projectiles. Rockets with motors (like these manufactured by Estes Industries*) are excellent study resources, but proper SAFETY PRECAUTIONS MUST be observed.

Comments

Altitude/height measuring devices are available in some laboratories, but they can also be manufactured locally by students.

Safety Precautions

Water rockets must *NOT* be pointed at any person or breakable object. Pursuing the inquiries outdoors is recommended.

References

Estes Industries, Box 227, Penrose, Colorado, 81240; various publications and rocketry materials.
Intermediate Science Curriculum Study, *What's Up?, Probing the Natural World/Level III*, 1972. Silver Burdett, Morristown, N.J., pp. 1–26.

11. Swinging Pendulums

Science Topic   The pendulum, conservation of energy; simple harmonic motion

Level   C:2–3   E:2–3   D:2–3   L:2–4

Overview

In this activity students examine the effects of variables on the swinging of a pendulum. It provides numerous opportunities to design and perform experiments using relatively simple materials.

Materials

Strings
Hooks or nails or masking tape
Bobs of various sizes, colors, shapes, weights
Timing device ($\pm$ 1 second) — watch or stopwatch

Suggested Activities

Pendulums of various kinds have been very useful to people over the years. Since the time necessary for them to complete one oscillation is rather constant, they have been used in governing devices that keep time. Also, pendulums have been used as a source of information providing Galileo and others with insights about matter and motion.

[An interesting way to initiate this inquiry is to have a student volunteer pull a large, massive pendulum bob suspended from the ceiling up to his or her chin before releasing it. Prior to releasing the bob, the student may be asked to predict to what position the pendulum bob will return after it is released and goes through one complete cycle. The student may test this prediction by standing in the same position from which the bob was released. Since there is relatively little friction in one swing, the bob will return to a point very close to the student's chin probably causing the student to flinch or to move back. Possible relationships and questions to be investigated can then be discussed. This same motivating "demonstration" can be conducted at the conclusion of investigative inquiry. Students can predict on the basis of their inquiry and then test the prediction with the massive pendulum bob.]

The time necessary for a pendulum to complete one oscillation is called its period (T). Pendulums can have different periods and in this inquiry we shall examine what variables influence or determine the period of a pendulum.

Examine the swinging of pendulums under different conditions. What are some of the ways in which simple pendulums may differ from one another? Length, material, color of string, method of attachment of string to ceiling, volume, shape, color, material of the bob, amplitude (at start), room temperature, fluid medium in which the pendulum swings, . . . What are the effects of these variables on the period of the pendulum? (To properly answer this question an experiment must be run in which variables are carefully controlled to enable only one to be varied and examined while all others are held constant. What are the effects of the variables you have outlined regarding pendulum characteristics? Select one of these variables for study. How do you think this variable will effect the period? Make a prediction and explain the rationale for your prediction. Design an experiment to test your prediction. How will you ensure accuracy in your measurements? Conduct your experiment and record your observations. What do you observe? Were your predictions correct? Explain. List factors that could have influenced the accuracy of your experiment. If you were to do the experiment another time, how could you increase the accuracy of your measurements? What effects, if any, would a magnetic field have on an iron pendulum bob swinging through it? On a magnetized bob? On a wooden bob? Explain. Test your prediction.

If you have been able to observe effects of one or more variables on the period of the pendulum, can you identify the mathematical relationship? Plot a graph of period versus the variable you have been changing. What mathematical relationship do you observe? If you suspect that there may be an exponential relationship, try plotting your variables on log-log graph paper (see special graphing technique X1).

How do your findings compare with those reported in physics books? Are there differences? If so, are these differences due to errors in data gathering techniques, or do the simple formulas in the physics books not account for some of the variables you have examined? For example, are mass, shape of the bob, and amplitude always irrelevant in determining the period of a simple pendulum as is implied in the textbooks?

Describe the force and motion relationships in the pendulum. Describe the velocity of the bob as it swings. Where is the velocity maximum? minimum? Describe the acceleration of the pendulum bob. What is the driving force that causes acceleration? Describe the forces on the pendulum bob. How is it that the books can say that mass "has no effect"?

Describe the energy exchanges that take place while the pendulum swings. Is there an exchange between potential and kinetic energy? How can it be explained? Does the pendulum stop swinging eventually? Would it do so in "force-free" space? Would it do so in an orbiting satellite? Explain.

Examine some commercial pendulum mechanisms. How are they used? How are they constructed? How do their properties compare with those of the pendulums you have been investigating?

Comments

This is an excellent activity to help students develop skill in designing experiments, controlling variables, and recognizing limits to the validity of simple generalizations that are useful and often found in introductory physics texts. The design of the experiment and the variables can be discussed with a class and then groups of students can examine the effects of different variables. Students may work in small groups and then share their findings with the large group in post-lab discussion.

Usually the pendulum experiment is conducted to verify the relationship: $T = 2\pi \sqrt{\ell/g}$; only the length of the pendulum string and the period are measured. However, the pendulum experiment can be used as an attractive exercise in which students can design experiments, control variables and develop a mathematical relationship prior to formal introduction of that relationship.

This kind of laboratory investigation will indicate that in the real world of experimental results, data do *not* always follow the simple relationships or algorithms outlined in introductory physics textbooks. For example, the kind of bearing on which the pendulum hangs and the amplitude can be found to influence the period of the pendulum. This inquiry provides an excellent opportunity to discuss the nature and value of simple algorithms in understanding the nature and the limits of such generalizations.

Reference

Williams, J. E., et al.: *Modern Physics,* 1980. Holt, Rinehart, and Winston, New York, pp. 106–107.

12. A Vibrating Spring

Science Topic   Simple Harmonic Motion, Energy Conservation, Elasticity, Potential energy, Kinetic energy

Level   C:2–4   E:2–4   D:2–4   L:2–4

Overview

A mass attached to a spring hanging vertically will oscillate in simple harmonic motion when it is displaced from its rest position and released. Inquiry into the motion can examine many characteristics of springs, simple harmonic motion, and energy exchanges (potential: gravitational and winding of spring;

kinetic: vertical and rotational motion). Inquiry can be conducted at a variety of levels of mathematical sophistication, conceptual, and logical development.

Materials

    Spring and support
    Weight set
    Metric ruler
    Timer

Suggested Activities

Suspend the spring vertically and hang a weight from it. Displace the lower end of the spring vertically and release it. Describe the motion that results.

You can acquire a more visible record of the motion by attaching a felt-tip pen to the lower end of the spring and by pulling a sheet of paper (mounted on a board) past the pen at a steady speed.

Is the "frequency" or the "period" of vibration constant? If so, how can these be changed? Does the period depend upon the "amplitude" of vibration or upon the size of the suspended mass?

Try graphing the period (T) versus the amplitude. Try graphing the period versus the mass of the suspended mass.

Can you identify mathematical relationships among these variables in terms of a formula? (See Special Resources *X1.*)

Can you find a mathematical relationship that includes the "spring constant" for this spring?

[The spring constant is "K" in the formula $F = -K \cdot \triangle \ell$ where F is the applied force and $\triangle \ell$ is the extension. See Activity *E1* .]

- -

Describe the velocity of the suspended mass during vibration. Where is the velocity of the suspended mass 0? Where is the velocity greatest?

How could you measure the maximum velocity of the suspended mass if you wanted to do so?

Describe the acceleration of the suspended mass. Is the acceleration constant or does it change?

If there is an acceleration, we know there must be an unbalanced "driving force". Describe the driving force.

Explain what causes the driving force.

- -

Describe the energy exchanges in the spring/mass system.

Where is the potential energy of the system greatest? Describe the forms of potential energy at that point.

Where is the kinetic energy of the system greatest?

Is energy conserved in the spring-mass system? Explain.

What are the effects, if any, of friction? Can they be observed in your system?

Predict how the gravitational energy lost by the falling mass will compare with the energy stored in the extended spring at the lowest point in the vibration.

Calculate the gravitational potential energy lost during the fall of the mass in one vibration.

Calculate the energy stored in the extended spring during the fall of the mass in one vibration.

How do your calculated energy values compare with your prediction? Explain why there are differences, if any.

Describe the several kinds of energy present when the mass is midway in its descent.

Calculate the quantity of each kind of energy and compare with the total energy at the top and bottom of each vibration. Explain relationships and hypothesize why there are differences, if any, from your predictions.

- -

Stop the spring from vibrating vertically and rotate the suspended mass so that it rotates when you let go.

Describe the rotational oscillations as precisely as possible examining the motion and the relationships as you have done earlier in this inquiry for vertical motion.

How is the rotational period/frequency related to the vertical frequency—if it is related?

- -

How is the rotational frequency of the spring-mass system related to the shape of the mass attached as weight?

Arrange several similarly weighted discs of different diameter and attach them to the mass successively to study the effects of shape and/or air resistance.

Repeat the inquiry with one or more of the discs rotating in water or other fluids. How does this affect the rotation?

- -

Pull the suspended mass aside and let the spring-mass system swing like a pendulum. Describe the motion that results. If you select the right combination of spring and mass, you can set up a very interesting exchange between pendulum-like swinging and vertical oscillation.

Can you predict how to select the right mass for a spring to maximize the exchange?

When these two kinds of motions are present, how do the frequencies in each mode compare?

Create some hypotheses that explain what you observe.

Comments

Energy stored in extended spring = applied force × distance moved.

$$E = F \times \Delta \ell$$

$$E = (k \times \frac{\Delta \ell)}{2} \times \Delta \ell$$

$$E = \frac{1}{2} k (\Delta \ell)^2$$

For a simple elastic spring with mass attached:

$$T \propto \sqrt{m}$$

References

Bolton, W.: *Physics Experiments and Projects, Volume 1, 1968.* Pergamon Press, New York, pp. 48, 49, 54, and 55.

Dillon, T. J. and Smith, M. K.: *Laboratory Manual, Concepts in Physics,* 1980. Harcourt, Brace and Jovanovich, New York, pp. 29–31.

Physical Science Study Committee: *Physics Laboratory Guide,* 1971. D.C. Heath, Lexington, MA., pp. 60–61.

13. Sliders and Rollers

Science Topic   Rotational Inertia, Angular Momentum

Level   C:2–4   E:2–3   D:2–3   L:2–4

Overview

This activity can be used with older students to introduce the formal study of rotational inertia and angular momentum. In an introductory course that does not include these topics, it can be used following the study of linear motion and free fall to show some new dimensions of motion and some new variables that have not yet been examined thoroughly. Students who have studied and understood free fall and Newton's Laws of Motion will normally predict that acceleration and final velocity will be independent of mass and variables other than friction. Thus a demonstration of this system will provide some surprises when objects of equal mass have noticeably different accelerations. This activity can be used for these students as an excellent relevant example of the importance of the experimental as well as the theoretical study of scientific relationships.

The activity can be used with younger students to examine the properties of objects that affect speed as they slide or roll down an incline. It provides a good opportunity for such students to control variables and to gather and interpret mathematical data. Instead of measuring velocity or acceleration, they can measure the time it takes for each object to fall a specific distance. . . .

Materials

Inclined track—(smooth piece of Masonite or other board preferably just over a meter in length)
Spheres, cylinders, hoops, blocks of assorted sizes and masses [Some of the spheres, cylinders, hoops, and blocks should have identical weight; some of them should have identical size]
Meterstick
Stopwatch (optional)

Suggested Activities

Does the final speed of an object sliding or rolling down an incline depend on the object's mass or shape? Predict which of these objects will slide or roll most quickly to the bottom of the incline. . . . Or will they all have identical accelerations and final speeds? Explain your predictions. . . .

[Doing this activity quickly leads to the recognition that the objects have markedly different accelerations and final speed.] What particular variables may have an affect on the final speed? Mass? Shape? Friction? Size? . . .

Design an experiment that examines the effects of these variables on speed. . . . Discuss experimental design with others to increase the likelihood that error will be minimal. Control variables by varying mass and keeping all other variables constant. . . . Then vary size and keep all other variables constant. . . .

If a hoop or cylinder slides down the incline on its face instead of rolling—how is the final speed affected?

What general relationships can you observe from analyzing your data? Do small rings roll faster than larger ones?

Discuss some possible explanations of these relationships.

Predict what will happen if you push these objects with equal speeds and let them roll or slide up the incline. Explain.

Test your predictions. . . .

Discuss the sliding and rolling objects in your inquiry in terms of the momentum and the energy that is present.

Does a rolling hoop have the same kinetic energy as one that is sliding on its side at the same speed? How can you test your prediction?

Reference

Williams, J. E., et al.: *Modern Physics,* 1980. Holt, Rinehart, and Winston, New York, pp. 47–51, 71–72, and 98–102.

14. Silly Silo

Science Topic   Circular motion, Centripetal force, Satellite motion

Level   C:3   E:2–4   D:2–4   L:2–4

Overview

Initial sections of this activity introduce the study of circular motion. Students empirically examine the relationship between centripetal force and satellite mass, frequency-velocity, and orbital radius.

Materials

Spring Scale
Rubber Stoppers or Wooden Spools
Meterstick
String
Short Glass, Metal, or Plastic Tube
Timing Device

Suggested Activities

A number of today's amusement parks have rides that spin people at high speed and then "hang" them above the ground without normal support. These rides have names like: "Silly Silo, Round-up, Rotor, and Cork-screw". What scientific principles can be used to explain how these rides work? How fast does the device have to spin to keep a person from falling?

Understanding the physics of circular motion can help in understanding and designing these amusement park rides. (Such understanding also helps engineers who do the important work of placing satellites in orbit above the earth).

To study circular motion set up a simulation of the "Silly Silo" or of a satellite by attaching a rubber stopper to the end of a string that passes freely through a tube and is attached to a weight on the other end (use more stoppers for the weight)—as shown in the diagram. Hold the tube in one hand and

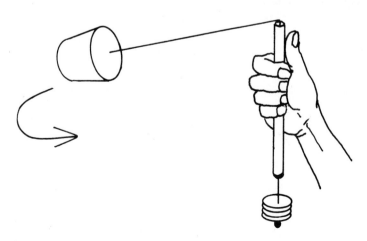

use it to twirl the stopper (satellite) around your head. Describe the motion you observe and the relationships that exist. What variables affect the motion of the satellite?

How can this apparatus be improved to get more quantitative information and to control these variables more easily? [Among other things, a spring balance can be substituted for the hanging weight, the number of satellite stoppers can be changed to vary satellite mass, and the radius of the orbit can be controlled and changed in discrete amounts by placing a marker (light alligator clips) on the string.]

Study the effects of specific variables such as satellite mass and orbital radius, and velocity on centripetal force [the force required to pull the inertial mass of the satellite out of a straight line path.]

To gather this information efficiently you may well want to assign responsibilities for different portions of this task among other students in your investigating team. What is the best way to make such assignments? In the process, how can the probability of sizeable experimental error be reduced? How many trials should be run for each variable?

What do graphs of centripetal force vs the other variables you have examined look like? What general relationships do you observe? Can you convert these relationships into a general mathematical formula?

This activity can be conducted with more sophisticated apparatus to reduce the probability of experimental error and to increase accuracy. Devices from your home or lab such as phonographs or air tables are among the resources you can use to design such apparatus.

- -

Using the mathematical formula developed that relates centripetal force to the other important variables in circular motion, predict the minimum speed "Silly Silo" or another amusement park ride will have to reach to keep from spilling out its human riders.

What is the effect of the weight of a particular person? Does a heavy person have to be spun more rapidly than a lighter person or are the effects of a person's weight or mass irrelevant to the determination of the minimum speed needed?

Go to an amusement park and check out your predictions—if you are able to do so.

How would your results differ if the amusement park were on the moon?

As an alternative, another interesting way to test your understanding and predictions about circular motion is for you to swing a bucket of water in a vertical circle. Can you do this without getting wet? Make a mathematical prediction about this and test it!

Apply your techniques to a toy car or an airplane about to do a loop-the-loop.

Comments

Prediction of minimum speed needed to swing a bucket of water overhead.

$$F \text{ centripetal} = m \frac{v^2}{R}$$

Weight of water bucket must be less than or equal to centripetal force needed to pull water and bucket out of straight line path.

$$\text{Weight} \leq m \frac{v^2}{R}$$

$$mg \leq m \frac{v^2}{R}$$

$$g \leq \frac{v^2}{R}$$

$$v^2 \geq gR$$

$$v \geq \sqrt{gR}$$

$$v \geq \sqrt{32.2\frac{ft}{sec^2} \times \sim 2.0 \text{ ft}}$$

$$v \geq \sqrt{\sim 64.4 \frac{ft}{sec^2}}$$

$$v \geq \sim 8\frac{ft}{sec}$$

[The minimum speed is independent of the mass or amount of water in the bucket, but is related to the radius of the circle or the length of rope used.]

References

Haber-Schaim, et al.: *PSSC Physics,* 1971. D.C. Heath, Lexington, MA, pp. 44–45.

Haber-Schaim, et al.: *PSSC Physics Laboratory Guide,* 1971. D.C. Heath, Lexington, MA, pp. 252–257.

15. Baseballs, Hula-Hoops, and Yo-Yos

Science Topic   Mechanics [all topics]

Level   C:1–4   E:1–4   D:1–4   L:1–4

Overview

Individual students select a familiar mechanical device or activity related to mechanics, analyze physical principles that underlie its use and answer interesting questions about its behavior. Inquiry should include the gathering of empirical data from experimentation with the device or activity, but it need not be limited to that. Students should be encouraged to review literature references that comment on the scientific concepts that are embodied in the device or activity.

Materials

A vast array of devices may be examined, but students will generally supply their own.

Items of laboratory equipment available in the lab may be used by students to pursue specific aspects of their inquiries.

Access to library references and journals can be an important part of this inquiry for some students.

Suggested Activities

In this activity you are to select an activity or a device related to mechanics that is of real interest to you. You will answer questions about its behavior and analyze physical principles that underlie its use. It might be efficient to select a device or activity with which you are already familiar, but that is *not* essential. Your inquiry may include a review of relevant scientific and technical literature that you can acquire, but if possible it should also include a study of some empirical data you have gathered while working with the device or activity.

As you look around the world in which you live there are many things you do and devices you use that function on a basis of scientific principles. Look around, be creative, and select a question to investigate that will give you new insights into something you do or use and the science on which it is based. Listed below are only a few of the many activities and devices that can be used in pursuing your inquiry.

Baseball—
  Catching ⎫
  Pitching ⎬
  Batting ⎭

Examine and describe energy exchanges and different techniques in those exchanges—such as running and moving the glove in catching; using different timing, weights of wood, swings in batting; effects of pitching techniques, spin, etc. . . .

Other sports activities—bouncing basketballs, super-balls, ping-pong, ice skating, hockey, golf, skiing, karate, judo, billiards, pool . . . track and field events, . . . jumping, . . . kicking a soccer ball, . . . football. . . .

Bicycle riding—
  Braking ⎫
  Stability ⎪
  Turning ⎬
  Acceleration ⎪
  Energy ⎪
    Consumption ⎭

Examine and describe the effects of different techniques and bicycle design on one or more of these problems. What design and speed combinations are optimal for long distance or for sprint racing. . . ? What are minimum stopping distances at different speeds? What are the force, speed, work ratios in different gear combinations? . . . Effects of tire balance/unbalance . . . air pressure. . . .

Other modes of transportation—boats, automobiles, . . .

Mechanical Appliances: pencil sharpeners, egg beaters, can openers, automobile jack, screw drivers, wrenches, hammers . . . (for what tasks is a heavy hammer best? . . . for what tasks is a light hammer best . . . ?) toilet paper dispensers, door knobs . . . nut crackers, . . .

Leisure time activities: Hula hoop, mechanical toys, skipping rocks, flying model planes, boomerangs, frisbees, yo-yos (describe/ measure-motion/energy exchanges . . . if yo-yo string is released when the yo-yo starts back up—what motion results).

To begin your inquiry you should formulate a question of interest about your device or activity and then design a scientific method to gather relevant data. You will subsequently analyze your data in an effort to answer your question. Or—instead, use your device or activity to provide evidence of a scientific principle or law that underlies its use. Your objectives, probable activities, material needs, method of reporting and target dates for this activity should be outlined as early as possible to facilitate effective planning.

- -

Were you able to answer the question you initially intended to examine?

How are your results consistent with and how do they differ from scientific principles—as you understand them. . . ?

How could you get more accurate and better data—if you had more time and resources?

What new questions and hypotheses has your inquiry suggested?

Based on your study can you formulate some recommendations for the design and use of your device or activity?

Comments

This activity is best run as an extended project with outside-of-class activity. Students will work individually or in small groups on different devices or activities of their own choosing. To facilitate teacher input and monitoring, it is recommended that student be required to prepare and subsequently update contracts for the inquiry they plan to conduct. Teachers are encouraged to solicit the support of persons with relevant technical expertise to supervise projects for a small number of students.

References

General:

How Things Work, 1967. Simon and Schuster, New York.

Walker, Jearl: *The Flying Circus of Physics,* 1977, John Wiley and Sons, New York.

Samples of many specific references are:

Bayes, J. H. and Scott, W. T., Billiard-ball collision experiment, *American Journal of Physics,* 197, 1963, p. 31.

Chapman, S., Catching a baseball, *American Journal of Physics,* 868, 1968, p. 36.

Gordon, J. M., Pedaling made perfect, *Engineering,* 526, 1971, p. 211.

Harter, W. G. (Class of), Velocity amplification in collision experiments involving superballs, *American Journal of Physics,* 656, 1971, p. 39.

Jones, D. E. H., The stability of the bicycle, *Physics Today,* 34, 1970, p. 23.

Kirkpatrick, P., Batting the ball, *American Journal of Physics,* 606, 1963, p. 31.

Wilson, S. S., Bicycle technology, *Science American,* 81, 1973, p. 228.

C Electricity

1. Sparks in the Night

Science Topic   Static Electricity

Level   C:1–3   E:1–4   D:1–3   L:2–4

Overview

The introduction to electricity and electro-statics provides a number of good opportunities for inquiry. Students can observe and grapple with the nature of electric charges before being formally introduced to them through readings or presentations in class. The activity described here should be used before formal introduction of the terms "positive" and "negative" to describe the two kinds of electric charge.

Materials

Vinyl and acetate plastic strips
Transparent tape
Wool and cotton cloth
Pith balls or small plastic spheres
Electroscope (optional)

Suggested Activities

When two objects rub together electrical effects can often be noticed. Under certain conditions when you walk across a rug and touch a doorknob you receive a noticeable shock. When you slide across the seat of an automobile and reach for the doorhandle, a shock is often the reward! Under certain circumstances when a cloud slides through the sky it becomes electrified and a big electrical spark (lightning) results. When you slide a comb through your hair, sometimes your hair seems to be attracted to the comb after you pull it away. In the dark of night, sparks can sometimes be seen jumping from bedroom blankets. How can these kinds of observations be explained? What is the nature of electrical charge?

Carefully observe the conditions under which charges develop (such as when combing your hair). What factors promote such "charging"? What can be done to reduce or eliminate the build-up of charge? What are the effects of moisture?

If we rub a clean plastic comb with a piece of cloth we often find that we can charge the comb sufficiently so that it will pick up tiny pieces of paper that may be nearby. Can you think of other ways you could try to charge the comb? Stick a piece of transparent tape across the entire length of a clean comb and then pull it off. Is this a way to charge the comb? If you can, charge the comb in this way, check to see if the tape has also acquired an electric charge sufficient to pick up the little pieces of paper (on the non-sticky side).

Over the years it has been observed that many common materials like glass acquire an electric charge when they are rubbed. You can examine the behavior of electric charges by briskly rubbing plastic strips that are easily charged with cloth (or in other ways such as the "stick tape method"). Hang a strip of vinyl and a strip of acetate by suspending them with masking tape from the side of a crossbar or table or doorframe . . . so they can swing freely. Charge them and then observe how they behave in the presence of other charged materials or strips you bring near them. Describe your observations. What conditions result in attraction between the object you bring near the hanging strip? What kinds of conditions result in repulsion? Investigate these materials and conditions to see if you can observe any patterns in the behavior of attraction and repulsion. What are these patterns? How can they be explained? How many kinds of charge have you been able to observe?

Charge one of the hanging strips by peeling a long strip of transparent tape from it. After you have done this check to see if there is any noticeable evidence of attraction or repulsion between the tape and the charged strip. Hang the transparent tape you have used and charge another tape in the same manner. Check to see if there is any evidence of attraction or repulsion between the two tapes. What do you observe? How can you explain your observations?

Hang a pith ball with a nylon thread from a ring stand or other support. Hang a second pith ball similarly from another support. Charge each of these balls by contact with a charged plastic strip. Bring the two balls near each other and observe what happens. Investigate how these pith balls behave under the influence of different charges.

How can a pith ball be discharged? Make some predictions and test them. Discharge one pitch ball and bring it in contact with the charged ball. What do you observe? How can your observations be explained? Are your explanations consistent with the explanations developed earlier? Describe experiments that will validate your explanations.

Use an electroscope to test for the presence of charge. Is the electroscope more effective than the pith ball you used? Explain. Use the electroscope to further explore the nature of charged objects. Will some objects charge or discharge an electroscope more readily than others? What kind of characteristics do these objects have in common?

Some observers have claimed that a large portion of falling snowflakes or raindrops are electrically charged. Study these charges and the conditions under which they occur. Can you observe any regularities? What factors (cloud type, height, temperature, raindrop size, . . .) affect the amount of charge? What hypotheses can you develop to explain your observations?

- -

Large numbers of investigations of the kind you have been conducting seem to result in identification of only two kinds of electric charge. These two kinds of charge were named positive and negative many years ago. Based on your observations, explain how objects that are positively and negatively charged attract and repel one another. Can charge somehow be "induced" in an electrically neutral doorknob or piece of paper? How can you explain the attraction you have observed between a charged object and an uncharged object?

Going back to examples at the beginning of this inquiry, can you now explain all your observations in terms of the two charge electrical model? When you walk across a rug and touch a doorhandle, how is it that a spark will sometimes occur between your hand and the door knob? Create hypotheses to explain this phenomenon. (You will almost certainly want to modify these hypotheses as you will learn more about electric charges and the flow of charge during your study of electricity.) What can you do to reduce the probability of getting a "shock"?

Now that you have a model for describing electric charge, can you hypothesize other ways that objects might be charged? If your goal is to rub off or to kick off elementary charges, might this be done with forms of energy other than the rubbing that was used here?

It has been obvious that a force exists between charged objects such as the pith balls you have been using. How can this force be described? How is it related to the amount of charge on the spheres? How is it related to the distance between the spheres? An examination of the electrical forces between charged particles reveals some very interesting relationships and is a worthwhile inquiry to pursue. Procedure suggestions for this inquiry are included in the *PSSC* and *Project Physics Handbook* references.

Comments

Dampness and atmospheric conditions can make a great difference in the ease with which experiments with static charges can be performed. Also, if the objects being used are dirty or greasy, charge will lead off rapidly and vivid effects will not be visible. Thus, it is important to use clean materials and to avoid excessive handling with greasy fingers. The plastic strips commonly used in these experiments can be cleaned by washing them with soap and water and then by letting them air dry thoroughly.

The last set of questions in the activity raise the question of examining how the force of electric attraction or repulsion between charged objects is related to the magnitude of the charge and the separation between the charges. Good inquiry oriented labs are included in the references for this section. These labs can be used *prior* to formal presentation of Coulomb's Law; from the data students can observe the inverse-square relationship between separation and forces. (Coulomb's Law inquiry provides another opportunity for students to use the logarithmic method of analysis of relationships outlined in Section X1; that technique is not referenced in most laboratory handbooks on this topic.)

References

Haber-Schaim, U., et al., *PSSC Physics Laboratory Guide,* 3rd edition, 1971, D.C. Heath and Co., pp. 64–69.

Modern Learning Aids, PSSC films—Coulomb's Law (# 0403) and Coulomb Force Constant (# 0405).

Rutherford, F. J., et al., *The Project Physics Course Handbook,* Holt, Rinehart, and Winston, 1970, pp. 242–246.

2. Metallic Conductors and Semi-Conductors

Science Topic   Resistance, Resistivity, Ohm's Law, Semiconductor/Diode

Level   C:1–4   E:1–4   D:1–3   L:2–4

Overview

In this activity students examine variables affecting the resistance of various metallic wires. Tasks can be shared and groups of students can concentrate on the effects of different variables. The activity can be conducted at various levels of sophistication and precision by students at different levels of development. Because of the length of this activity, students may return to it to pursue different phases at different times during the course of study.

Materials

A. Flashlight bulb and socket, 1.5 v cell(s), wire-spring, connecting wires, alligator clips (optional), diffraction grating (optional), assorted wires of different length and material (optional)
B. Voltmeter and ammeter OR Wheatstone bridge and galvanometer, wire or coils, of various length, gauge (diameter), and material such as copper and nichrome, 6v power supply, and connecting wires
C. Same as B above with ammeters of several ranges or Wheatstone bridge; resistance elements that can be immersed, thermistor ($\sim$ 100 Ω), beaker, bunsen burner with gauze, tripod, thermometer ($-10°C$ to $100°C$)
D. Voltmeter and ammeter OR Wheatstone bridge and galvanometer, commercial resistor, flashlight bulb, diode

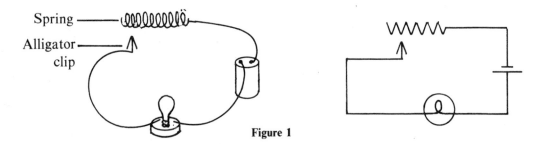

Spring

Alligator clip

Figure 1

Suggested Activities

Work has to be done to push water through a narrow pipe for the pipe offers "resistance" to the flow of water. Similarly, work has to be done to push electric charge through a wire or other conductor for it offers "resistance" to the flow of charge. A study of the resistance of an electrical conductor under various conditions provides information from which scientists can make inferences about the structure of the conducting material. Metallic conductors also enable engineers to design electric motors, radios, and many other useful devices. In this inquiry we will examine some of the characteristics of metallic conductors. Make some predictions about the characteristics or properties of a conductor that probably affect its electrical conductivity or resistance.

A. *Qualitative Inquiry*

When a bulb, cell(s) and wire spring are connected as in Figure 1, you can vary the length of the wire spring through which electrons must travel to complete the electric circuit. When the moveable alligator clip touches the conducting wire attached to the spring, the bulb should glow brightly. Then, slide the moveable wire down the spring and describe what happens to the intensity of the bulb.

Repeat the procedure, this time in a darkened area of the room and observe the spectrum of the glowing bulb through a diffraction grating. Describe the changes you observe, if any, in the intensity of the colors in the spectrum.

Substitute wires and coils having different lengths and made of different materials for your spring and study the effects of these changes on the flow of electric charge by observing the bulb and its spectrum. (You may wish to lay out lengths of different kinds of uncoated wire on a large box for further inquiry as in Figure 2).

What do you observe? Be as explicit and complete as you can.

From these descriptive observations what relationships may exist among the variables you have begun to examine?

What factors seem to affect the resistance of wire conductors?

What factors have we not examined?

What new questions have these observations raised for you?

Design some experiments that might answer some of these questions.

When looking through the diffraction grating at the glowing bulb were you able to associate color intensity with the temperature of the wire and/or with the amount of charge flowing through the wire in a period of time (current)? If so what relationships may exist?

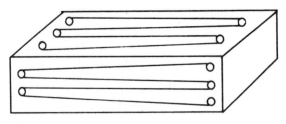

Figure 2

Would a spring like the one you have used in this inquiry be good for the commercial production of light dimming switches. If you were asked to design a light dimmer, what special concerns would you have?

B. *Effects of Length, Cross-sectional Area and Material*

Inquiry into effects of length, cross-sectional area, material, temperature and other variables on the resistance of a conductor can be examined with greater precision if the resistance is determined from measurements of current (I) passing through the conductor and the voltage (v) across it ($R = \frac{v}{I}$, Ohm's Law) as shown in Figure 3 or from use of a more accurate Wheatstone bridge arrangement.

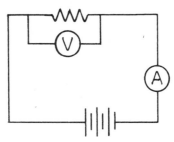

Figure 3

Being careful to control all other variables, study the effects of the variable you want to examine on electrical resistance by measuring the resistance of wire under several varying conditions. Constructing a box like the one pictured in Figure 2 will once again be helpful in examining the effects of length, cross-sectional area, and material on resistance. [Inquiry into the effects of temperature upon resistance is discussed in Section C below, and Section D presents information on inquiry into current-voltage (I-V) characteristics.]

Gather data as precisely as you can with several data points for each variable you are examining. Graph the data of resistance (in Ohms) vs. each variable you have examined (for example, resistance vs. cross-sectional area, holding other variables constant).

What relationships do the graphs show? Can you prepare a mathematical formula that relates resistance to length and cross-sectional area for the materials you have studied? How can the differences between materials be incorporated within your formula?

What are the effects of combining individual resistances in "series"? In "parallel"?

C. *Effects of Temperature*

Acquire resistance elements and a thermistor that can be immersed in distilled water. Set up a distilled water bath and vary the temperature between 20°–100°C. Determine the resistance of each of the elements over the range of temperatures. (There will probably be a wide range of currents).

Plot graphs of the Resistance vs. Temperature curves for each of the materials you have examined with a specific applied voltage.

What relationships are there?

The thermistor is a "semiconductor". Do you notice any special characteristics in the graph of R vs. T for this material?

Heat effects are normally quite significant in electrical resistance and can also be observed in the resistance of a light bulb under different voltage-current conditions (Section D below).

In terms of the structure of the materials you have been studying, prepare some hypotheses that may explain your results.

Predict what will happen at a lower temperature (such as in a solution of salt water with ice . . .). Test your predictions.

To extend your study, you may wish to investigate the resistance of the thermistor over a much wider range of temperatures using proper precautions and under the supervision of your teacher. Acquire a thermistor with much high resistance ($\sim 100\text{k}\,\Omega$ at $25°\text{C}$) and investigate its characteristics. Calibrate your thermistor and compare it with the calibration curve of the manufacturer. . . . Use it to investigate high temperature solutions like molten solder. . . .

D. *Effects of Applied Voltage*

In order to design electronic circuits to perform specialized tasks effectively, engineers must know the characteristics of commercially available circuit elements. One of the most important of these characteristics is the current the element will conduct under different applied voltages.

Using a circuit like that in Figure 2 or using a Wheatstone bridge to measure resistance, plot a current-voltage (I-V) curve for a commercial resistor, a flashlight bulb, and a diode. Make at least 7 measurements of current-voltage from a small fraction of a volt through 6 volts or more.

What kinds of relationship between current and voltage have you observed for each of the three elements? How can these relationships be explained? Is the brightness or color of the bulb related to its resistance? If so, how?

Plot a current-voltage curve for the diode after reversing its direction in the circuit. What similarities and differences do you observe with the first curve? Do the resistor and/or light bulb exhibit this kind of directional behavior? Can you propose an explanation for the behavior in terms of the structure of the diode-semi-conductor material?

You may wish to extend your study to examine current-voltage curves for other circuit elements. Compare your findings with those in a handbook.

Safety Precautions

If the characteristics of a thermistor are examined at extreme temperature ranges there is danger of serious burns. Thus extreme temperatures should be used only with great care and under the teacher's supervision.

Comments

B. For ohmic resistors at constant temperature:
   Resistance is directly proportional to length and inversely proportional to cross-sectional area

$$R \propto \frac{\ell}{A}$$
$$R = \rho\frac{\ell}{A}$$

C. A temperature below that of salt water with ice can be achieved with a dry ice and alcohol solution. Great care must be used in handling this mixture which can freeze flesh quickly.

References

Dillon, J., et al.: *Laboratory Manual, Concepts in Physics,* 1980. Harcourt, Brace, and Jovanovich, New York, pp. 91–95.

Elementary Science Study, *Batteries and Bulbs,* 1968. McGraw-Hill.

Williams, J. E., et al.: *Modern Physics,* 1980. Holt, Rinehart, and Winston, New York, pp. 404–411.

3. Charges in Solutions

Science Topic   Conductivity of Solutions; Electrolysis; Electrolytes

Level   C:2–4   E:2–4   D:2–3   L:2–4

Overview

In this activity variables affecting the conductivity/resistance of solutions are examined. Tasks can be shared and different groups of students can concentrate upon the effects of different substances or variables. The activity can be conducted at different levels of sophistication and precision as represented in this outline. Section A is a more qualitative inquiry appropriate for younger students and for those without great mathematical skill. Sections B and C present ideas for more quantitative inquiry.

Materials

A. flashlight bulb and socket
   10 1.5v cells
   beaker
   connecting wires

   salt   soap . . .
   sugar
   alcohol
   vinegar

B. 2 platinum electrodes
   distilled water
   beaker
   12v d. c. supply
   ammeter (0–2 A)
   voltmeter (0–5 v)

   milliammeter (optional)
   sodium chloride
   acetic acid
   copper sulfate
   zinc sulfate (optional)

C. Wheatstone bridge and
   galvanometer
        or
   ohmmeter or voltmeter and ammeter
   power supply
   thermometer or thermocouple
   (0–650°C)
   2 platinum electrodes

   crucible
   bunsen burner
   tripod
   sodium chloride

Suggested Activities

A study of the resistance or conductivity of a solution under various conditions provides information from which scientists can make inferences about the structure of that solution and many such solutions are present in modern electrical devices. In this inquiry we will examine some of the electrical properties of solutions.

Does tap water conduct electricity? Make some predictions about the electrical conductivity of water and other solutions and about what variables might affect that conductivity.

A. *Qualitative Inquiry*

When a bulb and flashlight cell are connected as in Figure 1 examine whether or not the bulb will be lighted. Make a prediction and then test your prediction. Does the number of flashlight cells in series providing energy in the circuit make a difference? Does the distance between the electrodes in the solution have an effect? Examine the effects of increasing the number of cells in the circuit and varying the separation between the electrodes. Observe what is happening very carefully. For example, look to see if there is any visible evidence of electrical activity on the electrodes.

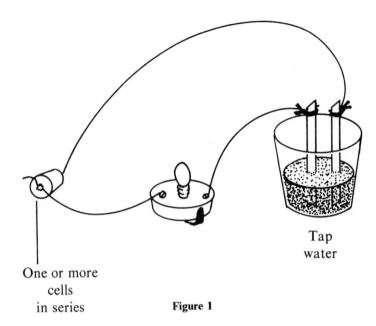

One or more
cells
in series

Tap
water

Figure 1

When different substances are dissolved in water, does the conductivity of the water change? Experiment with a variety of such substances (solutes). Use common household materials such as salt, sugar, alcohol, vinegar, soap, ... Does the amount of dissolved solute make a difference in the number of cells that are needed for the light bulb to glow? Does the kind of dissolved solute make a difference? What evidence of chemical and physical activity can be observed in the system (in addition to the glowing light bulb)? What are your observations? Explain your observations. Obviously, electrical charge is moving through the solution when the light bulb is on; how can this movement be explained? Create some hypotheses to explain this phenomenon; then design tests for your hypotheses.

B. *Quantitative Study of Conductivity and Electrolysis*

Does water conduct electric charge? Place two electrodes in beaker and connect through an ammeter to a dc supply as in Figure 2. The electrodes should be kept a fixed distance apart during this portion of the investigation in order not to introduce a new variable at this time. What is the current when there is no liquid in the beaker? Does the system conduct charge when distilled water is present in the beaker? Is there any evidence of reaction in the water or on the electrodes?

Examine the effects on charge flow of adding substances to the distilled water. Place, for example, some copper sulfate in the beaker. What happens to the flow of charge? What happens at the electrodes after a few minutes? Describe your observations carefully. How can these observations be explained?

In a metallic conductor the flow of charge is considered to be due to the movement of electrons. On the basis of your observations, hypothesize what is moving between the two electrodes in the solution enabling a current to flow in the external circuit. Design a test to examine the validity of your explanation.

What are the effects of voltage on the amount of charge flowing through the solution with a given solute? It might be interesting and useful to try to plot voltage vs. current curves for a particular solute. For a particular solute, is there a particular voltage below which no current seems to flow? Make some predictions and then test those predictions. How can your observations be explained in terms of the chemistry of the solution?

What is the effect on conductivity of the presence of different solutes? What other variables will affect the amount of charge going through a solution? Will temperature make a difference? You may find it interesting to measure the resistance of a solution of sodium chloride in water, for example, under different temperature conditions. What can you infer from your measurements? Pursue this inquiry for different electrolytes.

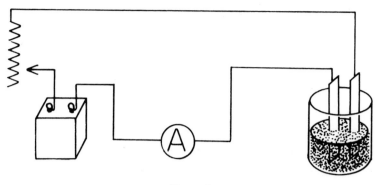

Figure 2

Note. When working with solutions and electrolytes, the term conductance is used more commonly than resistance. Conductance is the reciprocal of resistance.

Experiment with more than one substance in solution. For example, observe what happens in a solution of copper sulfate in distilled water (about .5m) when zinc sulfate is added. How does the presence of the zinc sulfate change the current-voltage graph?

To what special practical uses can your observation and inquiry be applied? Can you design an efficient way to plate copper onto an electrode? Can you apply what you have learned about electroplating to solutions containing other metals such as aluminum? What can be done to increase the quality of the bond between the electrode and the metal that you have plated out? If your findings are to be used in large scale industrial applications, what other variables would need to be considered? How could the process be made most cost and energy efficient?

C. *Effects of Temperature on the Conductivity of Sodium Chloride*

To examine the electrical conductivity of sodium chloride, place the electrodes in the crucible and pack sodium chloride tightly around and between them. (Good electrical contact is essential). Set up a Wheatstone bridge or ohmmeter in the external circuit to measure the resistance between the electrodes in the sodium chloride sample.

Measure the resistance at room temperature, then increase the temperature and observe how the resistance changes. If possible, make measurements up to the hottest temperature you can achieve with a bunsen burner (more than 600° celsius). Since there is a large temperature range in this inquiry, measurements may be taken in 50° intervals. Plot a graph of your results. What do you observe? How can these results be explained?

In inquiring about the conductivity of metals, metals are good conductors at low temperatures, and the resistance of a metal increases with increasing temperature. Apparently, there is a decrease in electron mobility with increasing temperature in metals. How do the results of inquiry into the conductivity of metals compare with your inquiry into the conductivity of sodium chloride? How can differences be explained? You may wish to examine the effects of temperature upon the conductivity of salts other than sodium chloride. How do you predict the results will differ?

Safety Precautions

In part C where the conductivity of sodium chloride is examined, there is a *DANGER OF BURNS* when making adjustments or measurements at high temperatures. Thus, caution and teacher supervision are very important.

Comments

In aqueous solutions, conduction of charge is due to the movement of ions and not "free" electrons. In metals electrical conduction occurs through the movement of "free" electrons.

References

Bolton, W.: *Physics Experiments and Projects,* Vol. 4, 1968. Pergamon Press, Inc., New York, pp. 9–16.

Haber-Schaim, U., et al.: *PSSC Physics,* 1971. D.C. Heath, Lexington, MA, pp. 409–410, 452–456.

4. Batteries, Bulbs, Motors, and Other Electrical Devices

Science Topic   Electricity, Electric Circuits

Level   C:1–4   E:1–4   D:1–4   L:2–4

Overview

During the study of electric circuits or after formal study has been completed, individual students may want to explore questions that go beyond the activities performed in class. Such inquiry can be brief or greatly extended. The activity should include the gathering of empirical data from experimentation with an electric device, but it need not be limited to that. Students should be encouraged to review literature references that comment on the scientific concepts embodied in the device. One or more portions of this activity demand caution in handling potentially dangerous electrical devices.

Materials

An array of different electrical devices may be examined; students may acquire some of these in the local community. Common items of electrical equipment in the laboratory such as meters, oscilloscope, and common circuit elements may be used by students to pursue their inquiry.

Access to library references in journals can be an important part of this inquiry for some students.

Suggested Activities

In this activity you are to select an electrical device or circuit element of real interest to you. You will answer questions about its behavior and analyze physical principles that underlie its use. Your inquiry may incorporate a review of relevant scientific and technical literature, but if possible it should include a study of some empirical data you have gathered while working with the device. There are many questions you may want to explore that go beyond the activities you have performed in the study of electricity. Be creative in selecting an activity that makes sense to you.

It is commonly said that flashlight batteries should be stored in a cold area or refrigerator to preserve long life. Is there any truth to this statement?

Does the temperature of a cell or battery while it is operating make a big difference in its performance? Does the temperature affect terminal voltage, the amount of current that will flow in a certain period of time, the energy the battery can deliver, or "life expectancy"?

What are the effects of connecting circuit elements like resistors, or capacitors, or coils, or cells, . . . in series? In parallel? Are the effects related to frequency when alternating voltage is applied?

What are the actual materials inside an electric cell or battery and how is it designed? Can you build a battery using the same or similar materials?

What is a "fuse" or "circuit-breaker"? How can you make one that will work effectively in a circuit made up of batteries and bulbs?

Can you light a normal bulb from your house with a number of flashlight cells? How many does it take? Specifically, what is inside a bulb? How is it designed?

How can you make a bulb from simple materials that will glow when attached to one or two flashlight cells?

What are the relationships between electric currents and magnetism?—Magnets, simple electromagnets, coils, motors, compasses, generators. . . .

If you have a simple motor, does its speed depend on the number of flashlight cells or on the voltage providing energy in the circuit? How is the load the motor will lift related to the applied voltage? What happens to the current in the circuit when the motor is under heavy load? How can this be explained?

Can you use a simple motor as a *generator* to provide energy for a circuit? Can you design and construct a generator that will energize an electric circuit?

What do the special electrical symbols used by electricians, engineers, and scientists mean? Acquire an electrical circuit diagram for a device or portion of a building and study the diagram to understand the information it contains. What can you learn about the device or building from the diagram? Check the actual device or building to verify the existence of the circuit elements identified in the diagram. If possible, check the accuracy of the diagram by testing individual circuit elements to see if they meet the specifications identified on the circuit diagram. CAUTION: ELECTRICAL DEVICES CAN BE VERY DANGEROUS. Perform these tests *ONLY* under the supervision of a person who is technically competent and responsible.

What principles or regularities can be observed in the device you have studied? How are your results consistent with and how do they differ from scientific principles—as you understand them? How could you get better data, if you had more time and resources?

What new questions and hypotheses has your inquiry suggested? Can you formulate some recommendations for the design and use of the device you have studied?

Safety Precautions

When working with very low voltages and devices that do not store charge, this kind of activity provides few hazards. However, some students may want to explore devices that operate on household voltages or have large capacitance. This kind of inquiry can result in high interest and meaningful learning; however, there must be very careful supervision by an individual knowledgeable about proper safety procedures and about the dangers that are present. Teachers are encouraged to solicit the support of persons with technical expertise to supervise projects for a small number of students, but IF SUCH SUPERVISION IS NOT AVAILABLE, THIS ASPECT OF INQUIRY SHOULD NOT BE PURSUED. It is *very* important to inform students of these dangers ahead of time and to specify limitations and proper safety practice.

Comments

This activity is best run as an extended project with outside of class activity. Students work individually or in small groups on different devices or activities of their own choosing. To facilitate teacher input and monitoring, it is recommended that students be required to prepare and subsequently update contracts for the inquiry that they plan to conduct.

References

How Things Work, Simon and Schuster, 1967.
Technical manuals.

5. Batteries and the Traveling Lady

Science Topics   Batteries

Level   C:1–3   E:1–2   D:1–2   L:2–4

Overview

Students examine performance characteristics of batteries under load in different environmental conditions. They compare performance across brands and conditions. They also examine consumer demands.

Materials

Assorted batteries; 9v. radio batteries are preferred (old batteries can be brought from home)
Multimeter
Some resistors
Refrigerator
Oven or other low-level heat source
Desirable: a radio-cassette recorder

Suggested Activities

Students are told the story of a lady who loves music and who needs a radio-cassette recorder throughout her exotic travels to hot and cold, humid and dry places throughout the world. Her radio needs batteries which perform reasonably well under a wide variety of weather conditions.

The radio only performs properly if the output voltage and current are between values that are specified or determined by students in the lab. Students are asked to think of other criteria which should be specified for these batteries. For example one may require that the batteries survive heat of 45°C or cold of −10°C for at least 10 hours. One might also require a minimum play-time that will not decrease much under different climatic conditions.

Students in small groups then decide which criteria they are going to test. They design experiments, carry out tests, and collect data, and make consumer judgements. In large group discussion the class can pool data and information about different kinds of tests and try to come to consumer judgments ("buy" or "not buy") with respect to specific brands and kinds of batteries.

You will want to measure the output voltage of batteries under load and determine how long the battery can sustain a certain current. Try to simulate the load of a radio-recorder with a simple resistor.

What are the strengths and weaknesses of this kind of simulation?

[The voltage and load current of radio are normally printed on a specification card on the radio. For example:

9v   [9 volts]
250mA   [250 Milliamperes]   ]

What happens to the battery current and output voltage under load over time? What are the effects of environmental conditions such as temperature and moisture? What are the effects of exposure to different weather conditions while the battery is being stored?

How long can a radio-recorder play on a specific battery (play-time)?
Are there differences between batteries with regard to play-time?
Can batteries endure temperatures of 45°C?
How long can batteries be stored without significant decreases in performance? (shelf-life)
What are the effects of different weather and temperature conditions during storage on the performance of a battery?

Does the play-time of a battery depend on whether the radio-recorder is being used for recording from the radio, playing tapes, or just listening to the radio?

Does a "frozen" battery look unusual inside compared to a "normal" one?

What generalizations can you make based upon your study?

How can you explain your results in terms of battery chemistry? Compare: different brands of batteries; different kinds of batteries; energy needs of different kinds of radio-cassette recorders.

Examine the effects of extracting currents higher than the maximum advisable current for the battery.

Safety Precautions

No hazardous problems are likely to occur, but student-planned tests should be approved by the teacher. Some treatments may cause a battery to leak acid, and in these circumstances the battery should be in a suitable container and the student and surroundings should be properly protected.

Reference

Williams, J. E., et al.: *Modern Physics,* 1980. Holt, Rinehart, and Winston, New York, pp. 389–391.

6. Motor Efficiency

Science Topic   Energy (Electrical and Mechanical), Efficiency, Conservation of Energy

Level   C:3   E:3–4   D:2–4   L:3–4

Overview

Students investigate the energy efficiency of electric motors. This activity is appropriate for use after students have been introduced to measurement of electrical energy in terms of current, voltage and time and to mechanical potential energy.

Materials

small motor	volt meter (0–10v)
rheostat	ammeter (0–10a)
3v power supply	

Suggested Activities

In modern times people must be especially attentive to misuse and waste of energy resources. We have heard that certain kinds of engines are inefficient. What about electric motors? How efficient are they? How much of the electrical energy that they consume is converted to mechanical energy? These are very important kinds of questions for modern engineers and consumers of energy. Do all electric motors have approximately the same efficiency? Does the efficiency of a motor depend upon the applied voltage, upon the speed at which it is turning, or upon its load? To examine these questions for an electric motor, clamp a small motor to a stand, and attach a light spool or drum to its shaft so that it can lift a small load attached to a light string when it runs as shown in Figure 1. A circuit diagram is pictured in Figure 2. Arrange the motor so that it can raise a load of known weights that you can vary in different trials. (You might use washers or some other form of standard weight.) You know from your study of mechanics that the work output of this motor as it lifts its load is equivalent to weight time height or mgh. (To determine work output in joules, mass should be measured in kilograms, g in meters per second squared and h in meters.) You also know from your study of electricity that energy consumed in an

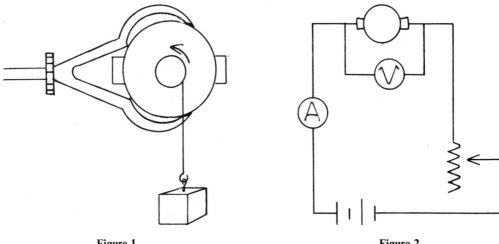

Figure 1   **Figure 2**

electric circuit in joules can be determined by multiplying the potential difference in volts times current in amperes times time in seconds, i.e., Energy = VIt. The efficiency of the system can be expressed as:

$$\text{Efficiency} = \frac{\text{Work output}}{\text{Work input}} = \frac{mgh}{VIt}$$

Examine the effects of different speeds of motor operation on the efficiency of the electric motor moving a constant load through a uniform distance. Plot a graph of this relationship. What do you observe? Is efficiency related to speed for this motor?

See if the efficiency of the motor changes in lifting loads of different mass at constant speed. Try to represent these relations in graphical form. What relationships do you observe? How can these relationships be explained? How do you explain the fact that the energy output is always lower than the energy input? Where does the lost energy go? Propose ways that the motor could be designed to be more efficient. Is there some way that the lost energy can be captured and used effectively?

Study other electric motors to determine their energy efficiency. Do motors vary substantially in efficiency? What are the characteristics of more efficient motors? Design motor testing procedures that can be used easily to compare the efficiency of different kinds of electric motors. Perhaps a brake can be rigged for laboratory testing purposes that will avoid the necessity of lifting weights over a uniform distance. (Consult engineering or technical manuals to see how this can be done for larger scale operation.)

- -

After examining the efficiency of your electric motor check to see whether or not your motor will convert mechanical energy to electrical energy when the system is reversed. Remove the battery from the electric circuit and allow the load to fall spinning the electric motor. Can you observe a meter reading that indicates that the mechanical energy is being converted back into electrical energy? (In this system, it may be helpful to replace the meters used in earlier parts of this inquiry with more sensitive meters.) How can the voltmeter reading in this system be increased? How is it related to the falling load that is spinning the motor? Determine the energy efficiency with the system now where the energy input is mechanical and the energy output is electrical. How does the efficiency compare with the efficiency when electrical energy was being converted to mechanical energy in the system? How can your observations be explained? What could you do to design a more efficient generator?

- -

How could you examine the efficiency of an electric fan? Conduct a study on the efficiency of fans or other "cooling" devices.

- -

Extend your study of the efficiency of electric motors to other kinds of engines. Perhaps you would like to design a system to study the efficiency of internal or external combustion engines. Acquire some technical manuals that indicate how these engines are tested commercially. Perhaps you can conduct or at least observe such tests. How does the efficiency of other engine systems compare with the efficiency of the electric motors you have studied? What are the characteristics of efficient engines? How can loss of energy be reduced when energy is converted from one form to another?

- -

Extend your study to examine the efficiency of transformers . . . solar collectors. . . .

Comments

Aspects of this inquiry, especially some of the extensions, are best run as projects outside of normal class activity. Some students may work individually or in small groups on motors or systems of their own choosing. To facilitate teacher input and monitoring, it is recommended that students be required to prepare and subsequently update contracts for the inquiry they plan to conduct.

References

Dillon and Smith, *Lab Manual, Concepts in Physics,* 3rd edition, Harcourt, Brace, Jovanovich, 1980, pp. 56–58.

Haber-Schaim, Uri, et al., *PSSC Physics Laboratory Guide,* 3rd edition, D.C. Heath and Co., 1971, pp. 78–79.

D Wave Motions/Light/Sound

1. Soda-pop Music

Science Topic   Sound, Resonance

Level   C:1–3   E:1–3   D:1–2   L:2–3

Overview

Blowing across the top of a bottle results in a sound. What factors determine the pitch and the quality or "timbre" of the sound?

Students compare the pitch of bottles with different shapes, top diameter, or length of water or sand column inside. A possible extension concerns an attempt to show the bottle sounds on an oscilloscope screen.

Materials

Bottles of different sizes, shapes, and kinds of glass
Water and/or sand to fill the bottles
Metric ruler
Optional: tuning forks
         microphone and oscilloscope

Suggested Activities

What determines the pitch and the quality of the sound made by blowing across the top of a bottle? [The phenomena may be demonstrated using some different bottles to show different pitches.] Students individually or in small groups are asked: to find relationships between bottle variables and pitch, OR to make a "water organ" using bottles.

What are the effects on pitch of length and the volume of the column of water in the bottle? The length and volume of the air column? Does the diameter of the bottle opening make a difference? What about the shape of the bottle? The kind of glass? How do sounds of the same pitch vary in quality and loudness from one bottle to another? If the bottle is filled with a different material such as sand (instead of water) does that affect the pitch or the quality of the sound?

Can you observe any simple relationships between the length of the air column and the pitch? Perhaps it would be helpful to graph the data.

How can the pitch of the sound be measured with precision? Measure the pitch of the sounds with as much precision as you can. When you have done so, you can look for mathematical relationships between the pitch of the sound and the length of the air column, etc. What mathematical relationships can you discover? From these relationships make some predictions about the pitch that would result from an air column of a length you have not measured. Then test your prediction.

What explanations can be developed for the relationships you have observed between pitch and the physical variables you have been examining? Try to set up an experiment to test one or more of your possible explanations. Perhaps you could arrange a tube in which you could vary the length of the air column with a piston or plunger in a very controlled way. What explanations of these phenomena are provided in textbooks on sound and music? Try to test some of these published explanations using apparatus in the laboratory.

Perhaps your attempts to explain relationships may be helped by examining a Kundt tube apparatus commonly used for acoustical demonstrations in a physics lab. The tube is plugged at one end and contains a light powder that collects in piles when the air in the tube is caused to resonate by an external source of sound. Examining the distance between these periodic piles and the ripples in the piles may shed light on "standing sound waves". Is there some relationship between observations with this apparatus and the phenomena you have been studying? Explain.

Use a pitch generator (tuning forks or an audio-oscillator and speaker) to determine the resonant frequencies of bottles with air columns of different lengths. How do the sounds (resonant frequencies) you can stimulate in each column (by placing the speaker over the column) compare to the sound when you blow across the column? What relationships exist?

When you tap your bottles with a metal object, they will resonate and emit a sound. How does the pitch or quality of that sound compare with the sound when you blow across the top of the bottle? What are the relationships that exist between the different methods of stimulating vibration and the sound produced?

Inquiry activities thus far have involved closed containers, that is, air columns closed at one end and open at the other. How do pitch and quality change when the air in a tube open at both ends is excited?

Investigate objects in your environment to see what statements can be made about the relationships between the resonant pitch of an object and its structure and material.

Investigate the construction of musical instruments and study the relationship of length and shape of air column and method of stimulation to the pitch and quality of the sound.

Safety Precautions

Experiments that may result in breaking bottles and cutting hands must be conducted with care. For example, be especially cautious in moving wet bottles and in holding tuning forks near the top of glass bottles or tubes (as in the resonance experiments). In moving the tuning fork near the opening of the bottle, students will often make contact between the vibrating tuning fork and the bottle causing the bottle to shatter.

Comments

This activity can be conducted at a descriptive level or it can be done very quantitatively. The pitch or frequency of a simple sound can be measured with precision relatively easily by comparison with standard frequency generators such as tuning forks or by analysis on an oscilloscope. The length of air columns can be varied and measured with precision if students are ready to do that. The resulting relationships observed between length of air column and resonant frequency can be compared with descriptions in texts on the physics of sound. Some students will find the extension of this inquiry to the study of specific musical instruments to be highly relevant and stimulating.

At a more descriptive level, the activity can easily lose its inquiry character on certain tasks such as preparing a "water organ" using bottles, if the students are not asked to make predictions and to test them and to explain observations and hypotheses. . . .

References

Johnson, Kenneth W. and Walker, Willard C., *The Science of Highfidelity,* Kendall/Hunt Publishing Company, 1977, (with laboratory manual).

Josephs, J. J., *The Physics of Musical Sound,* D. Van Nostrand, New Jersey 1967.

Tyndall, J., *The Science of Sound,* Philosophical Library, New York 1964.

2. Mixing Colors

Science Topic   Color

Level   C:1–2   E:1–3   D:1   L:2–3

Overview

This activity examines color properties of light. Students gather the descriptive information regarding the colors that result when colors of light are added together and they compare this information with results obtained when pigments are mixed. This activity may be of special interest for students with an artistic orientation. Their experiences are normally limited to working with pigments, and they often enjoy opportunity to do similar work with light.

Materials

Light projectors (flashlights will do)
Color filters (cellophane or other transparent plastic sheets will do)
Color wheel (optional)

Suggested Activities

How is a full range of color reproduced in a color TV? What kinds of special color effects can be produced in a theater, if the technicians are limited to just three colors in the spotlights. . . ? What happens when lights of different colors are mixed?

Most of you have observed what happens when you mix paints or crayons of different colors together. If you have not done this for some time, you may wish to do so as part of this activity. Be as thorough as you can so that you can make good generalizations from data and so that you can predict the colors that will result when specific colors are mixed. Most of you can recall that doing so results in color combinations that become darker as more colors are added.

If a red light is projected onto a screen and then a blue light is projected on the screen at the same time, what will the resulting color be? How does the result compare with mixing red and blue paint? What general patterns can you observe as you mix lights of different color? Can white light be produced when colored lights are mixed? Can white pigment be produced when colored paints are mixed?

Gather as much information as you can about color combinations that result when specific colors are mixed. How can your finding be organized simply so you can communicate your findings to artists, stage designers, and engineers who may wish to use them?

Can you mix lights similarly with only one light source? Predict the color of light on a screen when light passes through both a red *and* a blue filter before reaching the screen. Test your prediction. How can your observations be explained? What generalizations or principles can you state about these relationships?

Based on your findings, what recommendations would you make to people doing lighting effects in the theater? Locate a technical report that describes lighting techniques for the theater or a manual that describes the principles through which many colors of light can be presented on a color TV. How do the color descriptions in these books compare with your own findings? If there are differences, how may they have originated?

As you know, when white light refracts under the right conditions a color spectrum results. Use a prism (or a diffraction grating) and a source of white light (possibly sunlight) to examine the color spectrum with care. What do you observe? Can you arrange a second prism in such a way that the colors recombine to form a new beam of white light? Explain.

What happens if you observe colored objects through colored filters? How will objects of specific colors appear when viewed through filters of a certain color? For example, what color will a red ball appear to be when viewed through a red filter? What color will that ball be when viewed through a green filter or a blue filter? Study these relationships for objects of many colors and filters of many colors. What kinds of relationships and patterns do you observe? How can these observations be organized in a useful way? How can you explain what you have been observing? Can you explain some of your observations in terms of a particle model or a wave model of light?

Many interesting special inquiries can be pursued that relate to color effects in light. Edwin Land demonstrated that a full-color picture of an object can be created simply by taking two black and white photographs of the object, one through a green filter and one through a red filter. After processing the black and white transparencies the image of the object can be reproduced in full-color by simultaneously projecting both slides onto a screen. Red light should be projected through the slide made with the red filter and green light or white light can be projected through the slide made with the green filter. Can you reproduce the Land color effect? How can you explain what you observe in doing so?

Comments

An easy way to show the mixing of colors of light without projection equipment is to make a color wheel composed of sections of different colors. If the wheel is spun rapidly the colors seem to blend together and the reflected light arriving at our eye gives us a sense of one color. Acquire or have students make a color wheel and examine the effects of mixing different colors that are on the wheel. They can vary the amount of specific colors that are present on the wheel and see what effect this has on the resulting color combination when the wheel is spun much as they can do when mixing projected colors.

References

Land, E. H., "Experiments in Color Vision", *Scientific American,* 200, 84; May, 1959.
Surcliff, W. A. and Ballard, S. S.: *Polarized Light,* 1964. D. Van Nostrand, New York.
Williams, J. E., et al.: *Modern Physics,* 1980. Holt, Rinehart, and Winaton, New York, pp. 328–332.
Wood, E. A.: *Science for the Airline Passenger,* 1968. Houghton-Mifflin, New York.

3. How Tall Should the Mirror Be?

Science Topic   Reflection, Plane Mirrors

Level   C:2–3   E:2–3   D:1–2   L:2–4

Overview

The question addressed in this activity can provoke some interesting questioning and investigative activity that is relevant to the student. The activity can be used after laws of reflection have been introduced in an effort to test and apply what has been learned. Students who have "learned" the laws of reflection very often do not apply them properly in responding to questions raised about the necessary height of a mirror, and discrepancies can be observed quickly in activities with the materials. Pursuing the activity can result in more thorough understanding of the relationships involved in reflection from plane mirrors. The activity can also provide an interesting way to introduce the study of reflection of light before the property has been presented and developed in other ways. More advanced students can conduct the study with careful attention to quantitative measurements and make mathematical predictions and measurements throughout. Less advanced students can conduct the study in a more qualitative way. All students can sketch ray diagrams to explain their data.

Materials

One or more plane mirrors (pocketbook size is sufficient)
Masking tape
Meter ruler

Suggested Activities

If you were going to buy and install a plane mirror on your bedroom wall, what would be the shortest mirror you could buy that would enable you to see your whole body when you are standing on the floor in front of the mirror? Is a full length mirror necessary for you to see your shoes? Make some predictions and then test them by placing a plane mirror on the wall. If you have only a small mirror where must the mirror be placed in order for you to see your eyes? Where must the mirror be placed in order for you to see your shoes? How will your answers differ as you move away from the wall? What will happen at large distances? After making predictions conduct this inquiry with real materials and make measurements as accurately as you can. How can your observations be explained? Draw diagrams showing the path of "light rays" to help with explanation.

How must your answers to the question raised earlier change if the mirror is not precisely perpendicular to the floor? If the mirror is tipped at an angle of five degrees to the wall, how would this change your answers? Make predictions and again test them experimentally.

What about the location of your image in the mirror? When you are standing in front of the mirror does your image seem to be in front of the mirror, on the surface of the mirror, or some distance behind the mirror? How do the approximate distances from the mirror surface compare? Does the plane mirror magnify your apparent image? Does it make you look smaller? Explain your observations.

- -

The property of reflection from a plane mirror can be examined more carefully by locating the image of a nail or a pin placed in front of a plane mirror mounted on a table top. You can locate the position of the image by drawing rays on a piece of paper on the table along the edge of a ruler that points as precisely as possible from your eye to the point where the image seems to be. If you do this several times from different locations, the rays will intersect where the image seems to be. Where do the lines intersect? Where is the image pin located in relationship to the object pin? Rays reflecting from the mirror to your eye are marked on the paper. Now draw in the path of the ray before it reached the mirror and reflected. That is, draw a ray showing the path of the light from the pin to the mirror before the reflection occurred. What is the relationship of the angles between the "incident" rays and the mirror and between the corresponding rays of reflection and the mirror?

Your study of reflection might be expanded to look carefully at whether or not there is magnification in a plane mirror. Draw an object (for example, a triangle) on the paper in front of the mirror and locate as carefully as you can the images of the three vertices of the triangle. How does the size of the image triangle compare with the size of the object triangle? Are your results consistent with your predictions? Do you think there is much error in your experimental data? Describe the sources of this error and estimate how large the error is.

- -

In clothing stores mirrors normally run all the way to the floor. Such mirrors are quite expensive. Are they necessary? When a new store is constructed, could money be saved by purchasing shorter mirrors? Should shorter mirrors be installed? Would people like them?

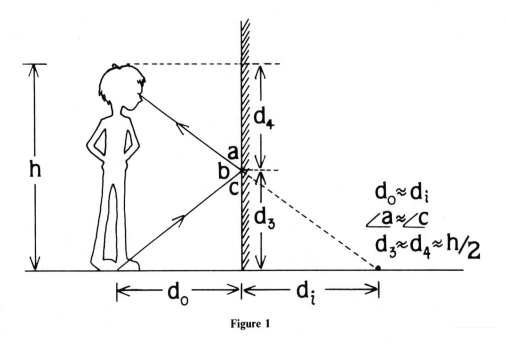

Figure 1

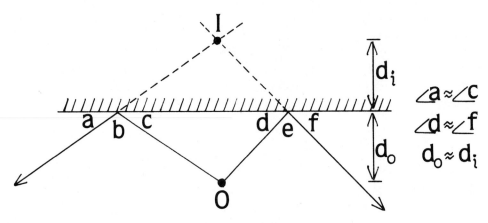

Figure 2

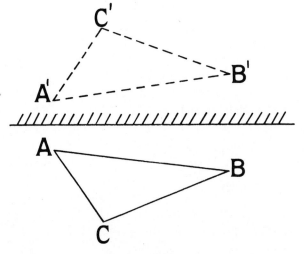

Figure 3

Comments

In setting up this activity, if the mirror being examined is not perpendicular to the floor, results will be noticeably different from a situation in which the mirror is flush against a perpendicular wall. Figure 1 shows a sketch of a ray diagram that might be used by a student to explain the location of the portion of the plane mirror in which he is able to see his feet.

Figure 2 shows a sketch of a ray diagram locating the image of an object pin placed in front of a plane mirror.

Figure 3 shows a sketch of a diagram used by a student to examine magnification in a plane mirror. Careful work will result in determining that the image size is approximately the same as the object size. However, it is common for students to have large error in this kind of study.

Reference

Haber-Schaim, U.: *PSSC Physics Laboratory Guide,* 3rd edition, 1971. D. C. Heath, Lexington, MA, p. 3.

4. A "Sharp" Photographer

Science Topic   Optics; lenses; depth of field; photography

Level   C:3   E:2–4   D:1–2   L:2–3

Overview

In this activity students investigate the distinctness of lens images as a function of other factors such as the radius of the lens opening (aperture), object distance, focal length of the lens, distance from the diaphragm to the lens, etc. It should follow the study of ideal lenses normally presented in an introductory physics course.

Materials

For each two or three students:

Lenses with different focal lengths

A diaphragm which can be opened and closed or several diaphragms of different diameters

A light source

A slide with two slits or two concentric circles

Ruler

Optical bench, if available

Suggested Activities

The problem of making portraits and pictures of objects at short distances from the camera with a desired "depth of field" is an important one for photographers. "Depth of field" is a term used by photographers to describe the range of distances from the cameras in which objects will have images that appear to be in sharp focus. Objects that are outside this range will have images that are blurred and not in sharp focus. Sometimes in making portraits, photographers want a narrow depth of field having only the principle object in clear focus with the environment blurred; at other times, when photographing landscapes, a photographer will want as large a depth of field as possible.

What factors determine the sharpness of the image that is formed on the screen? focal length of the lens? the object distance? the diameter of the diaphragm opening? the size of the object? the distance from the lens to the screen? the location of the diaphragm? Other variables? Be as precise as you can in describing the effects of these variables, if any, on the "depth of field".

How can you operationally define a "sharp" image?

Estimate the error in your measurement and its influence on outcomes.

How can your observations be explained? Try to interpret your findings using a diagram showing what happens to selected light rays.

What are the implications of your findings for the design of cameras and for photographers who want to be able to control the depth of field in their portraits and photographs?

What kinds of depth of field are desirable in photography? When would it be desirable to have a deep depth of field? When is a shallow depth of field more preferable? On what bases are your answers to these questions developed? Perhaps a survey of photographers or of photography books might be interesting in order to compare recommendations and to assess the basis on which these recommendations are made. Are the recommendations based on scientific principle, on aesthetics, or on some of both?

Examine the "depth of field" of a commercial camera. Perhaps you might be able to compare the "depth of field" of several cameras. How do the cameras compare on this variable? How do your results compare with the results you obtained when working with the simpler physics lab optical apparatus?

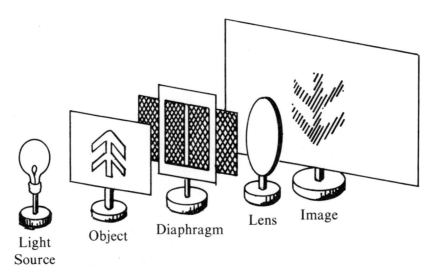

Light Source   Object   Diaphragm   Lens   Image

Comments

These inquiry activities should be preceded by more basic lab activities involving the study of properties of lenses, focal length, object distance, image distance, magnification, real and virtual images, etc.

After initial discussion the teacher demonstrates the equipment to be used and explains how the "in focus" range or the "depth of field" of a photograph can be defined. Students should participate in a discussion involving this definition to ascertain whether or not they understand the ideas involved. An alternative approach, of course, is to leave the task of designing an operational definition to the students as part of this lab activity instead of providing it. Students then investigate factors which might influence "depth of field". Some students may well be encouraged to examine the scientific and the artistic implications of this inquiry by reading manuals of photography and by talking with photographers.

References

Williams, J. E., et al.: *Modern Physics,* 1980. Holt, Rinehart, and Winston, New York, pp. 315–325.

How to Make Good Pictures, Eastman Kodak Co., 1972, p. 23.

5. Distance from the Light

Science Topic   Luminous intensity, photometry, inverse square law

Level   C:3   E:2   D:3   L:3–4

Overview

In this activity students examine the effects of distance from a source of light upon luminous intensity. The activity can be pursued with quantitative measurements, and from a graph of the results, an inverse-square relationship between luminous intensity and distance can be inferred. Thus, it is best used prior to the formal study of luminous intensity. Portions of the inquiry, of course, can be pursued at any time.

Materials

Light source
Light meter

Suggested Activities

When you are trying to read a book, the amount of light striking the page often makes a difference. Sometimes there is too much light and glare makes the page difficult to read; at other times a dimly lighted page is difficult to read. How does the amount of light reaching the page change as you move your book away from the light source? Is it a simple inverse relationship or is it a more complex or exponential relationship? Make some predictions based on your understanding of the nature of light.

An inquiry into these questions can be conducted relatively easily using a photoelectric lightmeter which measures the intensity of light falling on it. Light falling on a metallic surface in the photometer kicks off electrons; the intensity of the weak current is converted to a scale reading on the meter. Measure the intensity of light reaching the meter at different distances from the source of light. Naturally, the room in which you pursue the inquiry should be darkened to other sources of light as one control of variables. Read the luminous intensity from the meter at several distances from the source of light and plot a graph of intensity versus distance. What relationship does the graph show between these variables? If you suspect that there may be an exponential relationship, you may check that possibility out by using special graphing technique X1. You can also test predictions of the mathematical relationship using specific data points you have measured.

What are the effects on your graph or graphs of passing the light through color filters before gathering data? How do the graphs of red light and blue light compare with your graph of data gathered in white light? How can these relationships be explained? If you use a more intense light source, predict how this will effect the graph and the relationship of luminous intensity to distance. Test your prediction.

How can you explain the relationships between distance and luminous intensity that you have observed in this inquiry? What "model" of light best explains these relationships? (Particle, wave, other . . . ?)

Based on your inquiry, what recommendations would you make for the placement of light sources for energy efficiency and for reading comfort? What other inquiries should be pursued to properly make such recommendations? What other characteristics of light effect reading comfort besides luminous intensity? This kind of investigation will involve not only measurements of physical quantities but also an examination of psychological issues. What colors and intensities do different people prefer? Are there big differences between people? What do architectural handbooks on the design of library reading areas suggest? On what are these recommendations based? Can you make better recommendations based on your inquiries?

What relationships are there, if any, between the intensity of illumination with distance from a light source and the intensity of nuclear radiation with separation from the source of radiation? (See Activity E11.)

Comments

This inquiry provides a relatively simple way to gather data that will show the inverse-square relationship between distance from a light source and luminous intensity. The inverse-square relationship may be "discovered" or verified in several ways. One useful technique involves logarithmic graph paper and is described in Section X1.

Some teachers may object to using a light meter that is not fully understood by student users, and there are more basic photometric techniques that can be used if desired. Other simpler techniques, however, tend to take considerably more time in gathering data, and they also can involve abstractions that are difficult for many young students to understand. One experiment that is recommended is a PSSC investigation found in the reference. This PSSC investigation yields very few data points and often results in large measurement error but is an appropriate option. Note that it is written with the assumption that students have already been introduced to a particle model of light and have inferred an inverse-square relationship of luminous intensity from that model. The investigation seeks to gather data to verify or reject that assumption.

Reference

Haber-Schaim, U., et al.: *PSSC Physics Laboratory Guide,* 1961. D. C. Heath, New York, pp. 74–77.

6. Waves in My Coffee

Science Topic   Wave motion, water waves, ripple tank

Level   C:2–4   E:2–3   D:1–3   L:1–4

Overview

In this activity students explore various properties of water waves. They use a ripple tank and other wave media to better understand wave properties and they search for analogies between water waves and other wave media like light and sound. The activity can be used after wave motions have been introduced and students can explore some of the wave properties with which they are familiar by studying water waves in a ripple tank.

Materials   Ripple tank and associated apparatus

Suggested Activities

Have you ever stared bleary-eyed at your morning coffee and contemplated the waves in the coffee cup? Coffee dripping into a full cup off the side of a spoon can produce very interesting circular waves. What happens when these waves reflect from the edge of the coffee cup? Is the concave reflecting surface a good analogy of a concave mirror in light? Can you use the coffee cup to simulate the formation of a real image in light after it reflects from a concave mirror? What other wave properties can be observed in your coffee cup? *Caution:* In a bleary-eyed morning state, beware of falling into the coffee cup-ripple tank!

Ripple tanks enable us to improve our understanding of wave properties by studying water waves. We can then look for these properties in other wave media such as in light or sound or radio waves. Water waves are quite visible and relatively easy to study, but their wavelengths and other conditions of the water medium are very different from other kinds of waves such as electromagnetic media. You already know that wave disturbances reflect, refract, and have many other properties including: intensity, frequency-wavelength, interference, diffraction, dispersion. . . . Study as many of these properties as you can in the ripple tank water waves. Conduct these studies with as much precision as you can.

Describe what you have been able to observe. The PSSC Laboratory Guide and other lab handbooks provide explicit suggestions for the study of specific properties of water waves. Perhaps you might wish to refer to one or more of these as you conduct your inquiry.

Some of the many specific questions you may wish to investigate may include: when studying the property of refraction in water waves, can you observe evidence of internal reflection? Can you observe the refraction of different wave-lengths at slightly different angles (dispersion)? Can you set up a ripple tank arrangement that will simulate the refraction of light through a lens? What special questions does your ripple tank "lens" raise?

Comments

Some students very much enjoy extended study of wave phenomena in ripple tanks. However, getting "good" results, especially with refraction and diffraction experiments requires considerable care, patience, and clean water and apparatus (free of dust and grease). Thus, students can save much time if they are guided by suggestions on the proper care and use of ripple tanks. A good and fairly extensive source of such suggestions is found in the PSSC Laboratory Guide and Teacher's Handbook; the laboratory guide reference is cited below. In these activities different students in a class can be assigned to study different properties of waves in the ripple tank and their findings can be shared subsequently with other members of the class. Thus, it should not be necessary for all class members to spend large quantities of time on this particular inquiry, although some may very well wish to do so.

Film loops prepared from PSSC efforts are available on ripple tank phenomena. Presentation and discussion of some of these films can be very worthwhile since they show some wave properties more visibly than is possible for students working with conventional ripple tanks. Measurements made from the projected images of the film loops can also be used in class inquiry and discussion. The ripple tank film loops can be used in an inquiry mode without the use of actual ripple tanks, but in that event, more students will have difficulty understanding what the films represent. If there is no contact with actual ripple tanks, the activity is more likely to be an exercise in abstraction resulting in less than optimal understanding for some students.

Reference

Uri Haber-Schaim, et al., *PSSC Physics Laboratory Guide,* Third Edition, D. C. Heath and Co., 1971, pp. 13–23.

7. Polarized Sunglasses?

Science Topic   Polarization

Level   C:2   E:1–3   D:1   L:2–3

Overview

In this activity students explore the phenomenon of polarized light, for the most part qualitatively, and they search for hypotheses to explain their observations.

Materials

Two polarized lenses (lenses from polarized sunglasses will be sufficient)
Microwave transmitter/receiver and polarizing grid (optional)
Light corn syrup, cellophane or plastic wrap

Suggested Activities

When we go to the store to purchase sunglasses, we find that some sunglasses are advertised as being *polarized* and others are not. Normally, the polarized sunglasses are more expensive. Why should we spend extra money for polarized sunglasses? Do polarized lenses help us to see better? Conduct an inquiry to answer these questions.

What is meant by polarized and unpolarized light in the first place? Remove some lenses from polarized sunglasses or use other polarized materials. Place one lens in front of the other in front of a light source and observe the light source through the two filters; then rotate one of the filters and observe the variation in light intensity that results. On a bright day is reflected sunlight polarized? Is light coming from a cloudy sky polarized? Is light coming from a clear sky polarized? Do you observe similar levels of polarization from all areas of the sky? What do you observe? Are there any patterns or regularities that you can describe? Can you reproduce your findings experimentally in the laboratory?

Based upon your results what recommendations can you make for purchasers and for manufacturers of sunglasses?

It has been observed that many transparent materials can polarize light in various ways, and sometimes the polarization can be used commercially or in analytical applications. Scientists can determine weak spots in certain films or plastics by examining the polarization of transmitted light; they can measure the concentration of some liquids by examining the amount of polarization in the light they transmit. For example, place some cellophane or plastic wrap between two polarizing filters and examine its effects upon polarized light under various amounts of stretching. Place a container of light corn syrup (the kind you use on pancakes) between two polarizing filters and observe its effects on white light transmitted from a source on one side of the container. What are the effects of changing the thickness of the syrup container and the concentration of the syrup on polarization? Could you use this system to measure the quality or concentration of commercial syrups? Describe the color effects you have observed in the polarized light passing through the syrup.

Propose some possible models to explain how the materials you have examined can polarize light. What kinds of explanations do science textbooks provide? Are these kinds of explanations consistent with your own observations? Are these explanations easily understood? What kinds of questions do you have regarding the explanation of these phenomena?

Perform an inquiry on the polarization of microwaves using a microwave transmitter, polarizing filter, and receiver. What new insights does this inquiry provide?

You can read about many interesting applications of polarized light in other references. Among other things, honey bees and many other creatures use the polarization of light in the sky as an aid in flying and locating things. The Waterman and Lockley references below are especially interesting for persons interested in life science.

References

Lockley, R. M.: *Animal Navigation,* 1967. Hart, New York.

Shurcliff, W. A. and Ballard, S. S.: *Polarized Light,* 1964. D. Van Nostrand, New Jersey.

Waterman, T., "Polarized Light and Animal Navigation", *Scientific American,* 193, 88; July, 1955.

Wood, E. A.: *Crystals and Light,* 1964. Van Nostrand, Momentum, New Jersey.

8. Holes in the Sound?

Science Topic   Interference, Young's Experiment, Wave Properties of Sound, Light, and/or Microwaves.

Level   C:3–4   E:2–4   D:1–4   L:2–4

Overview

Students are introduced to the property of interference in waves by listening to the easily heard and
intriguing interference pattern around a standard tuning fork. Efforts to explain the observations can
lead to an examination of interference patterns from two point sources in other wave media including:
water, light, microwaves, et al. Following observation of the initial interference patterns in sound waves,
students individually or in small groups can pursue a study of interference patterns in one or more other
wave media and report their findings back to the large group. In that way, a sense of the common
elements of wave motions in different media and of the simplicity of physical explanation can be
appreciated.

Materials

    Tuning fork(s), compass (for drawing circles), ripple tank with two point source generator, power
        source, rheostat (for varying wave frequency), stroboscope
    Meter stick
    Line light source (clear, vertical filament light bulb), light barrier with double slit (can be made
        from microscope slide painted black)
    Two speakers, audio oscillator, oscilloscope (optional)
    Microwave experiment apparatus (optional)

Suggested Activities

    A. Sound

Very often when we observe things around us, we do not even notice some of the interesting details
that are there. For example, most of us have heard sound made by a tuning fork, but we have not noticed
the very interesting "holes" that can be heard when we move our ear around the tuning fork. To observe
these "holes" easily, all we really have to do after striking the tuning fork is to hold it vertically in our
fingertips and rotate it a short distance from our ear. Do this and describe what you observe.

While listening to the tuning fork, does the intensity of the sound depend on the position of the
tuning fork? Examine the arrangement of the system that provides the loudest and the softest sounds.
How can your observations be explained? Create some hypotheses that may explain your observations
about the variation of intensity in the sound pattern. Based on your hypothesis, predict whether or not
there would be changes in the pattern you can hear if you were to strike the tuning fork harder or not
so hard. Test your predictions.

Does the location of the "holes" or regions of high and low intensity sound vary depending on how
the tuning fork is held and rotated? Are there always the same number of spots of high and low intensity?
Again, make some predictions and test them.

Based on your understanding of the "holes" in the tuning fork sound, make some predictions about
how the pattern would change if you were to examine a tuning fork of higher pitch (frequency) or lower
pitch. With a higher frequency tuning fork, would you expect a larger number of "holes", the same
number, or a smaller number as you rotate the tuning fork one time outside your ear? Once again, test
your predictions. Are your predictions supported by your observations with tuning forks of higher and
lower pitch? Explain.

Diagrams of physical relationships are often helpful in our efforts to understand and to explain relationships. Perhaps you can construct a sketch of the sound disturbance or pattern around the tuning fork that can assist us in understanding the existence of spots of high and low sound intensity as we move our ear around the tuning fork. (Some people find it helpful to think of a tuning fork as generating circular sound waves that travel out separately from each of the two arms of the tuning fork. If we could visualize what the sound wave would look like at some instant looking down on top of the tuning fork in our sketch that might help.)

B. Water

Another method often used by scientists trying to understand a relationship is to try to "model" the phenomenon in a different medium. Thus, if we could set up a system to study water waves generated by two point sources close together, that system might provide an interesting analog or model of the tuning fork we are seeking to understand. This can be done relatively easily in a ripple tank. Set up a ripple tank to generate circular waves from two point sources and study the pattern in the water waves that results. What do you observe? Do you see regions of high intensity and low intensity in the wave pattern surrounding the two point source wave generators? Do you see regions of destructive interference (nodes)? What happens to the interference pattern when the frequency of the wave generators is increased? What happens when the frequency is decreased? How is the number and location of nodal lines dependent on frequency? Is the wave pattern generated in the ripple tank by two point sources a good model of the tuning fork phenomenon you have been studying? How is the water wave model similar to the tuning fork phenomenon? How is it different? Can you get some ideas from your observations of the ripple tank model that may enable you to find some new features in the sound patterns surrounding the tuning fork? For example, based on your study of water waves, can you detect a similar relationship between the number of nodal lines and relative frequency in the pattern of sound waves that surrounds the tuning forks of different frequency?

Pursuing the analogy between water waves and sound waves further, an experimenter might want to increase his or her understanding by attempting to create a sound interference pattern by setting up two electronically operated speakers to project sound in a particular direction. You may wish to do this. In doing so, you may wish to study the effects of several variables upon the interference pattern produced in the sound around the two speakers. What are the effects of speaker separation, loudness, orientation (physical placement), pitch, phase? (Reversing the wires to one of the speakers can cause that speaker to be 180 degrees out of phase with the other speaker. In a thorough study of the effects of phase, an electric device could be constructed to vary the phase difference between the speakers continuously to study its effects—An analogous study of phase change can also be studied in the ripple tank.)

In conducting this kind of study with great care, the experimenter might wish to study the sound pattern by moving some kind of hearing aid or horn or a microphone connected to an oscilloscope through that pattern to locate with precision the maxima and minima in the pattern. Such measurements might be used in combination with the ripple tank study to cross check mathematically the frequency generated by the audio-oscillator and the speakers. Can an interference pattern be observed with some speakers and speaker configurations and not with others? Can an interference pattern be observed with all frequencies? What if frequencies are mixed before leaving the speaker?

What are the implications, if any, for the design and placement of high fidelity speakers in your home or in an auditorium?

C. Light

Interference patterns in water waves can be studied relatively easily in a ripple tank, and the information gathered can be applied to the study of wave phenomenon in many other media. The water waves can provide insights into interference phenomenon that can then be tested in other media that are more difficult to observe, such as light and radio waves. Mathematical equations can be derived from the study of water waves in the ripple tank that relate separation between nodal lines and wave length or frequency in the wave medium. These mathematical relationships can then be used to measure wave length in media where the wave lengths are orders of magnitude smaller than they are in the water waves and sound waves. Perhaps you would enjoy using the ripple tank to derive or check out this kind of mathematical relationship. PSSC investigations 13 and 14[1] provide a good outline for this particular inquiry.

Study interference phenomena in other media. Setting up and observing interference patterns in light can be especially interesting. Light from a single vertical source passing through two very narrow vertical slits diffracts and interferes to produce a very interesting interference pattern. Observe the interference pattern for different colors of light. Can you observe different numbers of nodal lines per centimeter for different colors of light? Colored plastic strips or cellophane can be used to cover the bulb to produce "monochromatic" sources of light. How do the interference patterns compare in different colors? Are there more nodal lines per centimeter in red light or blue light? If the interference patterns observed in water waves from two point sources are a good "model" for light, which color, red or blue, has the higher frequency?

What kind of interference pattern do you observe in white light? How can you explain these observations? Measure the separation between the nodal lines (indirectly) and use the mathematical equation derived earlier in the ripple tank to determine the wave length of particular colors of light. PSSC Investigation 15[2] provides a good outline for the conduct of this inquiry (Young's experiment). Interference patterns in visible light can be found in a number of common places if we look for them. For example, we often see interference patterns in light reflecting from oil films. While we can find such films in a number of places, you may wish to study such an interference pattern by reflecting light from a film in the laboratory. How do you think this kind of interference pattern can be explained? What will determine the spacing between the nodal lines seen on the film? Will the color of light make a difference? Will the thickness of the film make a difference? Will the kind of material in the film make a difference? You may wish to make predictions and to test them experimentally. PSSC Investigation 18[3] examines a similar kind of interference pattern formed in the reflections of light from a thin layer of air between glass blocks. You may find it helpful to examine those patterns as part of your inquiry into interference.

D. Microwaves

Conduct the study of the interference pattern in microwaves using microwave transmitters and a microwave receiver. (The procedure for this experiment parallels the procedure followed in earlier sections of this inquiry.)

Based on what you know about interference, how could two point source radio transmitting towers be arranged to give optimal coverage to persons living along a coastal strip of land with greatest energy efficiency? What would be your wavelength preference, if any?

Comments

The drawing in Figure 1 shows an interference pattern in water waves in a ripple tank generated by two point sources. As the frequency of the water wave is increased (concurrent with decrease in wavelength) the number of nodal lines (destructive interference) increases and the separation between the nodal lines increases. Students can construct a diagram of this phenomenon by drawing circles around each of the two point sources (tips of the tuning fork); the separation between each circle will represent one wavelength, and the solid lines may represent wave crests. The drawing may also include dashed circles midway between each crest to represent wave troughs at the same instant. Students can then draw in the points where a crest from one source meets a trough from the other source resulting in cancellation and the formulation of a nodal line. Nodal lines can be sketched on the diagram.

Observation of interference patterns in light can be very exciting and stimulating for students. Most high school students can easily comprehend the qualitative relationship between color and frequency . . . (in blue light the nodal lines are more densely packed than in red light; thus, if the water waves are a good model for light, blue light has higher frequency and shorter wavelength than red light based upon

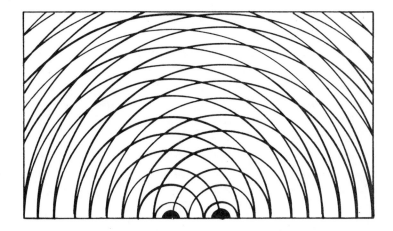

observations made in the ripple tank.) This experience is an important and helpful one and is highly recommended for all high school students in physical science. Some students will get great pleasure and sense of satisfaction from making mathematical measurements of the interference pattern and subsequently calculating the wavelength of red light and then other colors. With the most simple apparatus, one can compute the wavelength of red light to at least one significant figure and the correct power of ten. (The wavelength of red light is approximately 6.5×10^{-7} m.) While some students become very excited and motivated by this kind of measurement, others find the mathematics difficult to perform and understand. It is possible that these students ought to pursue the more qualitative parts of this inquiry.

If some students pursue the portion of the inquiry involving two speakers and audio oscillator, there are many variables that can make the experiment complex. Among these are diffraction effects, reflection of sound from other objects, and phase differences. The process of wrestling with these problems can sometimes be tedious, but it can be instructive as students work to understand and overcome limitations in equipment and experimental design. Students should not presume that all weighty problems can be resolved in one class period or even in a semester.

The experiments cited regarding interference in water waves and in light waves are written with a point of view that is consistent with the inquiry outlined here, and it will be helpful for teachers to consult that laboratory guide and relevant portions of the teachers guide. Microwave transmitters and receivers designed especially for use in physics laboratories normally are accompanied by manuals that include instructions on the conduct of experiments involving the interference pattern from two sources.

References
1. Haber-Schaim, U., et al., *PSSC Physics Laboratory Guide,* 3rd edition, D. C. Heath and Co., 1971, pp. 22–23.
2. Ibid, pp. 24–26.
3. Ibid, pp. 30–31.

9. A Funny Light Between My Fingers

Science Topic   Diffraction Effects

Level   C:3–4   E:2–4   D:2–4   L:2–4

Overview

This activity can be used to introduce the study of diffraction effects or to pursue the study broadly in a variety of wave media: light, sound, water, and microwaves. Students can concentrate their own attention on diffraction in one of these media, but the common elements of the property in different wave media are important to note.

Materials

> Line filament light bulb
> Speaker and audio oscillator
> Ripple tank with variable frequency
> Wave generator

Suggested Activities

When looking through light coming through two of your fingers pressed very closely together, have you ever wondered about the strange pattern that can be seen? Take another look. Hold two of your fingers parallel to a straight-filament light source or a fluorescent tube and examine the pattern carefully. What do you observe? How does the pattern change as you vary the width of the gap between your fingers?

What you have been observing is a "diffraction pattern" that occurs when light passes through a very narrow opening. *Diffraction* is the term used to describe the spreading out of a wave after passing through an opening that is small compared to its wavelength. The term is also used to describe how waves in different media bend as they pass around obstacles that are small compared to the wavelength. To better understand the diffraction of light, you may find it helpful to look at diffraction effects first in waves with longer wavelengths such as in water waves or in sound waves.

To investigate diffraction in sound waves, set up a small speaker powered by an audio oscillator. How does the spreading of the sound in front of the speaker depend on the frequency of the sound wave? Do some frequencies spread much more than others? Vary the frequency of the sound and listen to the pattern that results. Rotate the speaker or move your ear through the sound. (This study can be made more precise by using a microphone connected to an oscilloscope or by constructing a simple "ear trumpet" and listening through it.) What do you observe? The phenomenon you have been observing regarding the spreading of sound waves from a speaker has special implications for the design of high-fidelity speakers. If a room is to be filled with sound coming from one location, diffraction of sound around a speaker is very important, and engineers try to build speakers that will produce similar effects for sound waves over a wide variety of frequencies. Can you recommend a design for the construction of speakers that will result in the broad spreading of sound over a wide range of frequency? How are high fidelity speakers constructed to accommodate for the problems and phenomena you have been observing? You may wish to extend your study to diffraction around commercial high fidelity speakers and speaker cabinets. In designing a high fidelity speaker system, of course, there are other variables to consider such as the *quality* of the sounds being reproduced. Extend your study to examine some of these variables. What qualities do people like in high fidelity sound? How can these be best reproduced in a speaker?

Thus far, we have only examined the spreading of sound out from a speaker, but we can also examine how it diffracts around an obstacle. Take a thin piece of solid material like wood and mount it in front of your speaker. Probe the area beyond the obstacle with your "ear trumpet" and study the diffraction pattern that is present. Where are the regions of greatest sound intensity? Are there shadows or regions of silence in the sound? What patterns can you observe? Study these patterns in the presence of different frequencies and different sizes and configurations of the barrier. Can you detect any regularities in these patterns?

- -

Diffraction effects can be studied visually in a ripple tank. Set up a ripple tank to generate plane waves and observe how these waves pass through openings between barriers or around obstacles. Vary the width of the opening and vary the size of the obstacle; also, vary the wavelength to examine the effects of these variables on the diffraction pattern. (Naturally, it is important for an experimenter to control variables, that is to vary only one factor at a time while holding all others constant, in order to understand the effects of each variable.) Describe your observations carefully. What kinds of patterns do you observe? How does the pattern depend upon the frequency or wavelength of the water wave? How does the pattern depend upon the size of the opening or the size of the obstacle? Are there some conditions under which an obstacle would not cast a noticeable shadow, i.e., in which the waves diffract or bend quickly around the obstacle? Are there other conditions under which an obstacle casts a clear shadow? What relationships can you observe? What are the implications for diffraction in other media such as in sound waves where there is a relatively long wavelength and in light waves where there is a relatively short wavelength? If you have done portions of this inquiry with light waves or sound waves or micro waves, are the results of those investigations consistent with the observations you are making about water waves in the ripple tank? Can your observations be generalized to waves in other media?

- -

A more careful study of diffraction of light passing through a single slit can also be conducted by scratching a slit on a glass slide that has been painted black and observing a straight line source of light through the slit. The color of the light source can be varied by placing plastic or acetate filters around the light bulb. What are the effects of different colors of light on the diffraction pattern formed when light passes through a single slit? How does the diffraction pattern of red light compare with that of blue light? How do the patterns change when the width of the slit is changed? What happens in a diffraction pattern when the light passes through more than one slit such as through a diffraction grating composed of many very narrow slits that are very close together? These questions can be examined descriptively or in extensive quantitative detail. You may want to try to photograph diffraction effects.

Examine diffraction patterns when light passes through tiny holes. What are the effects of size of hole, distance from source, color of light, etc? Perhaps you would find it worthwhile to extend your study to the diffraction effects of lenses. Most information about the world around us comes through holes in our eyes and ears and through holes in telescopes, microscopes, cameras, etc. What problems are involved in receiving and processing information due to diffraction effects? What implications do your findings have, if any, for the design of optical devices such as cameras, microscopes, and light-projection equipment?

- -

Similar inquiry can be conducted into other wave media such as radio waves and micro waves. If you have access to micro wave transmitting and receiving equipment, you may wish to study diffraction effects as micro waves pass through openings that are small compared to their wavelength and as they move around obstacles. How do your observations about diffraction patterns in micro waves relate to your study of diffraction patterns in other media such as water waves, light, and sound? What implications do your results have for the design of radio transmitting and receiving equipment?

Comments

Figure 1 shows a sketch of diffraction in a ripple tank when plane waves pass through an opening in a barrier. With shorter wavelength, there is less bending of waves around the opening when the width of the opening remains constant. When students study plane waves in a ripple tank passing an obstacle with care, they can observe that when the obstacle is small relative to the wavelength the waves are disturbed relatively little; when the obstacle is relatively large, a shadow is formed as well as reflection effects.

The ripple tank study can be helpful to understanding, but achieving easily observed results requires special care and especially clean apparatus and water. Adjustments can be tricky! Some filmloops show these effects well, and, if available, they may be used by some students pursuing the study of diffraction in water.

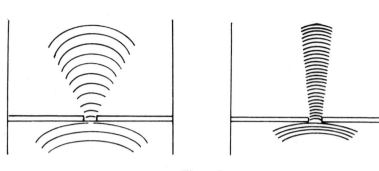

Figure 1

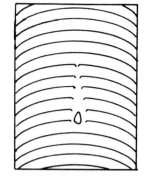

Figure 2

The PSSC Physics textbook referenced below provides a quantitative introduction to the property of diffraction in light and water waves but some students will find the presentation there to be too tedious for their level of mathematical development and uninteresting. Others may very well be anxious to pursue the inquiry in that kind of depth. The *Project Physics* reference, (pp 212–216) below provides some excellent suggestions for the study of diffraction in sound and for photographing diffraction patterns (pp 238–239).

The PSSC textbook also includes a relevant treatment of "resolution" or the diffraction effects of light passing through holes (pp 158–161). The *PSSC Laboratory Guide* includes an investigation of resolution that will also provide appropriate inquiry ideas for some students.

References

Haber-Schaim, U., et al., *PSSC Physics,* 3rd edition, D. C. Heath and Co., 1971, pp. 153–161.

Rutherford, F. J., et al., *The Project Physics Course Handbook,* Holt, Rinehart, and Winston, 1970, pp. 212–216, 238–239.

E Physical Properties

1. Springs—I

Science Topics Elasticity, Hooke's Law, Young's Modulus

Level C:1–2   E:2–3   D:2–3   L:2–3

Overview

This activity examines the stretching of a spring under various loads both below and beyond its elastic limit. Students examine the effects of length, tightness, material, gauge, etc. A similar study can also be conducted on other elastic materials.

Materials

Different kinds of springs
Wire for making springs (copper is suitable)
Other wire of different gauge and/or metal
Weight set (washers will do)
Metric ruler
Other "elastic" materials (optional)

Suggested Activities

What are some of the properties and characteristics of springs?

What variables affect the extension and/or compression of a spring? What are the effects of diameter, tightness, material. . . ?

To examine the effects of different variables upon extension (or compression) of the spring, construct springs out of wire using a pencil, bottle, broom handle or other object as a form. The different springs to be tested may vary in diameter, length, tightness, material, gauge, etc., and students must control variables to assess the effects of a particular variable, i.e., change only one variable at a time while holding the others constant to examine its effects.

What do you observe when a spring is stretched (or compressed) under different weights?

To study extension, hang a series of weights from a spring and record the extension (stretch) for each weight. (The spring can be hung from any convenient object and a paper clip can be used, if necessary, to attach weights to the spring; any appropriate unit masses such as washers or weight sets can be used.)

What does a graph of the stretching versus force applied look like? Is the graph linear in places? i.e., is "stress proportional to strain"?

Can you identify a mathematical formula that describes the stretching?

Does the spring always return to its original position when the weights are removed? Under what conditions will the spring return to its original position?

Can you locate the "elastic limit"?

Can you predict what the extension of the spring will be when a weight is added that is greater than those available to you?

What are the effects of temperature on the elasticity of the objects you have examined?

Use this kind of inquiry to examine the properties of wires or other elastic objects.

"Young's Modulus" is defined in some engineering and physics textbooks to quantitatively relate the variables you have been examining in this inquiry. More specifically, what is Young's modulus and how does it relate to the properties of materials and to what you have been doing in the inquiry?

Are rubber bands truly "elastic"?

What happens to a wire beyond its "elastic limit"? [In pursuing this inquiry, use caution to insure that breaking wires cause no injury to persons in the room. Special apparatus for this inquiry can be found in some physics labs and in some commercial engineering labs.]

What happens to a wire near its "breaking point"?

Create some hypotheses to explain your observations in terms of molecular or atomic structure.

Design and build a useful spring balance.

Comments

For less developed students, the graph of extension versus weight can be made of strips of ticker tape cut to match the actual extension in each trial.

The load applied is directly proportional to extension before the elastic limit is reached (Hooke's Law).

$$F \propto \triangle \ell$$

(Stress is proportional to strain)

$$F = k \triangle \ell$$

Beyond the elastic limit Hooke's Law does not apply.

References

Bolton, W.: *Physics Experiments and Projects, Volume 1,* 1968. Pergamon Press, New York, pp. 12–13.

Smith, C., "Investigating Springs", *School Science Review,* 57, 201; June, 1976, 762–764.

Williams, J. E., et al.: *Modern Physics,* 1980. Holt, Rinehart, and Winston, New York, pp. 142–44.

2. Springs—II

Science Topics Elasticity, Hooke's Law, Young's Modulus

Level C:2–4 E:2 D:2–4 L:2–4

Overview

Identical springs or identical rubber loops are connected in series or in parallel and their extension under load is examined. The activity can be conducted at varying levels of mathematical sophistication for students at different levels of development and skill.

Materials

Six or more identical springs or rubber loops
Weight set (washers will suffice)
Metric ruler

Suggested Activities

Predict the effects on extension under load when identical springs or rubber loops are connected in series or in parallel.

(Make comparisons where possible with one spring or loop.)

Conduct an experiment to test your predictions. (For more specific suggestions see Activity *E1*. Don't forget to control the variables in this inquiry. That is, change only one variable at a time while holding the others constant.)

Graph the data you have gathered; for example:

Extension versus applied weight
Extension versus number of springs or loops
Extension versus 1/number of springs or loops

Describe the graphs.

What do the data show? What general relationships do you observe?

From the graphs, determine mathematical formulas to describe the relationships, if you can.

Can you combine all formulas into one general mathematical relationship?

Were your original predictions accurate?

Can you use your findings to predict the extension with more springs or loops than you used in your inquiry?

How can the relationships between the series and the parallel data be explained?

How are these results related to the effects of length, cross-sectional area, and other variables for a single spring or loop?

In what way, if any, is the series and parallel connection of springs or loops related to the series and parallel connection of resistors in an electric circuit? Is the spring system a good analogy for electrical resistors in series and in parallel?

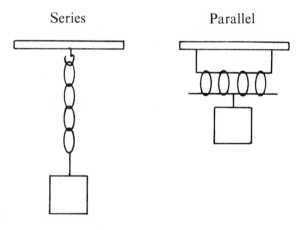

Series   Parallel

Comments

With one spring: a graph of extension versus load results in a positive linear relationship (below the elastic limit).

$$\text{extension} \propto \text{load}; \quad \triangle\ell = k_1 \cdot F$$
$$[\text{change in length}] \qquad [\text{applied force}]$$

With several identical springs in series and a constant load: a graph of extension versus number of springs results in a positive linear relationship.

$$\text{extension} \propto \text{Number of springs}: \quad \triangle\ell = k_2 L$$
$$[\text{length}]$$

With several identical springs in parallel and a constant load: a graph of extension versus number of springs is an inverse relationship; graph of extension versus 1/number of springs is positive and linear.

$$\text{extension} \propto \frac{1}{\text{number of springs}} ; \triangle\ell = k_3 \cdot \frac{1}{A}$$
$$\left[\frac{1}{\text{area}}\right]$$

Combining All

$$\text{extension} \propto \frac{\text{load x number of springs in series}}{\text{number of springs in parallel}}$$

$$\text{extension} \propto \frac{\text{load x length of spring}}{\text{cross sectional area of spring}}$$

$$\triangle\ell \propto \frac{F \times L}{A}$$

$$\triangle\ell = K \cdot \frac{F \cdot L}{A}$$

Reference

Williams, J. E., et al.: *Modern Physics,* 1980. Holt, Rinehart, and Winston, New York, pp. 142–44.

3. Sediment Drag

Science Topics   Sedimentation rate

Level   C:2   E:2   D:2   L:2–3

Overview

In this activity students investigate the effects of mass and shape on the settling rate of particles in quiet water.

Materials

Balance
Plastic modeling clay
Clock with second hand
Marble chips or stones of various sizes
Long plastic tube sealed at one end (2 meters $\times$ 50 mm are convenient dimensions, not critical)

Suggested Activities

What kinds of particles settle out fastest in still water, heavier or lighter ones? Why? [Aristotle or Galileo?]

Design and perform an experiment to test your prediction.

Weigh different-sized marble chips and measure time of descent in the water-filled plastic tube. Graph the results. What can you conclude from the shape of your graph? Why? [Weight or mass is not a predicting variable for settling rate.]

Does shape affect settling rate? Why?

Design and perform an appropriate experiment to test your prediction. (Use something easily shaped, like clay, and keep weight constant. Try different shapes.)

Based on your results, design a streamlined particle that would fall most rapidly. Then, test your prediction. Would your findings about streamlining apply to objects in other fluids like air? Would they apply to the streamlining of automobiles?

What generalizations can you make about the effects of shape and weight on falling? Explain in terms of physical concepts. How is it that the particles do not accelerate in accordance with Newton's second law? Challenge students to a "reverse drag-race"; which team can make the *slowest* falling shape?

Reference

Galindez, P., "Getting the Drop on Sediment", *Science Activities,* 14, 3; May/June, 1977, pp. 21–24.

4. Dancing Raisins

Science Topics   Density, buoyancy

Level   C:1   E:1   D:1   L:1–2

Overview

Since raisins are expected to sink in water, this activity engages students in seeking an explanation for an interesting, puzzling phenomenon. They observe and quickly speculate about what is happening, coming up with a variety of explanations.

Materials

Several raisins
Beaker or plastic cup (250 ml)
One teaspoon of baking soda
25 ml vinegar
Cylinder (25 ml)

Suggested Activities

Mix about 100 ml of water with one teaspoon of baking soda, and 25 ml of vinegar. Then add one or two raisins and observe carefully.

Describe and try to explain what is happening.

Comments

Adjust the vinegar concentration for a steady evolution of bubbles, taking care to prevent frothing. Allow students to speculate freely and avoid defining the problem for them.

After students have had enough time to observe the system and to speculate about it, initiate a class discussion to consider what problems the groups were trying to solve. If they were all working on essentially the same problems, why was this so? (No problem was initially defined.) The centrality of anomalies in initiating inquiry can be highlighted through this activity.

Compare observations of different students. Why are different observations reported by different students? Compare explanations offered for the phenomenon. Which explanations are "best"?

A well carbonated beverage or a mixture of zinc and dilute hydrochloric acid can be used in place of the acid-carbonate mixture.

Reference

Lawlor, F. X. and Lawlor, E. P., "Scientific Anomaly and Raisins in the Fizz Water", *The Science Teacher,* 44, 4; April, 1977, p. 44.

5. The Strange Diver

Science Topics   Density, buoyancy

Level   C:2–3   E:2   D:1   L:2–4

Overview

This activity explores the mechanisms underlying the well-known Cartesian diver phenomenon.

Materials

Dropper
Transparent glass or plastic bottle with tight-fitting stopper

While students initially may explore this phenomenon with a bottle containing one dropper, the photograph shows a variation of the activity with a bottle containing two droppers.

Suggested Activities

Present the dropper assembly. Press on the stopper or on the walls of the bottle until the diver submerges. Then release the pressure. What do you observe?

What happens as the stopper (or walls of the bottle) are pressed and released?

Can you make the diver float at any desired depth?

Does the diver's volume change? mass? density?

When is the diver's density equal to that of water?

Suggest an explanation for your observations.

Design and perform some tests to support or reject your explanation.

What effect would adding salt to the water have on the operation of the diver? Do some experiments to test your prediction. Is the temperature of the water significant? Why?

For more careful investigation, you can use a plastic syringe inserted through a stopper in a large test-tube nearly filled with water.

Will the diver work in other liquids?

Will the diver work with different sized droppers?

Can you make a diver from the head of a match?

Is the explanation for the match head diver the same as that for the rubber stopper?

Can you make a diver using small test-tubes?

Try replacing the dropper with a small aquarium fish. Based on your observations, can you get any clues about how fish control their swimming depth?

Comments

The dropper should contain an amount of water which will keep it initially submerged just below the surface of the water in the bottle. (It is convenient when setting up this apparatus to prepare the droppers in a pail of water so they can be adjusted easily, prior to putting them in the bottle.)

A change in air pressure, when transmitted to the column of air in the dropper, causes a change in the quantity of water in the dropper. The resulting change in the dropper's density causes it to move up or down in the water.

It is interesting to note that the Cartesian diver phenomenon is relevant to mechanisms used by divers, submarines, swimmers, and fish as they rise and descend in water.

References

Arnold, B. N., "The Cartesian Diver", *The School Science Review,* 60, 210; September, 1978, p. 128.

De Vito, A. and Krockover, G. H.: *Creative Sciencing,* 1976. Little Brown and Co., Boston, p. 67–8.

Nicholson, J. R. and Papazachariou, P., "Match-head Divers from Divers Match Heads", *The School Science Review,* 60, 213; June, 1979, pp. 760–1.

Tsab'a, M. "Fish Bladder Analogy", *The Science Teacher,* 47, 5; May, 1980, p. 45.

Ukens, L. L., "Making Cartesian Divers", *The Science Teacher,* 45, 1; January, 1978, p. 35.

6. What's in the Layers?

Science Topics   Density, solubility

Level   C:2   E:1   D:1   L:2

Overview

This teacher-conducted demonstration of immiscible liquid layers invites students to use density and solubility concepts to explain some unusual observations. One or more portions of this activity demand caution in handling potentially dangerous material.

Materials

Three large test tubes	Rubber stoppers
Syrupy phosphoric acid (H_3PO_4)	Pipettes
Concentrated phosphoric acid	Benzene

Iodine solutions of chloroform ($CHCl_3$) and carbon tetrachloride (CCl_4)

Aqueous potassium permanganate (All three solutions should have very light but approximately equal violet color intensity.)

[The carbon tetrachloride, benzene, and phosphoric acid solutions are for the alternative Part 2.]

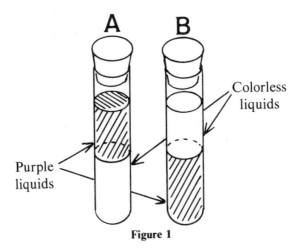

Figure 1

Suggested Activities

Here are some liquids in two tubes.

Tube A: chloroform and an aqueous solution of KMnO₄

Tube B: chloroform solution of Iodine and water

Are the colorless liquids the same? Are the purple liquids the same? Explain.

What simple experiments could you do to test your prediction? [Shaking, separation of layers, mixing in different combinations, odor. . . ?]

An extension of the inquiry, or an alternative, is to present a multi-layered array of liquids as shown in Figure 2.

How many different substances are in the tube?

Could the colored liquids be the same? the colorless liquids?

What might happen if we shook the contents of the tube and then let the liquids settle out again?

Is there more than one possibility?

How do you explain the appearance of the tube after shaking? [After shaking, two phases—aqueous and non-aqueous—settle out.]

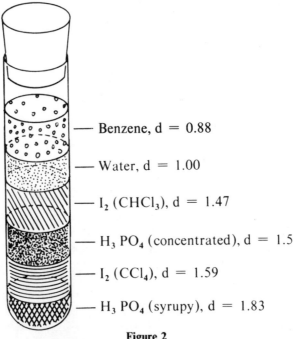

— Benzene, d = 0.88

— Water, d = 1.00

— I₂ (CHCl₃), d = 1.47

— H₃ PO₄ (concentrated), d = 1.5

— I₂ (CCl₄), d = 1.59

— H₃ PO₄ (syrupy), d = 1.83

Figure 2

Comments

In preparing the layers, use a pipette to transfer each liquid with a minimum of mixing.

Safety Precautions

Many of the solutions in this activity are very dangerous: flammable, explosive, toxic, carcinogenic. . . . Thus, they should only be handled by the teacher, using proper safety precautions.

References

Dunbar, R. E., "A Unique Density, Non-Miscibility Demonstration", *Journal of Chemical Education,* 12, 12, 1936, p. 589.

Hopkins, D. E., "The Relative Densities of Liquids", *The School Science Review,* 57, 198; September, 1975, pp. 141–42.

7. The Match-Stick Star

Science Topics   Capillarity

Level   C:2   E:1   D:1   L:1

Overview

This activity is a striking illustration of the effect of water soaking into spaces in wood fiber.

Materials

Five wood match sticks or tooth picks
Flat clean glass plate or other smooth clean surface
Dropper

Suggested Activities

Arrange five bent matches on flat, smooth, clean surface (a glass plate works well), to resemble a five-arm star.

Place a drop of water at the center and observe what happens. [The star opens like a flower.]

Suggest an explanation for what occurs.

Based on your explanation, what other materials could be used; what materials would not work?

Test your explanations.

Make stars from different materials and put a drop of water in the center.

Do the results support your explanation of why the star opens?

References

De Vito, A. and Krockover, G. H.: *Creative Sciencing,* 1976. Little Brown and Co., Boston, p. 42.

Ward, A., "Investigating Small Forces with Match-sticks", *The School Science Review,* 59, 209; June, 1978, pp. 712–13.

8. Getting Pure Water

Science Topics   Distillation

Level   C:2   E:2–3   D:1   L:2–3

Overview

In this activity students learn the principles for operating an efficient distillation apparatus, by actually coping with the practical problems of condensing the water vapor from a boiling mixture. They are given the opportunity to be creative in designing an apparatus to solve a problem.

Materials

Suction flasks	Test tubes
Beakers	Delivery tubes
Rubber tubing	Tripod
Clamp	Gas burner
Ice	Thermometer
A colored solution (such as methyl orange in water)	

Suggested Activities

Obtain a colored solution in a beaker. Try to construct an apparatus for "purifying the water". Decide what apparatus you need and request it from your teacher.

Is it possible to get pure water from the colored solution? How?

Suggest a separation principle or property or mechanism. [Differences in boiling temperature—boil; differences in freezing temperature—freeze; precipitation of dissolved substance—filter. . . .]

Which suggestion seems the most promising? Why?

Design an apparatus for getting pure water; draw and explain.

Use the apparatus to produce some pure water.

Evaluate the method. Is the water pure? Is the method efficient?

Suggest modifications to your separation system that will make it more useful and effective.

Design, use, and evaluate an improved apparatus.

Safety Precautions

CAUTION: Steam can cause bad burns. Check out all apparatus with the teacher before operating.

Comments

The task is one of designing a system to solve a problem. It is best if the written materials available to the student do *not* show a classical distillation diagram. The goal of the activity is to help the student *understand* the operation of a common laboratory apparatus. This inquiry activity may be conducted with different levels of teacher guidance. In an open mode, students should be allowed to actually try out different separation methods they suggest; they should be encouraged to think about the feasibility of their apparatus, both before and after it is tested. In a more guided mode, the following sketches represent stages in the development of an efficient apparatus using differences in boiling point as a separation principle.

After discussing the advantages and disadvantages of the method which seems best among those tried out by members of the class, the teacher can show a Leibig condenser and ask students to explain its operation and its relationship to the methods used in class.

Distillation is one of the most widespread separation procedures in industry and in research. Some well-known examples are to be found in petroleum refining, the oil industry, whiskey production, and water purification.

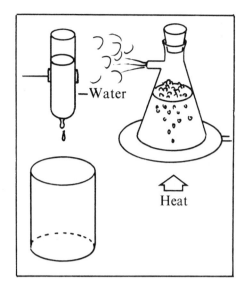

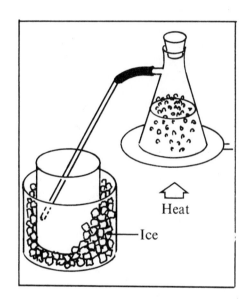

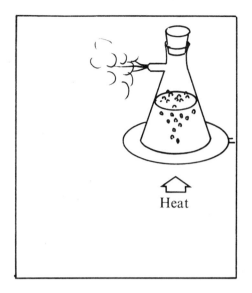

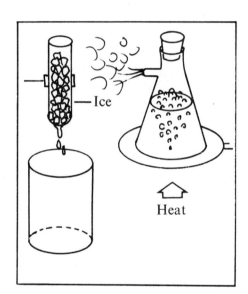

References

Science Teacher Education Project (STEP): *Through the Eyes of the Pupil—A Collection of Pupils' Writings,* 1974. McGraw-Hill, Maidenhead, Berkshire, England, pp. 15–18.

Sivan, R. J., editor: *Teachers Guide for Chemistry Take Shape, Book 1,* 1976. Bar Ilan University, Israel, pp. 28–29. (In Hebrew)

9. Separating Oil from Water

Science Topics   Mixture separation, immiscible liquids, density, air pressure

Level   C:2–3   E:2   D:1   L:2–3

Overview

In this activity students cope with the practical problem of separating oil from water; they design and try out separatory methods.

Materials

A mixture of light oil and water

Large test-tube and stopper assembly (see figure); the glass tubing should slide freely.

Separatory funnel with stopper

Suggested Activities

At home we sometimes need to separate liquids that are mixed together; fat from milk or from soup, water from gasoline or from kerosene. [Give each student or group a large test-tube containing equal volumes of oil (or other liquid immiscible with water) and water.]

Devise a method for separating the oil from the water—try to think of the most efficient way to do this. [Decant, use medicine dropper or pipette. . . .]

Try out your idea. How does your method compare with other proposed suggestions? What are its merits and associated problems?

Give each student or group a two holed stopper with two free moving (use glycerine) tubes of equal length; one tube is closed by a clamp.

Use the double-tube assembly to separate the liquids.

Predict the proper positioning of the tubes.

Which liquid will come out first?

Try out predicted position.

Modify positions if necessary.

Caution: Remove the tube assembly from the test-tube *before* changing the position of the two tubes. This is necessary in order to avoid spillage.

Explain why some positions work and others do not. What are the effects of air pressure?

What are the merits and problems associated with this system of separation?

Separatory funnels like this one are frequently used in scientific and in industrial laboratories and similar principles are used in the huge settling tanks found in many chemical plants (e.g., oil and soap, salt). [Give each student or group of students a small separatory funnel *with* its stopper.]

Use this separatory funnel to separate the oil and water.

Will the funnel work best when it is stoppered or unstoppered?

Try each way and explain the results.

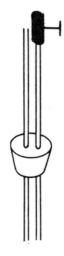

Comments

The task is one of designing a system to solve a problem. It is similar in intent to "Getting Pure Water", Activity *E8*.

The activity involves three stages: a) devising an "original" apparatus, b) discovering the "separating funnel principle" using a double tube assembly, c) using a separatory funnel.

Reference

Sivan, R. J., editor: *Teachers Guide for Chemistry Takes Shape, Book 1,* 1976. Bar Ilan University, Israel, p. 30. (In Hebrew)

10. What's in a Color?

Science Topics   Chromatography, mixtures, kinetic-molecular model

Level   C:2–3   E:2–3   D:1–2   L:2–4

Overview

Chromatography can be a very interesting and informative activity. In this activity, paper chromatography techniques are used to examine the composition of common materials. Students study the effects of different variables and develop and test hypotheses based upon a kinetic-molecular model.

Materials

Jam jars and bottle tops OR test tubes and petri dishes
Rubber bands
Medicine droppers
Common solvents: water, alcohol, acetone; dilute alkaline and acid solutions
Inks of various colors; food dyes
Various papers: Filter paper, toilet paper, napkins, tissue paper, newspaper, writing paper, paper towels
Extracts of various plant leaves such as spinach (optional)

Suggested Activities

Can you separate one color ink into several colors?
Can you separate mixtures of two or more food colors?
Simple chromatography techniques have been developed to help you do so. The differences in the velocity at which a substance (solute) in a solution can be transported and the total distance it travels across a surface (for example, paper) has become a powerful tool in the separation and identification of chemicals.

To use a paper chromatography technique, put a small amount ($\sim$ 1 ml) of a common solvent (water, alcohol, acetone, or . . .) in a small container. Cut a strip of paper somewhat longer than the depth of your container. With the medicine dropper, put successive drops of the substance to be separated or identified on the paper 1 cm from the end of the paper strip; wait until the previous drop has dried before applying each new drop. Hang the paper strip in the container such that the lower end with the substance on it is a few millimeters into the solvent.

What are the effects of using different solvents? Different solution concentrations? Different papers?

Separate extracts of leaves, grass, or vegetables in alcohol solution? What does the chromatogram tell you about the content of these materials?

What factors might be responsible for the separation patterns? Kind of paper? Kind of solvent? Design a series of experiments to find out the effect of each factor on the separation pattern. What are the effects of immersion time? What are the effects of vertical versus horizontal placement of the paper?

Which paper is preferable for a particular substance you have used? Which solvent? Other conditions? How can you be sure that a chromatogram shows all the colors present in a substance?

How can your findings be explained? Formulate hypotheses that will indicate how migration speed or distance travelled is dependent upon:

the density of the particular substance;
the size of the molecules of the particular substance;
the chemical characteristics of the substance;
the chemical and/or physical characteristics of the paper and the solvent.

Are substances that travel more slowly heavier? Are substances that travel slowly the same ones that don't travel very far?

Does molecular weight make a difference?

Design some ways to test your hypotheses.

Acquire a technical handbook on chromatography and develop and use more sophisticated techniques for the separation and analysis of a substance.

Carefully analyze the contents of some special substances of interest (like blood) with appropriate chromatographic techniques.

Safety Precautions

Lab coats will protect clothing from stains of inks and burns of alkaline and acid solutions if these materials are used. Acetone is flammable—avoid use in the presence of a flame.

Comments

This activity can be conducted at a number of levels of sophistication and complexity. For less developed students, materials and techniques can be quite simple. Solvents can be water and alcohol and variables can be controlled through fairly explicit instructions. More advanced students can be allowed to design their own experiments and controls (individually or in groups). In fact, class discussion of these variables and procedures (pre-lab as well as post-lab) can be very beneficial to the development of skills and understanding. Advanced students should be encouraged to propose hypotheses and ways to test them.

Chromatographic techniques provide excellent analytical tools for independent student projects.

References

Joseph, et al.: *A Sourcebook for the Physical Sciences,* 1961. Harcourt, Brace, and World, New York, pp. 296–297.

Macek, K., "Techniques of Paper Chromatography", *Chromatography: A Laboratory Handbook of Chromatographic and Electrophoretic Methods* (3rd edition), 1975. E. Heftmann (ed.), Van Nostrand Reinhold, New York.

Magee, R.: *Selected Readings in Chromatography,* 1970. The Commonwealth and International Library, Pergamon Press, New York.

Morholt, E., Brandwein, P. F., and Joseph, A.: *Teaching High School Science: A Sourcebook for the Biological Sciences,* 1966. Harcourt, Brace, New York, pp. 183–184.

Stock, R. and Rice, C. B. F.: *Chromatographic Methods,* 1974. Chapman and Hall, London.

11. Nuclear Radiation in My Bedroom?

Science Topic   Nuclear Radiation, Inverse-Square Law, Radiation Absorbers.

Level   C:2–3   E:2–3   D:2–3   L:2–4

Overview

Students examine the effects of distance from a radioactive source upon radiation intensity. They also examine the effects of different materials and material thickness as radiation shields or absorbers. The activity can be pursued with quantitative measurements using a Geiger counter, and from a graph of data, an inverse-square relationship between intensity of radiation and distance can be inferred.

Materials

Weak radiation source (a clock with radioactive luminous hands will be sufficient)
Geiger counter
Meter stick
Assorted sheets of materials (for use as radiation absorbers)

Suggested Activities

I have been told that the light coming from the luminous dial and hands of my bedside clock is the result of radioactive materials that have been placed there. My eyes detect the light coming from the dial; can a Geiger counter detect evidence of radioactivity as well? If so, how does the intensity of radiation vary with distance? Make a prediction and test that prediction using a Geiger counter. How does the amount of radiation reaching the Geiger counter change as the Geiger counter is moved away from the source of radiation? Is it a simple inverse relationship or is it an exponential or more complex relationship?

Measure the intensity of radiation at several distances from the source and plot a graph of intensity versus distance. Naturally, as in other inquiries, it is important to control variables in an attempt to understand the actual physical relationships. Thus, it is important to examine the nature of the background radiation that is present in the room when the special source you are examining is not there. With the Geiger counter at the setting you will use throughout your inquiry, record the background count and subtract this count from readings you take when you are examining radiation from your source. A good way to make these measurements is to record the number of counts (intensity) in an appropriate time interval. What relationship does the graph of intensity versus distance from the source show between these variables? (If you suspect there may be an exponential relationship, check by using special graphing technique X1. You can also test predictions of the mathematical relationship using specific data points you have measured.)

What are the effects of barriers placed between the source of radiation and your Geiger counter? Does the kind of material make a difference? Thickness of the barrier? Other variables? You may wish to conduct a careful inquiry into the effects of one or more of these variables. For example, keeping all other variables like distance constant, it might be interesting to plot a graph of intensity of radiation versus the thickness of cardboard by changing the number of sheets of cardboard used to shield the radiation.

If you were to use a more intense source of radiation, predict how this would effect the graph and the relationship of radiation intensity to distance. Test your prediction if you can.

How can you explain the relationships between distance and radiation intensity that you have observed in this activity? What "model" of radiation best explains these relationships?

Nuclear radiation is now commonly recognized to be harmful if certain low doses are exceeded. Is the amount of radiation that comes from the luminous clock dial harmful? Does the clock have any kind of marker indicating the nature of the radiation or whether or not it might be harmful? In past years many persons wore wrist watches with luminous dials. Are these potentially harmful with long-term use? What is the possibility that twenty years from now a study will claim that the radiation from the clock in my bedroom has been harmful? Can you make recommendations on the use of this kind of radiation based on your inquiry and search for information? Is relevant information available in your community or state on these questions?

Nuclear reactors are more intense sources of radiation than the relatively safe sources you have been examining. How do the properties of radiation intensity and shielding materials in a large nuclear reactor differ from the properties you have observed in your inquiry? What other sources of radiation exist in your home or community? What kinds of "radiation" may come from TV sets or microwave ovens or the sun? How can these be monitored? What levels of radiation are "safe"? Is the background radiation uniform throughout your community? Is it random?

Comments

This activity provides a relatively simple way to gather data that will show the inverse-square relationship between distance from a source of radiation and radiation intensity. The inverse-square relationship may be "discovered" or verified in several ways. One useful technique involves logarithmic graph paper and is described in section X1.

Levels of radiation present in older luminous clock dials and in the weak sources available for use in student laboratories have been considered safe when properly used. Proper safety precautions should always be taken when using even the weakest radiation sources. Students should be careful not to touch or ingest any sources and should always wash their hands after using radioactive sources.

When students inquire about sources of radiation in their community or state, about monitoring procedures, and about levels of safety, they will often discover that insufficient information is available. Locating information sources and determining what information *should* be available can be part of the inquiry.

References

Atomic Energy Commission, "Radioisotope Experiments for the Chemistry Curriculum" (Student manual 17311) Washington: Office of Technical Services.

Rutherford, F. J., et al.: *Project Physics Handbook,* 1970. Holt, Rinehart, and Winston, New York, pp. 321–332.

Stong, C. L., "How the Amateur Scientist Can Perform Experiments that Call for the Use of Radioisotopes.", *Scientific American,* N.Y., May 1960, p. 189.

F Heat/Kinetic-Molecular Model

1. Keeping Heat Together

Science Topics   Heat flow, heat exchange, conduction, convection, evaporation, radiation, conservation of energy.

Level   C:2–3   E:2–3   D:2   L:2–3

Overview

Students study heat exchange and related phenomena especially relevant to contemporary concerns regarding conservation of energy resources in the heating of homes and buildings.

Materials

Tin cans
Plastic
Large beaker
Clock timer or watch
Thermometers (two for each pair of students)
Beaker tongs or insulated mitts
Various insulation materials (cloth, styrofoam, wood, metals, plastics, commercial insulation materials)

Styrofoam
Glass cups
Tripod and wire gauze
Bunsen burner or alcohol lamp

Suggested Activities

Much of our personal energy consumption goes into heating (cooking, heating the home, heating water) and cooling (refrigeration and air conditioning). A good portion of this energy appears to be lost largely as a result of design problems in our homes and appliances. Much heat energy that could be retained is dissipated through chimneys, roofs, and windows. . . . In a time of declining energy resources and increasing energy costs, how can we become more energy efficient? To do so, we need to explore and understand the nature of heat flow from one body to another and we need to investigate the insulating properties of various materials and structural arrangements.

One way to investigate some of the relationships that are important is to examine the cooling of hot water in an open paper cup of water. Using water of about 80°C read and record the temperature of the water every 30 seconds. It may be helpful to plot a graph of temperature versus time.

Predict what you can do to increase the rate at which the water cools. Predict what you can do to reduce the rate of cooling. For example, what are the effects of stirring, inserting a spoon in the cup, using cups made of other materials, wrapping the cup in various insulating materials, blowing a stream of air across the top of the cup, insulating the top of the cup? Make some predictions about the effects of these procedures and test them. Comparing graphs of the cooling curves may be very revealing. How can the relationships you have discovered by explained?

What are the effects of the material of which the cup is made, the various types of insulation material, the various ways of insulating? How can you explain these effects?

These kinds of questions may be especially relevant if you want to keep a cup of coffee or cocoa as hot as possible. If you must stir it, what are the effects of the kind of spoon you use? Will plastic or stainless steel make a difference? If you must add sugar or cream, when should they be added so as to dissolve and yet keep the liquid at an optimum temperature for drinking?

What hypotheses can be formulated regarding the role of evaporation, conduction, convection, and radiation on the rate of cooling in the various arrangements you have studied in this inquiry? From what you know about these processes (or can read about them) make some predictions about new ways to reduce the rate of heat transfer from your cup of water. Will wrapping a container in aluminum foil reduce the rate of cooling of hot water noticeably? Can you measure the effects of aluminum foil on the transfer of heat in some other arrangement of materials? How do you explain your results? Should insulation in the home always have an aluminum foil barrier as well as other forms of conventional insulation materials? Compare the cooling rate of hot water in your best insulated system with that in a thermos bottle that can be purchased in a store. Are all commercial thermos bottles equally effective?

In your inquiry thus far, what variables have you not controlled? How may these variables have distorted the results you have obtained?

What implications do the results of your inquiry have for the design of energy efficient cooking procedures, refrigeration units, or homes generally? If one wants to boil a fixed amount of water what are the effects of pan size, shape, and material? What are the effects of amount of water, surface area, volume/surface area ratio? Should a lid be used? What are the effects of drafts? What are the effects of using a lot of energy to heat the water quickly versus a lower burner setting? Possibly you may wish to compare energy consumption using electricity, natural gas, and microwave stoves. What are the effects of cooking where there are drafts of air across the stove? Design an optimum cooking environment.

Another interesting extension of this activity is to examine and compare the efficiency of home heating systems such as hot air convection, hot water convection, forced hot water, steam heating, etc. How can the heating system in your school or home be modified to conserve energy, to make it more efficient while maintaining appropriate standards of safety and comfort?

What are appropriate temperature ranges that will enable optimal energy efficiency and yet not result in unnecessary human discomfort? What are the effects of lowering temperatures during non-working hours on energy consumption and efficiency? What variables need to be examined to properly answer this question?

Another interesting extension of the practical laboratory aspects of this activity is to examine the temperature gradient across an insulating medium or barriers. For example, what are the effects of inserting panes of glass on the heat lost through a window? A simulated window could be set up in the laboratory between a hot area and a cooler area and the temperature between successive plates of glass could be examined. The effects of the number of panes of glass, the thickness of the glass, and the kind of glass could be examined quantitatively. Similar temperature gradient studies could be run on a variety of different kinds of materials including insulating materials with heat applied at one side of the surface and temperature measurements made with thermometers at intervals across the material.

What are the effects of different commercial windows? Roofing materials?

Safety Precautions

Students heating water should use proper safety precautions; beaker tongs or insulated mitts may be used to handle hot beakers.

Comments

In classes with less sophisticated students, the teacher can specify procedures for one or two portions of this activity and then suggest that students might pursue their own ideas regarding ways in which one could keep water warm longer. This kind of relevant, practical activity can stimulate some students to do a lot of work outside of class.

Reference

Miller, F., et al.: *Concepts in Physics,* 1980. Harcourt, Brace, and Jovanovich, New York, pp. 195–196.

2. Warm Clothing

Science Topic   Heat flow, conduction

Level   C:2–3   E:2–3   D:2   L:2–3

Overview

Students study heat flow and conduction in textiles and fabrics particularly relevant to clothing. The activity can be conducted at a number of levels of sophistication.

Materials

Calorimeter or beaker or jar
Thermometer
Samples of textiles: wool, linen, cotton, nylon, . . .
Clock timer
Beaker, Bunsen burner, tripod and gauze, tongs or insulated mitts

Suggested Activities

Textiles and other fabrics differ in their ability to conduct heat or to insulate depending on the kind of fiber used and the way the fibers have been woven and treated. As you know, the clothing you choose to wear outdoors on a cold winter day should have very different characteristics than the clothing you wear on a very hot summer afternoon. How do these fabrics differ? Do they have different insulating characteristics?

One way to inquire about these questions is to fill a glass jar or beaker or calorimeter with hot water (approximately 80°C), put a lid (with a hole for the thermometer) on top and measure the temperature every one half minute until the temperature stabilizes. It may be helpful to plot a graph of temperature versus time. Subsequently wrap various kinds of fabric around the calorimeter or jar and compare the temperature loss across time with the standard developed when there was no cloth wrapped around the calorimeter. What are the effects of different fabrics on cooling time? During your inquiry into the effects of different fabrics, are you holding all other variables constant? What are some other variables that must be carefully controlled? Does the thickness of the fabric make a difference? Make predictions about the insulating properties of different fabrics and then test them. Which fabrics are the best insulators? Do they have any common structural similarities or differences that you can identify? What characteristics of a fabric seem to effect its insulating properties? What differences exist between "summer" and "winter" fabrics? Which fabric provides the "best" heat insulation?

If a fabric is wet, is there a difference in its insulating characteristics? Can your findings on the effects of moisture for one fabric be generalized to different kinds of fabrics or do they behave differently in the presence of moisture?

What kind of model can you construct to explain how heat is dissipated through an insulating barrier? Do any of the fabrics trap air in the fabric? If so, is it the fabric or the air itself that is the insulator? If air is trapped in the fabric and is prevented from circulating, does the fabric reduce heat loss (insulate) because it inhibits transfer of heat by conduction, convection, radiation, or some combination of the three? What kind of experiment would you design to test your explanation?

Do fabrics that are poor insulators always allow for good ventilation? Can you observe any similarities and differences in the structure and insulating properties of synthetic and natural fabrics?

How can your observations be explained? What are the possible effects of structure on insulating characteristics? What would be a good test for your hypotheses?

This inquiry might well be extended to examine the insulating properties of sleeping bags, shoes, and other items.

Another interesting extension would be to examine the traditional clothing habits of desert tribes, Eskimos, Indians, mountain peoples and so on.

I once heard that it was better to wear white clothing in the summer to "reflect" heat and to stay cool and dark clothing in the winter to absorb heat and stay warm. Is this "old wives' tale" valid? If we use identical fabrics except for color will there be noticeable differences in the rate at which heat dissipates and the water cools? Make a prediction and test it. What do you observe when you conduct the investigation? What do the data show? How can you explain your results? If you observed no noticeable differences, could you propose a more sophisticated test that may in fact show differences if they are present?

Safety Precautions

Students using hot water should use proper safety precautions; tongs or insulated mitts may be used to handle hot beakers.

Reference

Miller, F., et al.: *Concepts in Physics,* 1980. Harcourt, Brace, and Jovanovich, New York, pp. 195– –196.

3. A Freezing Problem

Science Topics   Phase change, heat transfer, heat of fusion, change of state

Level   C:2–4   E:2   D:1   L:2–4

Overview

Students investigate the question: Which freezes faster, hot or cold water?

Materials

Water
Beakers or other containers
Two thermometers
Ice cube trays or paper cups
Freezer or other source of temperatures below 0°C

Suggested Activities

My aunt once told me that hot water in an ice cube tray would speed up the making of ice cubes. Was she right? To make ice cubes quickly, is it better to fill the ice cube tray with hot water or with cold water prior to putting it in the freezer?

Design and carry out experiments to test your prediction.

Compare different designs used by members of the class and discuss the results obtained.

Work out a common experimental design and repeat the experiment.

Suggest hypotheses to explain the results.

Do impurities in the water make a difference? What are the effects of using distilled water? Does the volume and surface area of the ice cube tray make a difference? Does a freezer that is "frost-free" make a difference?

Comments

The problem, "which freezes faster, hot or cold water", presents an anomalous situation conducive to many inquiry activities: formulating hypotheses, designing experiments, controlling variables, explanation of relationships. There is no "textbook answer" to the problem, making it particularly suitable for unbiased research.

A decade ago, a young African student named Mpemba discovered that hot milk freezes into ice cream faster than cold milk. Mpemba's story is documented in the *Physics Education* references. Mpemba's story is a fascinating one and is highly recommended reading.

In order to stimulate student involvement and curiosity, students may be asked to carry out the experiment at home and try to arrive at an answer. Their findings can then be the basis for class discussion of the variables involved, possible reasons for disagreement, and possible explanations of the results.

In a second phase of the activity, students could repeat the experiment, with improvements suggested in the first class discussion.

The post-lab discussion should focus on the various investigative approaches, the "answers" to the inquiry based upon experimental results, explanations of the findings, and probable sources of error.

Typical student responses in the inquiry are reported in the article by Robert James.

References

Ahtee, M., "Investigating the Freezing of Liquids", *Physics Education*, 4, 6, 1969, pp. 379–380.

Deeson, E., "Cooler—Lower Down", *Physics Education*, 5, 1, 1970, pp. 42–44.

Firth, I., "Cooler", *Physics Education*, 5, 1, 1970, pp. 32–41.

James, R. K., "Which Freezes First, Hot or Cold Water", *The Science Teacher*, 44, 1; January, 1977, pp. 39–40.

Mpemba, E. B. and Osborne, D. G., "Cool?", *Physics Education*, 4, 3, 1969, pp. 172–175.

4. The Rising Tube Puzzle

Science Topics   Air pressure, surface tension

Level   C:2   E:1   D:1   L:2–3

Overview

This activity is based on the demonstration of a simple discrepant phenomenon which challenges students to seek a reasonable explanation.

Materials

Two test tubes of similar diameter such that one can be inserted into the other with minimal space between them.

Suggested Activities

A student or the teacher (demonstrator) shows a group two test tubes, the smaller of which narrowly fits into the larger. He or she fills the large tube with water to the brim and then inserts the empty smaller tube into the larger one.

What will happen to the smaller tube if the system is inverted? [It will fall out; it will remain stationary; it will rise.]

The demonstrator inverts the system; the smaller tube rises into the larger tube as water drips out.

Why does the inner tube rise? Suggest hypotheses to explain the "rising tube" puzzle. Test these hypotheses if you can. [Air in the inner tube pushes up more strongly than the force of gravity pulls the inner tube down; air cannot get in between the tubes; there is a force of attraction between the inner tube and the outer tube.]

Investigate the effects of some variables on the rising tube phenomenon: varying the relative diameter of the tubes; varying the liquid in the larger tube; varying the relative lengths of tubes; varying the temperature of the liquid; varying the material of which the tubes are made.

Safety Precautions

Care must be taken with the slippery glass tubes to see that they do not fall and shatter when inverted. [Have policy clearly established on the manner in which broken glass should be handled.]

Comments

The principle focus of this activity is the search for an explanation for a puzzling discrepant event.

The activity is open ended and several explanations which might be suggested may be supported by observations. Explanations should, as always, be considered tentative. Members of the group should argue the reasonableness of their explanations.

Reference

Andersen, H. O. and Koutnik, P. G.: *Toward More Effective Instruction in the Secondary School,* 1972. MacMillan, New York, pp. 62–63.

5. The Water Level Game

Science Topics   Air pressure

Level   C:2   E:2   D:1   L:2

Overview

This is a variation of the demonstration that water "seeks its own level".

Materials

Two transparent polyethylene bottles with caps
Cork borer
A 30 cm. length of flexible plastic tubing

Bore holes in the bottles with a warmed work borer slightly smaller in diameter than the tube; join the bottles (see figure). Half fill the bottles with colored water.

Suggested Activities

Give the assembly to small groups and ask them to see what they can find out about it. Initially the bottles are closed and the water level in one bottle is considerably higher than in the other.

Why are the levels different?

What will make the water levels change in the bottles? lifting?, lowering?, holding closer or further apart?

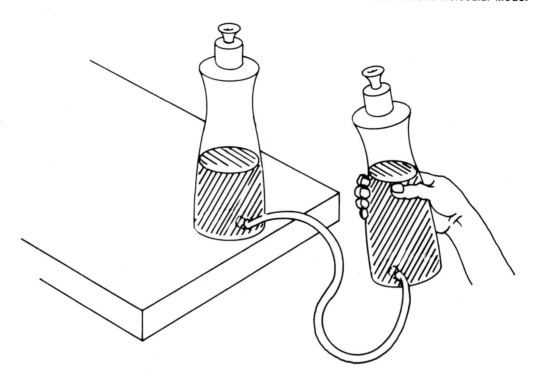

Test your predictions.

Why do the levels change? Sketch an explanation.

Can the water levels be changed if both bottles are closed? If one bottle is closed?

Were your predictions confirmed? If not, why not?

Equalizing water levels is frequently used in the laboratory to insure that a trapped quantity of gas is measured at atmospheric pressure.

Reference

Ward, A., "Water Seeking Its Own Level—Science or Kinetic Art?", *School Science Review,* 57, 198; September, 1975, p. 138.

6. The Suction Puzzle

Science Topics   Air pressure

Level   C:2   E:1   D:1   L:2

Overview

It is commonly thought that liquids are drawn up by "suction", implying a pulling force. This activity is designed to lead students to the realization that the "rise" of liquids is better explained by the "pushing force" of air pressure. It tests the notion that "nature abhors a vacuum".

Materials

Two plastic syringes (50 ml)

Connecting tube

Nail

Water

With a hot nail make a hole in the middle of the plunger of one syringe (see figure).

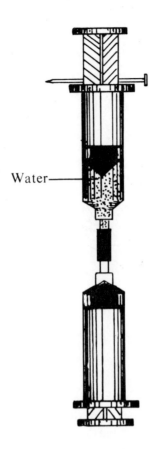

Water—

Suggested Activities

Show students the system described in the figure. How can we draw water from the first syringe into the second? Why should your idea work? Test your idea. If it doesn't work, try to explain why.

Comments

To prepare the system, draw water into one syringe from a beaker, insert the nail into the plunger, and then connect this syringe to the second one with a short length of firmly fitting tubing. Make sure there are no leaks!

Entertain all ideas for solving the problem. It will be clear that pulling the moveable plunger does not do the job—"suction" does not work!

Reference

Inversin, A. R., "Does 'Suction' Pull?", *The Science Teacher*, 44, 2; February, 1977, p. 38.

7. The Drinking Bird

Science Topics   Phase change, vapor pressure, static equilibrium, center of gravity, capillarity.

Level   C:2–3   E:1–2   D:1   L:3–4

Overview

The fascinating rhythm of the bird dipping its beak into a glass of water and then swinging upright raises questions related to many science concepts and provides opportunities to create and discuss explanatory models.

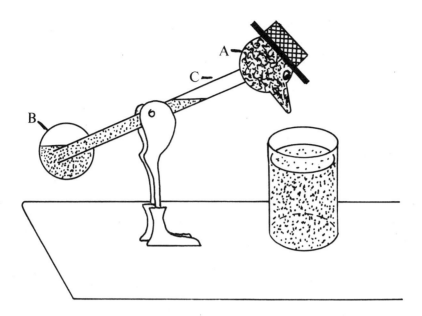

Materials

One "drinking bird" and a cup of water

Suggested Activities

Dip the bird's flannel-covered beak in a cup of water and then give it a slight swing. Soon the bird begins to tilt forward toward the water and the swing dies down. Suddenly it dips its beak into the water placed in front of it. Having satisfied its "thirst" it returns to the upright position and the whole process is repeated.

Observe and describe the drinking cycle using drawings.

Suggest an explanation for the birds' continuous cycle of dipping and rising.

What are some variables that might affect the bird's rate of dipping? [Position of pivot point, kind of liquid, room temperature, color of bird's parts, location indoors or outdoors (wind), relative humidity. . . .]

Test your predictions about the effects of some of the variables.

Will the bird bounce up and down forever? Explain.

Would your answer change if the cup of water were continually full or if it were a river?

Can the bird be a perpetual motion machine?

Safety Precautions

The liquids used in drinking birds are volatile and their vapors are toxic and sometimes flammable. The bird should be handled with care and should not be used near an open flame.

Comments

Glass bulbs A and B, connected by tube C, comprise a closed system containing a volatile liquid. The bird's head and beak are covered with felt-like material which must be kept wet. Tube C is pivoted on a pair of static plastic legs.

As the bird rights itself after dipping into the water, evaporation from the wet head causes cooling which reduces the vapor pressure in bulb A. Liquid is therefore pushed up from the bottom bulb; the center of gravity rises, eventually toppling the beak back into the water. The vapors in bulb A and bulb B make contact and liquid flows back to the bottom. Then the whole process is ready to start again.

Using a transparent bird, a large variety of inquiry questions may be posed. The W. E. Spooner reference lists 32 such inquiry questions.

A non-transparent type drinking bird may be preferred for inquiry activity since the mechanism is more obscure and students may suggest and discuss a wider variety of tentative mechanisms. This kind of discussion provides excellent opportunities to examine the probabilities of tentative models and explanations and to discuss the design of experiments to test explanations suggested.

References

Siddons, J. C., "Some Simple Physics Experiments", *The School Science Review,* 47, 162; March, 1966, pp. 471–2.

Smith, B. A., "Buoyancy", *The School Science Review,* 61, 217; June, 1980, p. 761.

Spooner, W. E., "Energy is for the Birds, Too", *The Science Teacher,* 44, 6; September, 1977, pp. 34–35.

Ward, A., "The Physics of the Goofy Bird", *The School Science Review,* 53, 194; March, 1972, p. 614.

8. The Balloon Fountain

Science Topics   Air pressure

Level   C:2   E:2   D:1   L:2

Overview

A series of operations involving inflating and deflating a balloon enclosed in a flask leads to many questions posed by the students themselves. They are challenged to come up with answers in terms of pressure relationships.

Materials

One large bottle (1000 ml)
Glass tubing
One balloon
One large beaker (1000 ml)

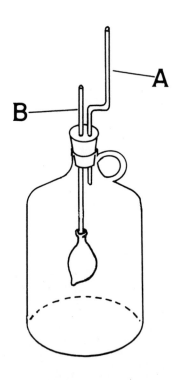

Suggested Activities

Construct an apparatus as in the drawing:
Then:

1. Leave tube A open to the air and inflate the balloon by blowing into tube B.
2. Before removing mouth from tube B, firmly press a finger against the opening of tube A.
3. Before removing finger from tube A, firmly press a finger against the opening of tube B.
4. Keep tube B closed, invert the bottle, and put tube A in a beaker of water.
5. Remove finger from tube B and observe carefully.

What questions do you have about what you observed?
Try to explain what happened at each stage.
Would adding more water to the beaker start the fountain effect again? Why?
Test your predictions.

Comments

Make all connections as air tight as possible.
Balloon inflates when air is blown into B, and A remains open.
Balloon remains inflated when mouth is removed while tube A is closed.
Balloon remains inflated when A is opened while B is closed—a small suction affect may be noticed when A is opened.
Water spurts into the flask when A is inverted into water and B is opened—water continues to enter the flask until the balloon is nearly deflated.

Reference

Barron, P., "Air Pressure and Balloons", *The Science Teacher,* 45, 5; May, 1978, p. 46.

9. Does Air Help or Interfere?

Science Topics   Diffusion, sublimation

Level   C:1–2   E:2   D:1   L:2

Overview

Diffusion, the spontaneous spreading of matter, is explained in the particle model in terms of the constant, random motion of particles. Many students have the preconception that the diffusion of a gas (such as ammonia) in air is mediated by air particles ("the air particles 'carry' the gas particles through the room"). This activity is designed to reinforce the idea of random particle motion.

Materials

A few iodine crystals
Two small test tubes (10mm x 75mm)
Plastic syringe (100 ml)
Stopper
Nail
Rubber band
Spatula
Alcohol burner

(A hole is made at the end of the plunger using a heated nail as shown in the figure.)

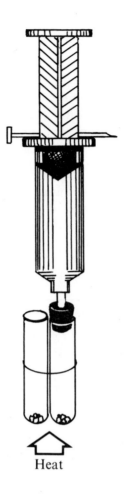

Heat

Suggested Activities

Does a gas diffuse faster in air or in a vacuum? [In air—air particle motion helps move the gas; in a vacuum—the movement of air hinders free movement of the gas (particle collisions).]

Design an experiment to test your hypothesis.

Discuss proposed experimental designs, their advantages and disadvantages.

In one convenient method, a partial vacuum is created using a syringe; iodine is convenient to use as the gas, for the solid sublimes and the vapor is easily seen.

A partial vacuum is created in one of the two tubes as follows:

The syringe is connected to the tube when the plunger is *in*.

The piston is pulled out and the nail inserted through the prepared hole in the plunger.

The pressure may be reduced to about 0.1 atmosphere, which is adequate for testing the hypotheses.

In performing the experiment, a few small iodine crystals are placed in each tube (try to have equal quantities). The pressure is reduced in one tube and then the tubes are fastened together by a rubber band. The iodine samples are heated *gently*. (An alternative to direct heating is to place the system in a warm water bath.)

Carry out the experiment and interpret the results. Are the results consistent with your hypothesis? [The iodine diffuses quickly in the evacuated tube, as evidenced by crystals formed on the cooler upper part. Although the iodine vaporizes in the open tube it does not reach the cool upper part nearly as quickly. Thus, there is a very noticeable difference in the quantity of sublimed iodine at the top of the two tubes. The violet color is also more intense at the bottom of the open tube]

Safety Precautions

Iodine must be handled with care. Dispense it with a spatula.

Waste iodine can be dissolved in methanol for future use. Use only a few crystals in each tube and heat directly with an alcohol burner only, in order to avoid escape of toxic iodine fumes.

Comments

This experiment could be presented as a demonstration, by preparing two large sealed ampules containing iodine crystals, one evacuated and one at normal air pressure. In that case it would be very important to insure that students understand the meaning of reduced air pressure in the evacuated tube and preferably the method of evacuation.

References

IPS Group, Educational Services, Inc., *Introductory Physical Science,* Prentice Hall, Inc., Englewood Cliffs, N.J., 1967, pp. 181–183.

*Sivan, R. J., "Gaseous Diffusion in Air and in a Vacuum", *The School Science Review,* 58, 155; June, 1977, pp. 750–751.

10. What Happened to the Ether?

Science Topics   Phase change, vapor pressure

Level   C:3–4   E:2   D:1   L:2–4

Overview

This simple experiment, showing that a solution has a lower vapor pressure than the pure liquid, affords opportunities to make predictions and formulate hypotheses. Portions of this activity demand caution in handling potentially dangerous material.

Materials

One wide-mouth bottle and tight-fitting cap
Two specimen tubes (about 4 cm long by 1.3 cm diameter)
Dry ether
Oil-soluble dye
Napthalene crystals

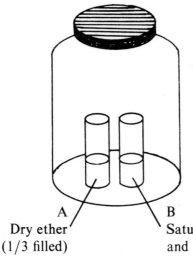

A
Dry ether
(1/3 filled)

B
Saturated solution of naphthalene in ether
and a trace of oil-soluble dye (1/3 filled)

Suggested Activities

Present system as shown in the figure. Invite students to ponder what, if anything, will happen in 2 or 3 days.

Predict changes that will occur in the system over time.

Explain the basis for your prediction.

Observe the system over a period of several days and describe your observations.

How can your observations be explained?

Predict the results you would expect with other volatile liquids and with water.

Repeat your observations using other liquids.

Explain differences in results when other liquids are used.

Predict the effects of temperature on the system. If you decide to test your prediction be extremely careful with explosive fluids like ether.

Safety Precautions

Ether must be handled with EXTREME care. Do not keep large quantities in stock. *Avoid open flames!*

Comments

The oil-soluble dye is used to visually differentiate between the two liquids.

Over a period of several days: the level in (A) drops, in (B) rises—after 2 or 3 days, depending on the temperature, all the ether is transferred to the solution.

The vapor pressure principle underlying this inquiry is applied in the use of antifreeze in automobiles and in salt to melt snow on the streets.

References

*Casey, M. T., "Two Simple Experiments to Show that a Solution Has a Lower Vapor Pressure than the Pure Solvent," *The School Science Review,* 47, 162; March, 1966, pp. 497–8.

Joseph, A., et al., *A Sourcebook for the Physical Sciences,* Harcourt, Brace, and World, Inc., N.Y., 1961, pp. 157–158.

11. Boiling by Cooling

Science Topics   Boiling, vapor pressure

Level   C:3   E:1–2   D:1   L:2–3

Overview

A puzzling phenomenon, seeing water boil as it is cooled, should stimulate generation of interesting hypotheses and application of kinetic molecular theory.

Materials

Large pyrex flask	Wire gauze
Rubber stopper	Towel
Bunsen burner	Ring stand

Suggested Activities

Place a large flask, ¾–filled with water and nearly boiling over a bunsen flame. After the water is boiling vigorously close the burner and tightly stopper the flask.

Is the water boiling now? Why?

What will happen if we cool the water quickly? Make a prediction and within a minute after the water has ceased to boil, invert the flask and hold it under cold running tap water. What do you observe now? Try to explain what you have observed. How does the cold water running on the flask affect the air above the water inside the flask?

What is in the bubbles that rise through water as it boils? What conditions are necessary for bubbles to exist in a liquid?

Can you suggest another way to make the water boil without heating it? Test your suggestion. [Can you reduce the pressure above the water by removing air?]

Continue the inquiry using a Buchner flask and after boiling, connect the closed flask to a water aspirator in the laboratory. Alternatively draw some hot water into a glass syringe, expel all the air, close the opening with a pinch clamp, and then pull out the piston to create a partial vacuum.

- -

Does it take more or less time to hard-boil an egg on a high mountain than at sea level? Explain. Explain why a pressure cooker shortens cooking time.

Safety Precautions

Use proper caution and care in handling the flask with boiling water and when cooling it under cold tap water.

Comments

When the flask with water at 100°C is cooled under cold water, the hot water begins to boil (large bubbles rise through the water).

It is interesting to note that sugar must be crystallized from solution after colored impurities are removed by adsorption on charcoal. The commercial process normally involves evaporation under reduced pressure at low temperature to prevent charring.

Reference

Baisley, D., "Boiling at Reduced Pressure", *The Science Teacher,* 47, 5; May, 1980, p. 45.

G Chemical Properties and Reactions

1. Mystery Powders I

Science Topics   Qualitative analysis

Level   C:1–2   E:1–2   D:1   L:2–4

Overview

This is an open activity in which students can make simple observations and combine them with elements of previous knowledge to make inferences about a group of "unknown" solids. They can also evaluate limitations about the number of inferences that can be made.

Materials

12 powders in plastic cups labeled 1–12:

Powdered Bromo seltzer®	Corn starch
Plaster of paris	Flour
Baking soda	Baking powder
Instant mashed potatoes	Free flowing salt
Coarse salt	Instant non-fat dry milk
Granulated pure cane sugar	Powdered confectioner's sugar

Three liquids in dropper bottles labeled A, B, C:

Water	Diluted vinegar

Very diluted iodine solution (in aqueous potassium iodide)

Burner or candle	Test tubes or aluminum foil (for cups)
Test tube holder	Wire gauze
Tripod	Magnifying glass
Wood splints	

Suggested Activities

Obtain unnamed white powders and colorless liquids, a test-tube holder, a burner, a magnifying glass, a set of test-tubes, a tripod and wire gauze. Find out whatever you can about the powders.

How can they best be described and classified?

Make some tentative hypotheses about the identity of some or all the solids. Make some tentative hypotheses about the identity of the gases evolved.

Test your hypotheses.

After the students have examined the powders and classified them, give them some "unknown" powders to identify. One or more of these might be mixtures of the original powders.

Comments

This inquiry, a variation of the Elementary Science Study (ESS) Mystery Powders activity, can be challenging at any level. As in the ESS activity, most of the inquiry can be conducted on wax paper on the table top without the necessity of using test-tubes and other specialized apparatus. (The powders can be handled using wood splints and plastic spoons.)

Twelve powders may be too large a number for some less advanced students to handle, in which case you can use a smaller number. Other powders and indicator liquids can be used in a similar way, to develop students' ability to make systematic observations and logical inferences. (A structured variation of an activity with common powders is described in the Deibler reference.)

References

Batoff, M. E., "Mystery Powders: An Intriguing 12", *The Science Teacher,* 40, 8; November, 1973, p. 42.

Deibler, R. W., "The Scientific Method", *Science Activities,* 14, 3; May/June, 1977, pp. 25–27.

Elementary Science Study: *Mystery Powders,* 1968. McGraw-Hill, Webster Division, St. Louis.

2. Mystery Powders II

Science Topics   Qualitative analysis

Level   C:2   E:1–2   D:1   L:2–4

Overview

This is a structured variation of Mystery Powders I. Students are given four unknown powders (A, B, C, and D) and three unknown liquids (I, II, and III) and use the results of their interactions as a guide to identifying mixtures of A, B, C, and D.

Materials

Four powders in paper cups labeled A, B, C, D:

Sugar	Laundry starch
Baking powder	Table salt

Three liquids labeled I, II, III:

Diluted vinegar	Water

Very diluted iodine solution (in aqueous potassium iodide)

Various mixtures of A, B, C, and D

Test tubes	Wood splints
Magnifying glass	

Suggested Activities

Give students solids A, B, C, and D in paper cups and dropper bottles containing solution I, II, and III. Ask them to devise a scheme to identify A, B, C, and D, using solutions I, II, and III. Then give them mixtures and ask them to identify the components—which have been made up from the solids A, B, C, and D.

Comments

Students may need some guidance as to quantities.

They should use very small quantities of solid (to just cover the bottom of the test-tube) and about 10 ml of liquid to determine relative solubility.

It is possible that students may not be able to identify some mixtures with certainty. Encourage students to consider the limitations of their techniques and ways to improve them.

References

Elementary Science Study: *Mystery Powders,* 1968. McGraw-Hill, Webster Division, St. Louis. Whitmer, J. C., "Kitchen Chemistry", *Journal of Chemical Education,* 52, 10; 1975, p. 665.

3. Mystery Powders III

Science Topics   Chemical reactions

Level   C:2   E:1–2   D:1   L:2–3

Overview

This is an open-ended activity rich with opportunities for making careful observations and pursuing unusual ideas. Manipulating two unknown white powders in a plastic cup, thinking about what happens and dreaming up unusual things to do with them enables students to be unusually inquisitive and imaginative. One or more portions of this activity demand extreme caution in handling potentially dangerous material.

Materials

Plastic cups or dishes   Wood splints
Powdered potassium iodide (KI)
Powdered mercuric nitrate ($Hg(NO_3)_2$)

Suggested Activities

Provide cups containing two (separated) white powders. Using *only* the wood splint to manipulate the powders, record your observations and learn as much as you can about the powders.

What do you observe?

Does everyone have the same observations? Why?

Are the observations dependent upon the way the powders are manipulated?

Was there a chemical reaction? What is your evidence?

Do such powders usually react?

How can you explain the reaction that may have occurred between these powders? [kinetics, ions, equilibrium, catalysis. . . .]

Design and carry out tests to identify the powders.

Safety Precautions

Unknown solids may be dangerous. CAUTION: Do not taste or touch with bare hands! [Mercuric nitrate should be handled carefully]

Reference

Bixby, L. W., "Twenty-two Pathways to Conclusions", *Chemistry,* 38, 5; May, 1965, p. 25.

4. The CO$_2$ We Breathe

Science Topics   Carbon dioxide, respiration

Level   C:2   E:2   D:1   L:2–3

Overview

In this activity students try to find out if we inhale or exhale more carbon dioxide. It affords opportunity to design an experiment and apply elementary principles of air pressure, after discussing the role of CO$_2$ in respiration.

Materials

    Clear limewater (Ca(OH)$_2$)   Rubber tubing
    Glass tubing   T-tube
    Two Erlenmeyer flasks (250 ml)

Suggested Activities

Carbon dioxide (CO$_2$) is a constituent of the air we breathe; it is also a product of respiration. Examine the effects of breathing and a bubbling carbonated beverage on limewater. (Limewater is often used as a test for CO$_2$, but other indicators like bromthymol blue (BTB) can be used.)

Predict whether we inhale or exhale more CO$_2$. What are your reasons?

Design an experiment which could provide the answer. What are the advantages and disadvantages of your design? Compare your design with the designs of others.

Here is a simple apparatus that will help test your prediction.

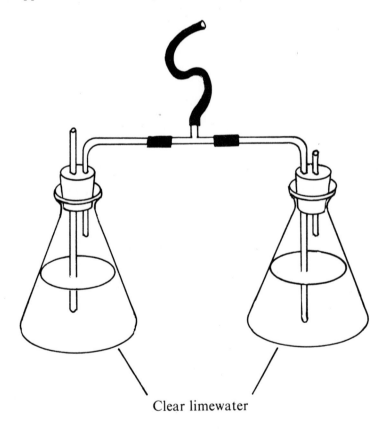

Clear limewater

Inhale and exhale alternately through the rubber tube attached to the T-tube; do this for one cycle. What is happening?

Trace the movement of the air that you inhale and of the gas that you exhale.

Describe the pressure throughout the apparatus during inhaling and exhaling.

Now inhale and exhale alternately and observe what happens.

Do the results support or refute your prediction? Do we exhale or inhale more CO_2? Explain.

Reference

Faraday, M.: *The Chemical History of a Candle,* 1963. Viking Press, New York, pp. 91–93.

5. A Dying Candle

Science Topics   Hydrocarbon combustion

Level   C:2   E:1–2   D:1–2   L:2–3

Overview

A candle is extinguished by being covered with jars of different size. This simple activity easily involves predictions and hypotheses, consideration of relevant experimental variables, and designing experiments to refute or confirm hypotheses.

Materials

Candle
Jars of assorted sizes
Clear limewater (optional) $(Ca(OH)_2)$

Suggested Activities

Predict what will happen when a jar is placed over a burning candle. Test your prediction and observe what happens.

What factors will affect the amount of time the candle burns after the jar is placed over the candle?

Specifically what are the effects of jar size, if any? What are the effects of the height of the candle, if any? Make measurements that are as precise as possible. It could be very helpful to display your data on a graph. If you find a new jar, can you predict candle burning time accurately from your graph? Try it.

What sources of experimental error are present?

Does it make a difference if a jar is used a second time immediately after a candle has been extinguished with it?

Can you identify any combustion products? Does a limewater test indicate the presence of carbon dioxide?

How can these phenomena be explained? [One hypothesis might be that oxygen is depleted; another is that a product of burning extinguishes the flame when a certain concentration is reached. . . .]

Design and conduct some experiments to test your hypotheses.

Based on your experiments, which of your hypotheses is the most plausible?

Are there any other products of combustion you may not have identified?

Design experiments that would detect additional products such as water and carbon.

Write equations for complete and partial combustion.

What is a flame and how is it maintained?

Observe a burning candle and describe it very carefully. . . .

What is the "fuel" when a candle burns?

Formulate an explanation for flame structure.

Comments

    This activity is a stimulating introduction to the study of hydrocarbon combustion.

    For a very stimulating opening activity with candles, give each student or group a candle, a match, a piece of window screen, and the task: find out all you can about the nature of a burning candle.

References

    Dietz, P., et al.: *Chemistry, Experimental Foundations,* Laboratory Manual, 1975. Prentice-Hall, Englewood Cliffs, New Jersey, pp. 1–4, 101–105.

    Faraday, M.: *The Chemical History of a Candle,* 1960. Viking Press, New York.

6. How Does the Burner Burn?

Science Topics   Combustion

Level   C:2   E:2   D:1   L:2–3

Overview

    The Bunsen burner can be used to investigate the conditions necessary for combustion—fuel, air (oxygen), kindling temperature, as well as aspects of the combustion process itself. A series of questions about the operation of the burner can be used to elicit student hypotheses and experimental tests. Many of the findings can be applied to combustion processes in the environment (stoves, automobiles, candles, etc.).

Materials

Bunsen burner	Beaker (1000 ml)
Erlenmeyer flask (250 ml)	Cobalt chloride paper
Clear limewater	Glass tubing
Matches	Copper screen

Suggested Activities

    What happens to fuel when it burns?

    What are the products of combustion?

    What is the composition of the fuel?

    Why won't fuel burn without igniting it?

    Does a flame have different parts? What are they?

    How can you make a yellow flame? A blue flame?

    Which is hotter, a yellow flame or a blue flame?

    What new questions does this inquiry raise in your mind?

    What new experiments do they suggest?

    How does what you have learned about the Bunsen burner flame relate to other sources of combustion like candles, matches. . . ?

    Try to find out as much as you can about combustion by using a Bunsen burner.

Safety Precautions

    Remove all flammable liquids! Very hot glass causes burns; place hot glass on an asbestos plate to cool. In case of skin burn, wash with running cold water and seek medical aid.

Comments

Students should first be allowed to inquire freely with the burner using proper safety precautions and then discuss their findings relative to the questions posed. Which questions were answered and what is the evidence? Which were unanswered or were answered only tentatively? What further experiments are needed?

Seven guided activities are outlined in the Engleber reference. These can be used as a second stage of inquiry in an attempt to get more information.

Reference

Engleka, K., "Bunsen Burner: More Than a Flame", *The Science Teacher,* 42, 8; October, 1975, pp. 41–42.

7. The Cloud Puzzle

Science Topics   Combustion, phase change

Level   C:2   E:2   D:1   L:2–3

Overview

Students inquire about the cloud that forms on the outside of a container of cold water as it is heated with a burner flame. Initial explanations are commonly disproved.

Materials

Beaker or pan of cold water   Tripod
Burner and hot plate   Asbestos gauze
Cobalt chloride paper

Suggested Activities

Ask student or group to heat a beaker of cold water and observe any changes on the outside of the container during the first few seconds.

What forms on the outside of the container?

Explain where the material on the outside of the container comes from. [the air?, a product of combusion?, the pores of the container? . . .]

How can you test your hypotheses? [use alternative heat sources (e.g. hot plate); heat the empty container (for a few moments only); direct flame into an empty cold beaker; test cloud with cobalt chloride paper]

Deduce products of the burning from the accepted model for a combustion reaction of the fuel with oxygen.

Comments

The cloud that forms on the outside of a container of cold water as it is heated with a burner flame is often identified as water condensing from the air. When experiments are performed to confirm this hypothesis however, it must eventually be discarded and a new hypothesis developed. The degree of confidence in alternative hypotheses will depend on the nature of the proposed experiments and their results.

Investigation leads relatively easily to the notion that the cloud material is a product of combustion.

Clouds of moisture appear all around us. In many cases the moisture is due to the production of water in combustion processes. On winter days, heavy fog is seen around automobile exhaust pipes. Moisture condenses in rooms where portable fuel-burning heaters operate. The combustion of fuel in supersonic aircraft produces huge quantities of water and carbon dioxide which emitted in the upper atmosphere may have far-reaching and possibly harmful effects on global climate. (This phenomenon has been called the greenhouse effect.)

Reference

Kronick, B. D., "On Hypothesis Testing", *The Science Teacher,* 41, 9; December, 1974, p. 55.

8. The Rising Water Puzzle

Science Topics   Combustion, composition of air

Level   C:2–3   E:2   D:1   L:2–4

Overview

A burning candle on a weighted cork in a dish of water is extinguished when covered with a flask. Students observe the changes in this system and attempt to formulate an explanation which can account for all of their observations.

Materials

Small birthday candle standing on a narrow side of a rubber stopper
Shallow dish
Water
Matches
Flask (250 ml)

Suggested Activities

Set a small candle in a shallow dish of water, light the candle and when it is burning well, cover the candle with a flask.

What are your observations? [Bubbles appear when the flask is inverted into the water; water rises as the candle burns; the flame grows dim and is extinguished; water continues to rise for a moment after the candle is extinguished; condensation appears on the walls of the flask.]

How can you explain what you have observed? Why are bubbles released? Why does water rise while the candle is burning? Why does water continue to rise after the candle is extinguished? Why is there condensation on the walls of the flask? [Student explanations may include: Something is removed from the air—oxygen; something is added to the air—product of burning, carbon dioxide; carbon dioxide is soluble in water; as the air cools, the pressure is lowered and water rises; water condenses on the walls of the flask because. . . .]

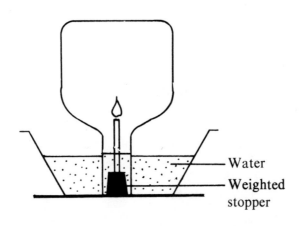

Water
Weighted stopper

Design and conduct some experiments to test your hypotheses. [Cover the candle with a beaker, add limewater; cover the candle with a beaker and test the condensate with cobalt chloride paper; burn a candle in pure oxygen; extinguish a candle with carbon dioxide.]

Explain how your experiments support or refute interpretations.

Comments

This activity is related to hydrocarbon combustion. However, explanations may take into account *two* sets of factors. One set involves the pressure-temperature-volume relationship of the trapped air. The other involves the gases in the combustion reaction. Do these factors reinforce each other or oppose each other during this event? This question can become the major focus of the inquiry.

This activity is particularly appropriate for large group discussion of alternative explanations and the development of experiments to test these hypotheses.

References

CHEM Study, *Chemistry: An Experimental Science Teachers Guide,* 1963, W. H. Freeman and Co., San Francisco, pp. 26–28.

Fowles: *Lecture Experiments in Chemistry,* 1957. G. Bell and Sons, London, p. 62.

*Woodburn, J. H., "Discover and Describe", *The Science Teacher,* 38, 9; December, 1971, p. 40.

9. Does Sugar Burn in Air?

Science Topics   Combustion, heat conduction, catalysis

Level   C:2–3   E:2   D:1   L:2–4

Overview

The atomic composition of sugar would lead us to expect that it burns readily in air, but that is not so. However, if the sugar is rubbed with cigarette ashes or with a number of solids, it then burns readily.

Materials

Several sugar cubes   Tongs
Bunsen burner   Asbestos pad
Powdered solids: cigarette ashes, Al, Fe_2O_3, MnO_2, graphite, talcum, instant coffee, nutmeg, cinnamon, dirt

Suggested Activities

Ask students whether or not they think a sugar cube will catch fire in a flame and why. Hold the cube in the Bunsen burner flame. [The sugar decomposes but does not burn.] Rub another cube in cigarette ashes and then hold it in a flame. [The sugar burns readily.]

What factors are necessary for burning to take place?

Which of these may be missing in the case of the sugar cube?

What is the role of the cigarette ashes? [Apparently it serves as a catalyst lowering the kindling temperature.]

Do you think other powdered solids might make the sugar burn?

Based on your observations with many powdered solids, do you still think the cigarette ashes are a catalyst?

What might be some properties of those solids or factors that would cause the sugar to burn? [small particle size, ability to absorb heat, melting point, decomposition point. . . .]

Another possible explanation is that a thin film of liquid from the heated sugar coats the ash particles, enabling the kindling temperature to be reached before the heat is dissipated in the melting process (see reference).

Safety Precautions

Do *not* use powdered solids which are strong oxidizing agents (e.g. $KMnO_4$, $KClO_3$!)

Reference

Smith, D. D., "The Burning Sugar Cube", *Journal of Chemical Education,* 54, 9; 1977, p. 552.

10. Campers' Dilemma

Science Topics   Combustion, heat transfer, specific heat

Level   C:2   E:2   D:1   L:2–3

Overview

Presentation of a practical camping problem invites creative problem solving based on elementary science concepts.

Materials

Candles   Matches
Paper bags   A wire coat hanger
A very large leaf (capable of holding liquid)
A piece of curved tree bark (capable of holding liquid)

Suggested Activities

Two students went on a camping trip. It was cold and they wanted some hot cocoa. They did have a small can of instant cocoa, but no cooking utensils were available. There was a brook nearby and they had started a small campfire. How could they obtain hot water, using materials that were on hand? (some paper bags, leaves, tree bark, a coat hanger, and other natural items you would find in the woods). Design a set-up for warming the water. Explain why you think your method will do the job.

Test your method. If it doesn't work, try to explain why and continue looking for a solution to the problem. Try out all your ideas.

Comments

There are three conditions necessary for burning: fuel, oxygen, and kindling temperature. In order to prevent the container from burning, it must be kept below its kindling temperature. The leaf and bark are not suitable because of their low heat conductivity. A paper bag is thin enough to conduct heat from the candle to the water, which has a high specific heat, so that the water can be warmed without the paper reaching its kindling temperature.

Reference

Washton, N. S.: *Teaching Science in the Elementary and Middle Schools,* 1974. David McKay Co., Inc., New York, pp. 107–109.

11. Copper Black

Science Topics   Oxidation of metals

Level   C:1–2   E:1–3   D:1–2   L:2–3

Overview

The blackening of copper when it is heated is usually interpreted in several ways by students who have not yet studied the oxidation of metals. The different explanations can be refuted or confirmed by simple experiments suggested and carried out by the students themselves.

Materials

    20 cm length of stiff copper wire
    Gas burner   Crucible
    Clay triangle   Tripod
    Copper powder   Balance
    Tongs

Suggested Activities

Hold a piece of stiff copper wire in a gas burner flame until it glows red and then remove the wire from the flame. Carefully observe what happens to the wire.

How can you explain what you have observed? What might the black substance be?

Design and conduct experiments to test your hypothesis.

This inquiry can be extended by pursuing questions such as: How do other metals behave when heated? [Mg, Zn, Pb, Fe, Ag] Investigate reactions of metals with oxygen. [Mg, Zn, Pb, Fe] Can the black substance be reconverted to the original copper?

Safety Precautions

Copper wire should be held by tongs or in some other safe way; do not touch the hot wire!

Comments

Students will probably suggest one or more of the following hypotheses to explain the blackening upon heating: the copper combines with something in the air; it decomposes, leaving a black substance; it changes into a black form of copper; it collects soot from the flame. . . .

Experiments to test the hypotheses may include: heat the copper in the absence of air; weigh the copper before and after heating (use powdered copper); heat the copper indirectly (no contact with the flame).

An increase in mass supports the hypothesis that copper combined with something. It does not support decomposition and structure change hypotheses. No change in color when copper is heated in the absence of air indirectly supports a combining hypothesis. Change in color by indirect heating refutes the soot hypothesis. The fact that a black substance rubs off the copper wire neither supports nor refutes conclusively any of these hypotheses.

In order to detect a mass change it is necessary to heat copper powder. When heated in a crucible the black substance forms on top while the powder portion underneath remains unchanged. This fact supports the combining hypothesis.

A neat way to probe the necessity of air is to heat a piece of copper foil that has been folded into the shape of an envelope. The outside blackens while the inside retains the copper color.

The phenomenon can be presented in an introductory study of chemical change, leading into topics such as oxidation of metals, activity of metals, and burning.

In this activity the blackening of copper is shown to be due to reaction with oxygen in the air. This kind of reaction of metals is very common. Most metals do not retain their luster after some exposure to air. Some, like aluminum, become coated with a protective (oxide) coating. Copper, in addition to reacting slowly with oxygen, reacts with carbon dioxide to form green copper carbonate; this is what happened to the Statue of Liberty. The rusting of iron is also a reaction of the metal with oxygen which is speeded up in a moist atmosphere. The corrosion of metals affects their strength and other important properties, e.g. electrical conductivity. Special efforts must be made to prevent or retard these processes, e.g. painting, greasing, waxing, etc. (See Activity H2.)

Reference

Bradley, J., "The Copper Problem", *The School Science Review,* 45, 156; March, 1964, pp. 364–368.

12. Dancing Metal

Science Topics   Reactions—alkali metals with water

Level   C:2–3   E:1–4   D:1–4   L:2–4

Overview

The vigorous reaction of an alkali metal with water is commonly demonstrated in the study of elementary chemistry. This reaction can be related to many topics, such as chemical families, the activity series of metals, oxidation-reduction, reaction rates and the collection of hydrogen. In this activity, the reaction takes place at the interface between water and kerosene, allowing students to safely make a large number of interesting and puzzling observations which stimulate them to raise many questions. After formulating tentative hypotheses, they can suggest and carry out simple procedures for testing them. This activity is an excellent introduction to the study of some of the topics listed above. It is quite open ended, and has many possible extensions. One or more portions of this activity demand extreme caution in handling potentially dangerous material.

Materials

One test tube about 1/3 full of water
A smaller test tube about 3/4 full of kerosene
1/2 cm cube of freshly cut sodium (oil is removed by absorption into filter paper)

Suggested Activities

Obtain a test tube about 1/3 full of water and a smaller test tube about 3/4 full of kerosene in which a 1/2 cm cube of freshly cut sodium is immersed. Carefully pour the contents of the smaller tube (including the sodium) into the larger tube.

What are your observations? [Periodic rising and falling of sodium in kerosene layer, gas formation at kerosene-water interface, streaks or streams in the water layer (schlieren), change in size and shape of sodium cube, change in temperature of kerosene, formation of new solid, irregular rate of gas formation at the interface. . . .]

What questions do your observations raise? [With what is the sodium reacting? Is a gas released? If so, what is its identity? Why does the sodium rise and fall? Why does the kerosene temperature change? What does the schlieren streaming indicate? What does the solid formation indicate? Why does the sodium appear to cease reacting from time to time?]

Develop a good hypothesis that will explain what is happening. [Sodium reacts with water, releasing hydrogen, or oxygen. Sodium reacts with water *and* kerosene, releasing carbon dioxide. Sodium rises and falls because of changes in density due to gas bubble adherence to and release from the solid. A water soluble product of the reaction causes the schlieren (streaming). Sodium becomes coated by a reaction product and this diminishes its contact with water at the interface. A solid reaction product accumulates at the interface, diminishing sodium contact with water.]

Suggest and, if possible, carry out some experiments to test your hypotheses. [Collect gas and test. Measure temperature change in the two layers. Test acidity, basicity, conductivity of water layer. Repeat experiment with other metals (alkali metals, alkaline earth metals). Repeat experiment with other liquids floating on water (e.g., butanol, petrol ether, paraffin oil—do *not* use halogen compounds). Repeat experiment with other liquids place of water (e.g., methanol, ethanol, glycerol).]

Write an equation for the reaction of alkali metals with water.

Extensions of the inquiry include:

Compare reactions of lithium (if available), sodium or potassiuim at the water-kerosene interface with reactions of these metals in water.

Interpret the differences that can be observed with different alkali metals.

Investigate the reaction quantitatively. Determine the ratio of moles of metal to moles of hydrogen. (See Johnston, T.C.)

Correlate "dancing frequency" of the sodium cube with the relative densities of various non-polar liquids used with water.

Safety Precautions

Students should wear eye protection and be warned of the dangerous nature of alkali metals because of their extreme reactivity. Sodium must be handled *only* with forceps and on a *dry* work surface.

The kerosene and sodium should be *slowly* and *carefully* poured into the water.

Great care should be taken in removing any unreacted sodium by removal with forceps and placing it in methanol.

Any student-planned work should be approved by the teacher before the work is started. Alternatively, the teacher may be the only person to pour the kerosene and sodium into the students' test-tubes containing water.

Comments

This activity is likely to be most successful with students who know the least initially about the reaction between alkali metals and water. The activity is also an excellent introduction to the study of the alkali metals as a group in the periodic table. When the activity is used with students who are already familiar with the basic reaction, it is probably best to emphasize an investigation of the effect of several variables on the activity of the metal at the interface.

It is possible that the sodiium will cease to react after a time if it becomes "insulated from the water". In this case, you will probably find that the sodium will completely disappear after several days. This is an interesting case of "slowing" a normally violent reaction.

References

Alyea, H. N. and Dutton, F. B., "Tested Demonstrations in Chemistry", *Journal of Chemical Education,* 1962, Easton, PA, p. 27.

Johnston, T. C., "Collection of Hydrogen from the Reaction Between Sodium and Water", *The School Science Review,* 52, 179; December, 1970, pp. 414–415.

*Sivan, R. J., "The Controlled Reaction Between Sodium and Water—An Inquiry Experiment", *The Chemical Bond,* 4, 3; 1977, pp. 30–31. (In Hebrew.)

13. Heating Sulfur

Science Topics   Allotropic forms of sulfur, oxidation of sulfur

Level C:1–3   E:2   D:1   L:2–3

Overview

Observations of changes in sulfur when it is heated pose interesting questions which can be investigated by a combination of simple experiments, application of the atomic theory, and data from the literature. One or more portions of this activity demand extreme caution in handling potentially dangerous material.

Materials

Powdered sulfur   Test tube
Test tube holder   Bunsen burner
One-holed stopper
40 cm glass tube (to use as an air condenser)

Suggested Activities

Obtain a test tube about ⅓ full of powdered sulfur. *Slowly* heat the solid to boiling (move the tube in and out of the flame) and observe carefully *all* the changes in the appearance of the sulfur as well as viscosity changes.

Observe changes in the sulfur as it is heated and then as it cools down. [Progressive darkening of the sulfur after it begins to melt. Increase in viscosity and then decrease before boiling. Crystallization of yellow sulfur along the wall of the test tube as the system cools.]

Is the dark material another form of elemental sulfur? Is it an oxidized form of sulfur?

Why does the viscosity change? [The sulfur atoms rearrange; smaller molecules form larger ones. . . .]

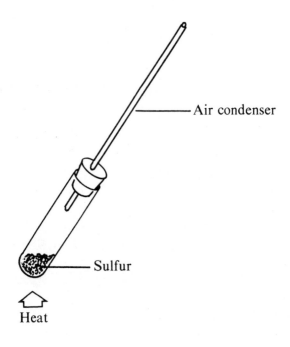

Air condenser

Sulfur

Heat

Investigate the mass of the system before and after heating.

Compare your explanations with the explanation in the literature.

Investigate the properties of solid sulfur which has been crystallized from carbon disulfide solution and from a melt.

Find relationship between crystal forms and spatial arrangement of molecules.

Safety Precautions

Caution students to avoid inhaling gases at the mouth of the test tube. Molten sulfur can cause serious burns. In case of burn, wash immediately with running cold water and get medical aid. Use carbon disulfide in a hood away from flames; avoid skin contact with liquid and inhalation of vapor.

Comments

The color and viscosity changes observed when sulfur is heated are not typical of physical changes which occur when most substances are heated. For this reason, students are challenged to propose original explanations for the changes.

Given the molecular formula of solid sulfur, S_8, students can be challenged to interpret the changes observed in terms of bond breaking and bond making.

Elemental sulfur is mined on a large scale in Louisiana. The Frasch process for bringing the deep sulfur deposits to the surface involves heating and cooling the element as it is done in this inquiry. Students who have investigated heated sulfur will find considerable interest in applying their knowledge to the understanding of the Frasch process.

Sulfur is a basic raw material in the production of sulfuric acid, one of the most widely used industrial chemicals.

References

*Herdman, G. A., "Observing the Changes Which Occur on Heating Sulphur", *The School Science Review,* 59, 209; June, 1978, p. 670

Johnstone, A. H. and Morrison, T. I.: *Chemistry Takes Shape, Book 1,* 1964. Heinemann Educational Books Ltd., London, p. 64.

Mahan, B.: *University Chemistry,* 1965. Addison Wesley Publishing Co., Inc., Reading, MA, p. 524.

14. Mysterious Solid

Science Topics   Periodic table, chemical properties, physical properties

Level   C:2–3   E:2–4   D:1–2   L:1–4

Overview

In this activity students engage in careful observation and interpretations to identify a chunk of solid material. The activity will probably conclude with some degree of uncertainty, depending upon the sophistication of the students and the tests performed. This is a typical kind of activity performed by chemists; it involves consideration of what determines "proof" in a scientific investigation.

Materials

A small piece of solid (silicon)

Common laboratory apparatus and reagents

Suggested Activities.

Here is an interesting solid. Try to find out everything you can about it, so that you will be able to identify the solid. Observe its properties carefully. Consult handbooks. Design and conduct needed tests. Check all experimental procedures with your teacher before conducting tests.

Safety Precautions

Do not allow students to proceed with experimental work before they get your approval regarding the meeting of safety requirements.

Comments

The activity can be used at any time of the school year and at many levels of sophistication. It is particularly appropriate during the study of the periodic table. Few, if any, students will recognize the material as silicon. If students suggest tests requiring apparatus which is not available, the teacher or a handbook can serve as a source of experimental data.

References

Metcalfe, H. C., et al.: *Modern Chemistry,* 1970. Holt, Rinehart, and Winston, New York, pp. 468–470, 556–560.

*Talesnick, I., "Periodic Table", *The Science Teacher,* 40, 2; February, 1973, p. 57.

15. Carbon and Colored Solutions

Science Topics   Adsorption, activated carbon

Level   C:1–2   E:2   D:1   L:2–3

Overview

The use of activated carbon to remove color from solutions can highlight methods of scientific investigation: the demand for evidence for every statement, the need for controlled experimentation and separation of variables.

Materials

Ink	Test-tubes
Methyl orange solution	Medicine dropper
Litmus solution	Burner
Funnel	Test-tube holder
Filter paper	Activated carbon
Dilute copper sulfate solution	
Dilute solution from charred sugar	
Dilute cobalt chloride solution	

Suggested Activities

Add a pinch of activated carbon to a test-tube containing one drop of ink in about an inch of tap water. Boil, filter, and describe the filtrate. [colorless] How can you explain what you have observed?

Dilute ink as before (no carbon) and boil. [colorless] Do your new results cause you to want to change your explanation? Why? What can be done to see whether the carbon or the boiling causes the solution to become colorless? Shake dilute ink solution with activated carbon (do not heat it) and filter. Describe the filtrate. [colorless] [Discuss the need for separation of variables.] How can you tell if the carbon or the boiling affected the color and not the filtration alone? [Discuss the need for a control.]

Filter dilute solutions of ink in tap water and in distilled water. Describe your observations and explain the importance of this step.

Does activated carbon remove color from all solutions? Repeat the investigation with other colored solutions: methyl orange, litmus, dilute solution from charred sugar. Is a generalization warranted? Explain. Predict and then investigate the action of activated carbon on solutions of copper sulfate and cobalt chloride. Was your prediction correct? Explain what has happened.

What is activated carbon? Does it wear out? How does it work? If it does wear out, can it be reclaimed?

Comments

Colored solutions of ink are boiled with activated carbon and filtered. The activity proceeds in steps—at each step students are asked to make an hypothesis or a prediction. Both expected and unexpected results highlight various aspects of scientific investigation.

Activated carbon is commonly used in aquarium filters. It is widely used in industry to remove colors and odors from commercial products. The general method is to filter a solution through large blocks of activated carbon, which absorbs the large molecules responsible for odor and color. The desired product is recovered from the filtrate by evaporation of the solvent. This procedure is used in sugar refining.

References

Joseph, et al., *A Sourcebook for the Physical Sciences,* Harcourt, Brace, and World, Inc., N.Y., 1961, p. 198.

*Mackean, D. G., "Learning by Mistake", *The School Science Review,* 45, 157; June, 1964, pp. 707–708.

16. A Mystery Tablet

Science Topics   Acids and bases, carbon dioxide

Level   C:2   E:2–3   D:2   L:2–4

Overview

Investigating Alka-Seltzer® tablets allows students to experiment imaginatively with home materials and to design and carry out experiments to resolve a puzzling observation.

Materials

Alka-Seltzer® tablets ground to a fine powder
Red and blue litmus paper
Clear limewater (aqueous $Ca(OH)_2$)
Wooden splints
pH paper (4.5–7.5)

Suggested Activities

Obtain an envelope containing two Alka-Seltzer® tablets ground to a fine powder, one strip of red litmus paper and one of blue. Take these home and find out everything you can about the unknown powder. You can do anything you want except put the powder into any liquid you cannot normally drink.

What did you observe? [Did all students find that blue litmus turned red in a solution of the powder? Seek out the perplexed students and encourage them to stand by their observation that red litmus turned blue in the solution.]

How could different students observe different color changes with the same powder? What variables might affect the action of the solution on litmus? [kind of liquid, concentration, temperature, time of reaction]

Design experiments to test the variables using appropriate controls. [Use pH paper to test the effects of reaction time. Each student or pair can test the pH after specified time intervals from the moment of mixing the powder with water up to about seven minutes] Construct a graph of average pH versus time. Explain the shape of the graph. What gas is evolved? [test for CO_2, H_2, O_2] Interpret observations in terms of a reaction between a base, HCO_3^- ion, and an acid.

- -

This powder is frequently found in the home. What do you think it is? What evidence do you have to support your identification?

Look at the ingredients listed on a box of Alka-Seltzer® tablets and try to explain your experimental results in terms of the chemical content of the tablets.

- -

Carry out a similar investigation of effervescent denture cleaning tablets to see if they release bubbles of oxygen as claimed.

Reference

Johns, K. W., "Explore, Invent and Discover With Alka-Seltzer Tablets", *Science Education,* 54, 3, 1970, pp. 241–242.

17. Acids Turn Litmus Red?

Science Topics   Acid-base indicators, acidity in aqueous solutions

Level   C:2   E:2   D:1   L:2–3

Overview

This activity deals with the role of water in acid-base reactions by comparing the behavior of blue litmus in pure acids and in their aqueous solutions.

Materials

Tweezers	Glass rods
Filter paper	Litmus paper
Glacial acetic acid	Syrupy phosphoric acid
Concentrated acids: H_2SO_4, HCl, HNO_3	
Dry solid acids (e.g. benzoic acid, tartaric acid)	

Suggested Activities

Dry a strip of blue litmus paper over a flame or in an oven; handle with tweezers. Spot one end with a moist glass rod (use freshly boiled distilled water) and quickly blot in a fold of filter paper to absorb excess moisture. Spot both the moist and the dry ends of the litmus paper with glacial acetic acid. [The dry end remains blue, the wet end turns red.]

Describe your observations and suggest an explanation.

What is litmus and why does it change color? Suggest some experiments to test your explanation.

Spot moist and dry litmus paper with other concentrated acids (H_2SO_4, HNO_3, syrupy H_3PO_4, HCl). Are the results consistent with your hypothesis? How can discrepancies be explained? Find out about the composition of the concentrated acids you tested, using handbooks and other resources.

- -

Predict results of spotting dry blue litmus paper with a solution of HCl in toluene. [no change in dry blue litmus paper] Suggest reasons why a solution of HCl in toluene doesn't affect the color of blue litmus.

What will happen if you touch dry blue litmus paper with a solid acid? Check your prediction. Explain.

Develop an hypothesis to explain how bases turn red litmus blue. Design and perform experiments to test the hypothesis for bases (dry ammonia, solid hydroxides for example).

Safety Precautions

Dispense concentrated acids in small quantities only and *caution students* to avoid contact with skin and clothing and to avoid inhaling any fumes. Wash affected areas immediately with plenty of water. Have Na_2CO_3 solution available to neutralize spilled acid.

Comments

In absorbing excess moisture from the wet end of the litmus paper, the dry end should not be enclosed in the filter paper fold in order to prevent moisture from reaching the dry end through the filter paper.

This procedure works well with concentrated H_2SO_4, but the moist end soon disintegrates; the paper survives longer if the wet end is less moist, being firmly pressed several times in a filter paper fold.

References

*Adair, A., "Do Acids Turn Blue Litmus Red?", *The School Science Review*, 45, 156; March, 1964, p. 412.

Andrew, H. G., "Litmus", *The School Science Review*, 44, 153; March, 1963, p. 338.

18. The Quantities Puzzle

Science Topics   Le Chatelier's Principle

Level   C:3   E:1   D:1   L:3–4

Overview

The familiar iron-thiocyanate equilibrium demonstration can be conducted in a discovery mode as an exercise in concept development *before* students have acquired the concept of equilibrium. The activity is conducted in general terms, referring to the iron (III) and thiocyanate solutions as Solutions A and B.

Materials

Solution A: a few ml of 0.2 M $Fe(NO_3)_3 9H_2O$ (80 g/liter)
Solution B: 0.2 M KSCN (19 g/liter)
Beaker (250 ml)
Solid Na_2HPO_4
Five test tubes
Two medicine droppers
Boiling water bath
Ice bath

Suggested Activities

To 100 ml distilled water, add 12 drops each of solutions A and B. Then divide this solution among five test-tubes.

What do you observe?

What evidence is there of a chemical reaction between A and B?

What could happen if several more drops of A were to be added to the original mixture? [darker, lighter, no change] How could each of the possible changes be explained? [darker—the original mixture contains an excess of B; no change—the original mixture contains an excess of A; lighter—dilution?] Have the class vote on a prediction. Subsequently add more drops of A [color darkening can be observed.]

What could happen if several drops of B were to be added to the original mixture? How could each of these possible observations be explained? Have the class vote on a prediction. [Since darkening caused by adding A was probably interpreted as due to an excess of B in the mixture, most students will vote that addition of B will cause no change in color.]

Subsequently add drops of B [color darkening can be observed.]

We have a dilemma. How can the mixture contain both an excess of A and an excess of B?

After students suggest ideas, introduce equilibrium concept and explain color changes in terms of Le Chatelier's Principle.

- -

Investigate the effect of putting the mixture in a boiling water bath and then in an ice bath. Since the reaction $Fe^{3+}(aq) + SCN^-(aq) \rightarrow FeSCN^{2+}(aq)$ is exothermic, interpret changes in terms of Le Chatelier's Principle.

Investigate the effect of removing one of the reacting ions through reaction with another substance ($Fe^{3+}(aq)$ combines with $HPO_4(aq)^{2-}$ to form $FeHPO_4^+(aq)$). How can the results be interpreted in terms of Le Chatelier's Principle?

Comments

As indicated in the overview, this inquiry activity is written with the assumption that students have not previously acquired an understanding of the equilibrium concept.

References

CHEM Study Teachers Guide, Chemistry: An Experimental Science, 1963, Freeman and Co., San Francisco, pp. 281–283.

*Driscoll, D. R., "Invitations to Enquiry: The Fe^{3+}/CNS^- Equilibrium", Journal of Chemical Education, 56, 9; 1979, p. 603.

19. What Are the Products?

Science Topics   Quantitative analysis of a chemical process

Level   C:3   E:3   D:3   L:3–4

Overview

The activity guides students in the laboratory analysis of a chemical reaction which enables them to 1) hypothesize about possible products, 2) make tests for their presence, 3) hypothesize about possible equations for the reaction and 4) design an experiment to identify the reaction which actually occurs.

Materials

Crucible	Clay triangle
Tripod	Gas burner
Solid sodium bicarbonate	

On request by the student: balance, limewater, medicine droppers, cobalt chloride paper, litmus paper, and other simple items (e.g., wooden splint, corks, water, etc.), tongs

Suggested Activities

Sodium bicarbonate, $NaHCO_3$, is a familiar chemical in your home. Heat some in a test tube. As a chemist, what kinds of questions about sodium bicarbonate might interest you?

On the basis of what you already know about sodium bicarbonate and your observations, what are some possible products when you heat sodium bicarbonate?

Plan and carry out an experiment or experiments to test your suggestions.
Summarize what you have learned about the heating process thus far.

It has been suggested that the white solid remaining in the tube, after strongly heating the sodium bicarbonate, may be one of three substances:

1. $NaOH(s)$, sodium hydroxide
2. $Na_2CO_3(s)$, sodium carbonate
3. $Na_2O(s)$, sodium oxide

This means that one of the following three reactions probably occurs on heating the bicarbonate:

1. $NaHCO_3(s) \rightarrow NaOH(s)$ + _____
2. $NaHCO_3(s) \rightarrow Na_2CO_3(s)$ + _____ + _____
3. $NaHCO_3(s) \rightarrow Na_2O(s)$ + _____ + _____

Complete and balance these equations on the basis of your experiments thus far.
Suggest a quantitative experiment to determine which of the reactions actually occurs. What calculations are necessary?
Carry out the experiments, summarize your quantitative results, and then decide which equation most probably represents the reaction when sodium bicarbonate is heated.

Mole relationships between materials involved in chemical processes is a real research tool and not just the subject of practice exercises in chemistry class! A classic example is Fischer's stoichiometric investigations of the esterification of sugars in the elucidation of their structure. This activity is an elementary example of this kind of investigation.

Safety Precautions

Exercise caution when handling a hot crucible! Use tongs.

Comments

The activity is presented in the form of a guided inquiry. However, in many of the steps the student is free to make any suggestions and the class can discuss the reasonableness of various suggestions. The experiment is carried out in a crucible for heating solids. Students should understand why it might be preferred to some of their own suggestions.

The choice between the three suggested equations for the reaction is based on the mass ratio of the solid after and before heating the crucible. The ratio obtained should be close to:

$$\frac{\text{formula weight } Na_2CO_3}{2(\text{formula weight } NaHCO_3)} = \frac{106}{168} = 0.63$$

Reference

Novick, S., "An Inquiry Experiment for High School Chemistry", *CHEM 13 News;* November, 1975, p. 6.

20. Finding the Relative Atomic Mass of a Metal

Science Topics   Relative atomic mass; mole concept

Level   C:3   E:3   D:3   L:3–4

Overview

This activity involves students in analyzing experimental data to yield information about relative atomic masses after formal introduction of empirical formula and mole concepts. One or more portions of this activity demand extreme caution in handling potentially dangerous material.

Materials

Lithium metal	Erlenmeyer flask (250 ml)
Filter paper	Balance ($\pm$ 0.01 gram precision)
Knife	3 M HCl
Tongs	Graduated cylinder (100 ml)
Medicine dropper	Phenolphthalein indicator
Burner	Wire gauze
Tripod	Evaporating dish

Suggested Activities

Information about relative atomic masses of elements enable chemists to translate quantitative relationships from microscopic to macroscopic levels of analysis. How were relative masses originally determined? Given a sample of lithium metal, how could we find its relative atomic mass through inquiry in the laboratory?

Small groups devise procedures to solve the problem.

Suggestions are presented and critiqued in class discussion. Examine: a) the experimental and conceptual reasoning, b) the feasibility of the method and c) the expected accuracy.

If the relative atomic mass of one atom is known, how can it be used to determine the relative atomic mass of another element? [Law of constant proportions.]

How can lithium be combined with another element? Does lithium react with water?

What are the products of the reaction of lithium with water?

How can the product of the reaction above be converted to a compound between lithium and another element? [neutralize LiOH with HCl and evaporate to dryness]

What assumption must be made about this compound? [known combining ratio of elements]

How can the known relative atomic mass of this second element help to find the relative atomic mass of lithium? [constant ratio Li/Cl]

Outline a detailed experimental procedure.

Perform the experiment. [Review the notes by R. Arlotto, *TST*, 1974.]

Perform the calculations.

What is the relative atomic mass of lithium based upon your experiment?

Compare results of different groups.

Compare results with accepted value.

Discuss errors.

Safety Precautions

Students *MUST* wear goggles! Lithium metal should be handled with extreme care, avoiding skin contact. Prepare small pieces of freshly cut metal, absorb oil with filter paper and place a dry piece of lithium in a weighing bottle for each student or group. Addition of lithium to water should be carefully supervised! When trimming the lithium, dispose of scraps of the metal by placing them in methanol.

Perform this activity only with adequate ventilation. Do not inhale spray. When lithium reacts with water, the reaction is exothermic; the flash gets HOT!

Comments

The method to be used to find the relative atomic mass of lithium is based on the following scheme:

a. χ grams of lithium react completely with water, forming $LiOH_{(aq)}$.
b. $LiOH_{(aq)}$ is converted to $LiCl_{(aq)}$ by adding 3M HCl until the phenolphthalein-LiOH solution turns colorless.
c. y grams LiCl are recovered and weighed. (1 gram lithium metal yields about 6 grams LiCl.)
d. Calculations:

χ gram Li combine with $(y-\chi)$ grams Cl; assuming a 1:1 combining ratio (LiCl), and knowing the relative atomic mass of Cl (35.5),

$$\frac{\text{relative atomic mass of Li}}{35.5} = \frac{\chi}{y-\chi}$$

$$\text{relative atomic mass of Li} = \frac{\chi}{y-\chi} \cdot 35.5$$

The experimental apparatus is simple and the procedure straightforward and relatively short. Comparing results of students determinations with the accepted value affords a good opportunity to discuss sources of error.

Reference

Arlotto, R., "Three Simple Stoichiometric Experiments for Introductory High School Chemistry", *The Science Teacher,* 41, 5; May, 1974, p. 51.

21. Blowing Up Balloons with Moles

Science Topics Stoichiometry, mole concept, oxidation-reduction

Level C:3 E:2–4 D:2–3 L:3–4

Overview

In this activity students are asked to predict the relative volumes of hydrogen gas released by reaction of different masses of magnesium with a fixed volume of 1M HC1. The "discrepant event" of ballons inflating to unpredicted relative volumes forces students to think through the molar relationships involved and to realize the meaning of limiting quantity in a chemical reaction.

Materials

Clean magnesium ribbon
1M HC1
Three beakers (600 ml)
Three flexible balloons (capable of inflating easily to about 1.2 liters)

Graduated cylinder (100 ml)
Three Erlenmeyer flasks (250 ml)

Suggested Activities

Three flasks, each containing 100 ml 1M HC1 have three identical balloons taped to the mouths of the flasks as shown in the figure. Each balloon contains a weighed mass of clean shiny magnesium ribbon:

	Flask No. 1	Flask No. 2	Flask No. 3
Mass of Mg	1.2 grams	0.6 grams	2.4 grams

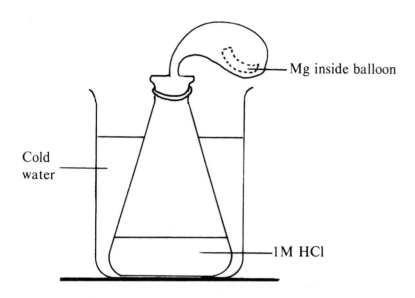

Predict what will happen when the magnesium is tipped into the acid. After the reaction is complete, will the balloons inflate to the same volumes or to different volumes?

Which balloon will be largest and which will be smallest?

[The most common prediction is No. 3 > 1 > 2 with volumes proportional to the mass of magnesium.]

Tip the magnesium into the acid and observe what happens in each case. Were your predictions confirmed? If not, try to figure out why.

[Some students will notice there is a considerable amount of ribbon left unreacted in flask No. 3. Analyzing the problem in terms of moles provides an explanation:

	Mg +	2 HCl	$MgCl_2$ +	H_2
No. 1	0.05	0.1	0.05	0.05 (no excess reactant)
No. 2	0.025	0.1	0.025	0.025 (0.05 moles HCl in excess)
No. 3	0.1	0.1	0.05	0.05 (0.05 moles Mg in excess)]

What else could we measure to support this explanation?

[Weigh Mg left in No. 3. Its mass should be 1.2 grams; titrate the solutions after reactions subside—No. 1 and No. 3 should be nearly neutral and No. 2 should contain 0.05 moles HCl.

Evaporate the solutions and weigh the residue. Residues No. 1 and No. 3 should weight 0.05 moles $\times$ 95 $\frac{grams}{mole}$ = 4.75 grams; residue No. 2 should weigh 0.025 moles $\times$ 95 $\frac{grams}{mole}$ = 2.38 grams.]

Comments

If the activity is conducted as a demonstration, set up the flask balloon assemblies in advance, so that the reactions can be initiated by simply tipping the magnesium ribbon in the balloons into the acid.

The flasks are placed in cold water in order to cool the mixture and prevent reaction of magnesium with hot water.

Reference

Dillard, C. R., "Two Lecture Experiments Demonstrating Limiting Quantities", *Journal of Chemical Education,* 49, 12, 1972, p. A 695.

22. Hydrocarbon Misfit

Science Topics   Structure of benzene, organic molecules

Level   C:4   E:1   D:1   L:3–4

Overview

The classical problem of the benzene structure can be tackled by students as an introduction to the unique chemistry of benzene and its derivatives. The anomaly between benzene's observed properties and some possible structures leads to a search for alternative structures and finally to the realization that a revision of the bonding model itself is needed.

Materials   Ball-and-stick molecular model sets

Suggested Activities

Some 130 years ago (about 1850) a new hydrocarbon was isolated from coal tar. Its molecular formula was found to be C_6H_6.

How many different (isomeric) models can you build for benzene which conform to the bonding rules for carbon and hydrogen? "Chemists of the last century showed that when a hydrogen atom of benzene is replaced by chlorine atom, one and *only* one isomer is obtained." Which, if any, of the models you have built as possible structures for benzene is consistent with this finding? Why?

Can you build a model for benzene which would yield only one isomer of C_6H_5Cl? Is this model consistent with the fact that benzene does *not* readily undergo addition reactions? "Modern X-ray analysis indicates that the benzene molecule has a *planar* ring structure and that the nuclei of the carbon atoms in the ring are *equidistant* from each other." Are these findings consistent with any of the structures you have suggested for benzene?

At this point the problem of benzene's structure remains unresolved. The classical valence model yields no structure consistent with all the evidence. A revision of the model is needed, and the concept of electron delocalization can be introduced as one such revision.

Comments

This activity is appropriate for advanced secondary science students and for some college students. They should know that carbon atoms form rings as well as chains, that the maximum number of hydrogen atoms in such chains is given by the formuls C_nH_{2n+2}, and that hydrocarbons containing less than the maximum number of hydrogen atoms are said to be unsaturated, readily undergoing addition reactions.

Reference

Wood, G. N., "Rediscovery in a Course for Non-Scientists", *Journal of Chemical Education,* 52, 3; 1978, pp. 177–178.

Chemical Dynamics

1. The Mini Volcano

Science Topic   Decomposition, Oxidation-reduction

Level   C:2–4   E:3   D:3   L:2–4

Overview

The spontaneous decomposition of ammonium dichromate is a somewhat spectacular phenomenon, sometimes called the "ammonium dichromate volcano." Based on initial observation of the "mini-volcano," several reasonable explanations are developed. These lead to the design of some simple experiments which could refute or support the hypothetical explanations. The activity can be extended considerably, depending on the level of the students involved. One or more portions of this activity demand extreme caution in handling potentially dangerous material.

Materials.

   granular ammonium dichromate ($(NH_4)_2Cr_2O_7$)
   Bunsen burner
   tripod
   asbestos, wire gauze

Suggested Activities

Heat about 5g. of ammonium dichromate on a square of asbestos, using a gas burner until the reaction starts. Then remove the burner. What do you observe? What questions and problems do your observations raise in your mind?

   Is oxygen consumed in the reaction?
   Is the mass of the solid product greater than, equal to, or less than that of the reactant?
   Is ammonia a major nitrogen-containing product?
   Is water a product? hydrogen?
   What is the composition of the solid product?
   What are some properties of the solid product?
   Why must the solid be heated for the reaction to begin? at what temperature does the reaction
      begin?
   Is the reaction reversible?
   How do other ammonium salts behave on heating?

How can the phenomenon be explained?

Is the reaction an example of burning, decomposition or change in structure? Design some experiments to test your explanations:

Heat the dichromate in the absence of air;
Weigh the solid before and after the reaction. (How can loss of the product be avoided?)

- -

Determine the formula of the green product.
Determine moles of gas evolved per mole of reactant, mass of water produced, mass of ammonia produced
Discuss the spontaneity of the reaction in terms of energy and entropy.
Discuss the reaction in terms of oxidation-reduction.
Compare your interpretations with the literature.
Predict and possibly observe how other ammonium salts and other dichromate salts behave on heating. Use proper SAFETY precautions.

Safety Precautions

Chromates and dichromates are known carcinogens. This inquiry must be carried out under strict supervision. Ammonium dichromate should be heated only in a fume hood which is operating properly. Wear eye protection! Stand away after the "volcano" becomes "active". Do not inhale fumes.

Comments

The ammonium dichromate "volcano" is a classical demonstration, but the reaction is ideally suited for stimulating curiosity and offering opportunity to engage in authentic chemical research activities. The Finholt reference provides an excellent discussion of how this phenomenon can be used for inquiry activities. If you decide to use this phenomenon with your students, you should read the reference carefully and observe SAFETY precautions.

The activity can be used at an introductory level, highlighting the distinction between observation and interpretation and the difference between burning and decomposition.

With more advanced students the scope of treatment will depend on the amount of time available for experimentation and the timing within the curriculum. Possible emphases are: the behavior of ammonium salts (descriptive chemistry), oxidation-reduction reactions, and why reactions occur (energy-entropy).

References

Finholt, J. E., "The Ammonium Dichromate Volcano as an Introductory Laboratory Project," *Journal of Chemical Education,* 47, 7, 1970, pp. 533–535.
Williams, I. W., "Experiments with Ammonium Dichromate," *The School Science Review,* 50, 172, March 1969, pp. 591–593.

2. Costly Enemy

Science Topic   Oxidation, Corrosion, Environmental Pollution

Level   C:2–3   E:2–4   D:1–2   L:2–4

Overview

In this activity students investigate environmental conditions which inhibit or stimulate corrosion. The activity can be extended to include many kinds of corrosion prevention practices such as galvanization, coating with other metals, painting, oiling and greasing, etc. Corrosion prevention measures can illustrate important principles of physics and chemistry.

Materials

Small sheets of iron, copper, aluminum, zinc. . . .
(sizes from 1cm $\times$ 1cm to 20cm $\times$ 20cm are appropriate)
Sulfuric acid
Hydrochloric acid
Sodium chloride
Sodium hydroxide
Distilled water
Oil, grease, detergent, glassware, some heavily corroded objects
Multi-meter to measure the voltage drop across metals in a solution or to investigate the effects of corrosion on electric conduction

Suggested Activities

Despite the development of new alloys and the replacement of metals by plastics, corrosion remains a common and expensive problem in the world today. News reports have indicated that air pollutants are rapidly destroying some works of art that have survived from antiquity. The problem is a familiar one with the materials we commonly use. Automobiles, for example, frequently develop very serious body corrosion problems due to road salt while the engine may continue to function well.

Examine some corroded objects to see what kind of damage has resulted. Understanding the causes and the scientific principles that are involved in corrosion can help in the development of methods to inhibit corrosion.

What characteristics can you observe in corroded pieces of iron? How do the properties of the material change as corrosion progresses? Presumably, corrosion will affect different metals in different ways. Compare corrosion effects on different metals. Where on an object does corrosion most commonly occur? For example, what parts of an automobile show the greatest effects of corrosion? What inferences can you make from these observations about the effects of environmental conditions on corrosion? What other evidence is there of corrosion caused by substances in the environment of your community? What surface conditions promote corrosion? Do surfaces that are smooth or rough, clean or dirty corrode at different rates? Make some predictions about the effects of these conditions and test them. Do metals corrode at different rates in the presence of similar materials? For example, will a piece of iron corrode more quickly in tap water, distilled water, or in boiling water? How important is air in the corrosion process? Other substances? What happens, for example, to different metals in salt, alkaline, and acid solutions?

Studying these questions necessitates designing an experiment or experiments in which you control variables, that is, examine the effects of varying conditions on one variable while you try to hold all the other variables constant. To do this, you may wish to set up a rack of bottles in which one metal or series of metals is immersed in a series of different kinds of solutions. (Perhaps the rack might even be set up in the form of an array or matrix.) What are the effects of differing concentrations of materials that cause corrosion? What are the effects of pH?

Does an object lose or gain weight during the corrosion process? Make some predictions and test them. Explain your observations.

What are the effects of corrosion on the electrical resistance of a piece of metal? How does the potential difference between metals in solutions vary as corrosion progresses? One kind of industrial environment can be simulated by putting metals in the exhaust gases from a furnace that may be used in your school's art department or machine shop. What fumes are present in the exhaust gases from the furnace? What are the effects on corrosion?

Thus far, we have raised questions that can be examined using simple conditions in the laboratory. However, pollution problems and conditions are complex. It might be worthwhile to study the effects of industrial pollution by exposing metals to water taken from different polluted and non-polluted sources. What are the effects of moisture or weak acids in the atmosphere? Perhaps you could simulate various atmospheres with different levels of acid rain.

What hypotheses can be formulated regarding corrosion causing agents in the atmosphere and in water? Design ways to test some of these hypotheses. What factors promote corrosion and what factors inhibit corrosion?

Study the effects of various methods of inhibiting corrosion. Based on your earlier investigation, it should be possible to arrange surface conditions and environmental conditions in ways to reduce corrosion problems. Investigate the effects of anti-corrosive paints, oils, and other agents that are sold commercially. Read and analyze some technical manuals that describe anti-corrosion procedures. For example, what are the effects of the presence of a sheet of copper on the corrosion of an iron sheet in a salt solution? What about steel and zinc? (These concerns need to be addressed in the construction of commercial pipelines.) Try protecting steel nails by coating them with various materials such as paint, grease, etc. and examine the effects of these protective coatings when they are exposed to conditions that promote corrosion.

How effective are commercially sold rust-proofing treatments for automobiles? Do they live up to the advertising? Does corrosion continue underneath a protective coating? How can rust proofing procedures be improved?

Can the right kinds of electroplating of one metal on another inhibit corrosion? What kinds of metal coatings are likely to be most helpful? What questions do you have that still need to be answered regarding these relationships?

Comments

To initiate this activity, the students may be asked to bring some corroded objects to class. The nature of corrosion may be discussed briefly or more thoroughly depending on the level of sophistication of the students. The damage resulting from corrosion to cars, tools, metals around the home that need regular polishing (such as silverware) provide interest and relevance. The choice of inquiry activities pursued may depend on the interests of students expressed in class discussion. Some activities should be selected which can show results in a relatively short period of time (within a week or so). Other studies may extend over a more natural corrosion period of some weeks while other topics become the center of class study.

Corrosion in the real world involves many factors and complex processes. This kind of investigation provides an excellent opportunity to help students see the need to simplify the number of variables being examined in order to better understand complex relationships. Decisions must be made about variables "that will not be examined at this time while we focus on simpler issues and relationships." Students individually or in small groups may choose to examine the effects of only *one* variable while holding other variables constant. Other students or groups might be assigned to examine the effects of different variables or even interaction effects among selected variables.

This activity provides excellent opportunities to help students with problems in the control of variables and in the design of experiments. For example, shall we conduct this activity only in water solution, only in the air, or in an environment where the air is very humid? The possibility of setting up a rack of bottles or closed test tubes in a two-dimensional or three-dimensional array can help students come to understand ways in which the effects of relevant variables can be examined under different conditions. For example, samples of different metals could be immersed in different kinds of water in an array as shown in Figure 1.

	tap water	salt water	distilled water	HCl pH 5.0	[additional solutions of specific pH]
aluminum					
copper					
iron					
lead					
steel					
zinc					

Figure 1

References

Nuffield Foundation. *Nuffield Secondary Science.* 1976. Longmans, London.

Metcalf, H. C., et al.: *Modern Chemistry,* 1970. Holt, Rinehart, and Winston, New York, pp. 444–453.

3. Fickle Aluminum

Science Topics   Activity series, catalysis

Level   C:3   E:2   D:1   L:2–4

Overview

Although aluminum ranks quite high in the electrochemical series, its reactivity is lessened by a protective surface oxide film. Aluminum's activity can be restored by catalytic removal of this film.

Materials

Commercial aluminum foil
Petri dish
Test tubes

Molar solutions of:

copper (II) sulfate pentahydrate ($CuSO_4 \cdot 5H_2O$)

sodium chloride (NaCl)   sodium sulfate (Na_2SO_4)

potassium chloride (KCl)   hydrochloric acid (HCl)

copper (II) chloride ($CuCl_2$)   sulfuric acid (H_2SO_4)

copper (II) nitrate ($Cu(NO_3)_2$)

Suggested Activities

Pour some copper sulfate solution into a Petri dish containing a piece of aluminum foil. [No reaction is visible.] Add some sodium chloride solution to the solution in the petri dish. [Vigorous reaction occurs.]

What do you observe?

Why did the reaction not proceed until the salt was added? [Catalytic removal of protective oxide film.]

What ions are effective in removing the oxide film from aluminum?

Design an experiment to answer this question.

Test combinations by adding appropriate solutions to samples of aluminum foil in separate test-tubes.

Cu^{2+}, SO_4^{2-} $Cu^{2+}, SO_4^{2-}, K^+, Cl^-$

$Cu^{2+}, SO_4^{2-}, Na^+, Cl^-$ Cu^{2+}, SO_4^{2-}, Na^+

Based on your observations, which ions appear to be necessary for removal of the oxide film? Explain your observations.

Test your hypotheses by adding Cu (II) Cl_2 solution to a piece of foil in a test-tube.

Test your hypotheses by adding various acids to aluminum foil in order to produce hydrogen.

Use the following combinations of ions with aluminum foil:

H^+, Cl^- $H^+, Cl^-, Cu^{2+}, No_3^-$

H^+, Cl^-, Na^+ H^+, SO_4^{2-}

$H^+, Cl^-, Cu^{2+}, SO_4^{2-}$ H^+, SO_4^{2-}, Cu^{2+}

$H^+, SO_4^{2-}, Na^+, Cl^-, Cu^{2+}$

Comments

Following the initial presentation and discussion of the catalytic action of sodium chloride, the inquiry can be carried out as a class laboratory exercise.

Zinc chloride and mercury (II) chloride (caution, handle with care!) also catalyze oxide removal from aluminum.

Reference

Lloyd, G., "Removal of the Oxide Film on Aluminum", *The School Science Review,* 60, 211; December, 1978, pp. 308–309.

4. How Strong Are Acids?

Science Topics   Acid strength

Level   C:2–3   E:2   D:1–2   L:2–3

Overview

While a conceptual treatment of acid strength requires a quantitative understanding of chemical equilibrium, an *operational* understanding can be developed at an elementary level. This activity can be quite open-ended with students suggesting alternative ways to test the strength of acids.

Materials

> Solutions of various acids (e.g. hydrochloric, sulfuric, nitric, phosphoric, citric, benzoic), all 2 normal
> 2N NaOH
> pH paper
> Distilled water
> Various metals (e.g. Mg, Zn, Cu)
> Boiling chips
> Test tubes

Suggested Activities

Here are some acids of different "strength". How might we define the "strength" of an acid and how might we determine the order of their strength?

Design an experiment to measure acid strength.

Carry out experiments, making careful and accurate observations.

What can you infer from your experimental results?

Compare the results obtained using different methods.

Do all groups using the same method agree on the order of the acid strength?

Explain discrepancies.

In the light of your results and experiments, comment on the adequacy of your definition of acid strength. How could it be improved?

Safety Precautions

Even dilute acids should be handled carefully. Protect clothing and skin, eyes, table-tops, etc. Specify precautions for students orally and in writing. Do not use very active metals such as lithium, sodium or potassium.

Comments

This activity is suitable for students who have learned operational definitions of acids: reaction with metals, carbonates, bases, and indicators.

To begin, students should be given a set of test tubes and samples of a number of acids. A good starting set would be: hydrochloric, sulfuric, acetic, and citric acids.

Before distributing additional material, have groups of students work out an experimental procedure to solve the problem, and then conduct a class discussion on the merits of suggested procedures. This discussion should deal with factors such as control of variables, accuracy, safety, simplicity of design and performance. Based on this discussion, a number of methods may be developed. Probably the simplest and most easily controlled is the following: add equal lengths of clean magnesium ribbon (about 2 cm) simultaneously to equal volumes (half a test tube) of the acids (2N) and measure the time for the magnesium to dissolve in each acid. Temperature change can also be noted. Compare results obtained with different methods and examine reasons for discrepancies in post-lab discussion.

References

Parry, R. W., et al., *Chemistry: Experimental Foundations,* 1970. Prentice-Hall, Inc., Englewood Cliffs, N.J., pp. 297–302.

*Vernon, E. J., "An Elementary Class Experiment to Compare the Strengths of Acids", *The School Science Review,* 49, 169; June, 1968, p. 855.

5. The Acids Puzzle

Science Topics   Acid-carbonate reaction, reactions between ions

Level   C:2   E:1–2   D:1   L:2–4

Overview

Strong acids react vigorously with carbonates, releasing CO_2 gas. This inquiry is initiated by the reaction of HCl with calcium carbonate ($CaCO_3$); the ionic equation for the reaction is:

$$2H^+(aq) + CaCO_3(s) \quad\underline{\quad\quad}\quad H_2O(l) + Ca^{2+}(aq) + CO_2(g)$$

However, calcium carbonate appears to react differently with another common strong acid, H_2SO_4. The activity centers around the search for an explanation of the anomaly.

Materials

Test tubes
Medicine dropper
Several calcite crystals
2 M HCl
1 M H_2SO_4
Limewater (aqueous solution of $Ca(OH)_2$)
(Other acids and carbonates)

Suggested Activities

Drop a small piece of marble or a calcite crystal into 2 M HCl in a test tube. Observe the reaction with care.

What gases might be evolved?

Test for possible gases (suspend a drop of clear limewater above the reaction mixture; a glowing splint; a lighted match).

Based on your knowledge and observations of acids, write the ionic equation for the observed reaction.

What might happen if the marble (or calcite crystal) were to be added to an equal volume of 1 M H_2SO_4?

Test your prediction and observe carefully.

Why does the initial evolution of gas die away very quickly? Is there evidence of any reaction afterward?

Suggest an explanation for the different behavior of marble (or calcite) in the two acids (HCl and H_2SO_4).

- -

Predict the rate of evolution of CO_2 when H_2SO_4 reacts with crystals of other carbonates.

Predict the rate of evolution of CO_2 when marble (or calcite) reacts with other common acids (e.g. HNO_3, H_3PO_4, CH_3COOH).

Predict the rate of evolution of CO_2 when H_2SO_4 reacts with powdered $CaCO_3$.

Test your predictions.

What factors determine the rate of evolution of CO_2 from carbonates reacting with acids?

Safety Precautions

Keep acids off skin, clothing, table tops, etc.

Comments

Calcite crystals (calcium carbonate) are transparent, becoming opaque after initial reaction with H_2SO_4 though the solution remains clear during reaction with HCl. If these crystals are unavailable, you can substitute small pieces of marble. A white precipitate forms around the marble when H_2SO_4 is added.

Demonstrating the reaction in transparent cells on an overhead projector facilitates observation of details which are normally difficult to see (for details, see reference). If you use this approach, be certain that the students understand what you are doing, the nature of the cell, and the materials added.

References

Driscoll, D. R., "Invitations to Enquiry: The Calcite/Acid Reaction", *Journal of Chemical Education,* 56, 10; 1979, p. 672.

6. A Solution Puzzle

Science Topics   Reactions between ions, solubility

Level   C:2   E:2   D:1   L:3

Overview

Students identify four "unknown" ionic solutions after consulting a handbook to identify the properties of the four solutions.

Materials

Test-tubes
Four solutions in bottles labeled I, II, III, IV:

     I—0.1 M $BaCl_2$ III—0.5 M H_2SO_4
     II—0.1 M $MgSO_4$ IV—0.5 M Na_2CO_3

Suggested Activities

"The labels have fallen off these four bottles—I've called them I, II, III, and IV. We know the four solutions are: $BaCl_2$(aq), H_2SO_4(aq), Na_2CO_3(aq), and $MgSO_4$(aq) and we need to identify them with certainty. We have *no* additional chemicals, but we can consult the literature to find properties of the compounds in these solutions. How can we determine which solution is in which bottle?"

Design a procedure to identify the solutions.
What information do you need?
How can you be sure to identify each solution with certainty? Explain.
Carry out the experiment according to your procedure, record observations and record your conclusions about the identity of I, II, III, and IV.

Can you suggest an alternative procedure *without* any additional materials?
Can you suggest an alternative procedure using additional materials?
Carry out the tests using an alternative procedure and account for any evidence that seems to contradict the previous conclusions.

Comments

In order to identify unknown ionic solutions students need to know some of their characteristic properties. They can be given solubility tables and reminded of the acid-carbonate reaction. Alternatively, individuals or small groups could design an experimental procedure for solving the problem and then look for the required data on properties in the literature. They could also discuss the advantages and disadvantages of different designs.

Since this activity involves combinatorial thinking, it could also be used as a task to assess logical skills for individual students.

Similar activities can be designed using different sets of solutions (see the CHEMStudy reference).

References
    CHEM Study, *Chemistry: An Experimental Science, Teachers Guide,* 1963, W.H. Freeman and
        Co., San Francisco, pp. 683–691.
    de La Matter, D., "What's the Solution", *The Science Teacher,* 45, 4; April, 1978, p. 51.

7. The Disappearing Precipitate

Science Topics   Relative solubilities, K_{sp}

Level   C:3–4   E:1–2   D:1   L:2–4

Overview

Both silver chloride and solid silver chromate form when silver ions meet chloride and chromate ions simultaneously. However, the relatively greater solubility of the "insoluble" silver chromate allows the silver chloride to be separated out.

Materials

    0.5 M sodium chloride (NaCl)
    0.5 M silver nitrate (A_gNO_3)
    0.25 M sodium chromate (Na_2CrO_4)
    Nine large test tubes clamped along the length of a ring stand. (The three bottom tubes contain the
        three solutions.)
    Graduated cylinder (.100ml)

Suggested Activities

Announce that you will combine equal volumes of the three solutions in all possible sequences of combining (six in all). Stir after adding each solution. After observing the results of mixing, encourage students to discuss possible chemical explanations in small groups before conducting a class discussion.

Naturally, the level of explanation, whether in terms of relative solubility, equilibrium or solubility products, will depend on the student level of development and background.

Observe carefully. Tabulate the formation of precipitates for each combination. What precipitates are formed? Why does a precipitate form and then disappear when another solution is added? How could you dissolve the final precipitate which was formed?

Test your predictions. If a prediction is not confirmed suggest a possible reason. Is there a competition involved in these phenomena? What particles are competing?

- -

Solutions often contain a variety of cations and anions. Selective precipitation of desired salts depends on relative solubilities (which are dependent on temperature) and relative ion concentrations. These principles are applied, for instance, in fractional crystallization of salts from sea water.

Observe successive addition of a series of anions to a solution containing silver ions, to form a series of decreasingly soluble silver salts or increasingly stable silver complexes. (See Schwenk for details.)

Predict or interpret results in terms of Le Chatelier's principle, solubility products, or equilibrium constants.

References

CHEM *Study Teachers Guide: Chemistry: An Experimental Science,* 1963. Freeman and Co., San Francisco, p. 319.

Schwenk, J. R., "The Chemistry of Silver: A Demonstration Sequence", *Journal of Chemical Education,* 36, 1, 1959, p. 45.

*Woodburn, J. H., "Discover and Describe", *The Science Teacher,* 38, 9; December, 1971, p. 40.

8. The Orange-Yellow Puzzle

Science Topics   Le Chatelier's Principle

Level   C:3   E:2   D:2   L:3–4

Overview

This activity pre-supposes that students have already conceptualized Le Chatelier's Principle. Thus, they may be able to propose a reasonable explanation for the inter-convertability of the chromate and dichromate ions, applying their knowledge in the areas of equation writing and chemical equilibrium. At a more advanced level, they may also consider what might be reasonable structures for the two chromium-containing ions, applying a model of molecular structure. One or more portions of this activity demand extreme caution in handling potentially dangerous material.

Materials

Test tubes	Spoons
Common laboratory reagents	Water
Solid potassium chromate (K_2CrO_4) and potassium dichromate ($K_2Cr_2O_7$)	

Suggested Activities

Obtain small quantities of potassium chromate (K_2CrO_4) and potassium dichromate ($K_2Cr_2O_7$). What procedures could change chromate ion to dichromate ion and vice versa?

Run one of these procedures and observe the outcome. Some procedures are to prepare equivalent solutions and test equal volumes with controlled quantities of acids, bases, salts, oxidizing or reducing agents; heat the solids. What do you observe?

Suggest a way to resolve the problem and to facilitate the change based on your observation.

Can the method be justified by additional experimentation?

Is there a relationship between the method and equilibrium principles? What are the equations that are involved in the conversion of chromate to dichromate and vice versa? How does Le Chatelier's Priniciple apply?

- -

Barium chromate is insoluble while barium dichromate is soluble [include data from literature]. How could we dissolve a precipitate of barium chromate? Test your suggestions.

Safety Precautions

Chromates and dichromates are known carcinogens. Solids and solutions containing these ions should be handled with care and under supervision. Avoid skin contact.

Comments

This well-known chromate-dichromate acid-base controlled equilibrium is one of a number of reactions which are illustrative of Le Chatelier's Principle. The problem is presented in an open-ended mode and is appropriate for group discussion. It allows for the use of a considerable range of knowledge and skills. Students should be free to suggest any initial experimentation which seems reasonable to them. Subsequent discussion can focus on why some procedures would be more reasonable than others (e.g. using acids and bases versus using oxidizing agents). Consult the references for more complete details.

References

CHEM Study: *Chemistry: An Experimental Science, Laboratory Manual,* 1963. Freeman and Co., San Francisco, pp. 53–54.
Ibid.: *Teachers Guide,* pp. 350–352.

9. The Red-Blue Puzzle

Science Topics   Interactions between cobalt ions, chloride ions and water molecules, transition metal complexes

Level   C:3–4   E:2   D:1–2   L:3–4

Overview

Cobalt chloride paper is frequently used to test for the presence of water. In this activity, students search for an explanation for the color change when the paper is moistened. Observations of cobalt chloride under various conditions can be used to support or refute tentative explanations. The activity can be related to complex formation and students can find support for their explanations by searching the literature on the subject.

Materials

Two strips of filter paper	Test tubes
2% solution of cobalt chloride	Water
Asbestos wire gauze	Methanol
Dilute hydrochloric acid	Ethanol
Dilute sulfuric acid	Gas burner
Sodium chloride	Tripod

Cobalt chloride hexahydrate ($CoCl_2 \cdot 6H_2O$)
Crystals of anhydrous calcium chloride ($CaCl_2$)
Crystals of anhydrous potassium carbonate (K_2CO_3)

Suggested Activities

Cobalt chloride paper is commonly used by chemists to test for the presence of water. What is an explanation for the color change when cobalt chloride paper is moistened? To pursue the inquiry, examine cobalt chloride under different conditions:

Place one drop of cobalt chloride solution on two strips of filter paper. Place one of the strips on a hot surface.

Heat a few crystals of solid cobalt chloride in a test tube.

Add a few large crystals of anhydrous potassium carbonate to a test tube containing cobalt chloride solution; to a second sample of the solution add a few calcium chloride crystals.

Why does the warm paper turn blue? [cobalt chloride loses water, or reacts with paper, or. . . .]

Why is solid cobalt chloride reddish and not blue? [the solid constains water, $CoCl_2 \cdot XH_2O$, or. . . .]

Which observations support your hypotheses?

If water molecules are removed from cobalt ions in solution, do you think they are replaced by something else? Why?

Do you think chloride ions can replace water molecules in cobalt chloride? What observations support your answer?

Can you suggest other ways to produce the blue color in cobalt chloride solution? [add chloride ions: NaCl, HCl—dilute, concentrated, sulfuric acid-dilute, concentrated, heat the solution]

Search the literature for the formulas of the complex ions involved in this activity.

$$[Co(H_2O)_6^{2+}, CoCl_4^{2-}]$$

What binds water molecules or chloride ions to cobalt ions?

An interesting application of the ideas developed in the inquiry is to perform the following demonstration. Prepare a fairly concentrated solution of $CoCl_2 \cdot 6H_2O$ in isopropanol (about 1g/10ml). Add water drop by drop, avoiding excess, until the color changes. Carefully heat the solution and then cool in an ice bath. Repeat the cycle. Ask students to interpret changes. ($CoCl_2 \cdot 6H_2O$ + isopropanol $\rightleftarrows$ $CoCl_2$ + isopropanol $\cdot 6H_2O$.)

The cobalt chloride system is sensitive to concentration and temperature changes. A mixture of the two complex ions, $Co(H_2O)_6^{2+}$ and $(CoCl_4)^{2-}$ produces an intermediate violet color in the equilibrium system. Prepare a stock solution of cobalt chloride, diluted with concentrated hydrochloric acid until an intermediate violet color is produced. Test the effect of concentration changes by adding water and hydrochloric acid to equal volumes of the stock solution. Test the effect of temperature change by immersing equal volumes of the stock solution in boiling water and in ice water, and then reverse the tubes. Interpret in terms of Le Chatelier's Principle.

Comments

Students usually have some experience with the use of indicator paper. Generally, they cannot investigate the nature of the specific interaction responsible for the characteristic color change of the paper. In this activity, they have the opportunity for such an investigation.

The role of water and its competition with chloride ions in complex formation can be developed in this inquiry (some teacher guidance will probably be needed in this process). Alternatively, students can offer their own explanations for the blue color appearing in the cobalt chloride solution and then find the accepted explanation and its supporting evidence in the literature.

The key interaction in solution is:

$$Co(H_2O)_6^{2+}(aq) + 4Cl^-(aq) \rightarrow CoCl_4^{2-}(aq) + 6H_2O$$

red   blue

The key interaction in the solid state is:

$$Co(H_2O)_6\,Cl_2(s) \xrightarrow{\text{heat}} CoCl_2(s) + 6H_2O$$

red   blue

Reversible color changes due to combination with water are widely used as indicators of moisture and humidity. Such indicators, including cobalt chloride, are frequently incorporated in silica gel pellets. Acid-base indicators operate on a similar principle, except that hydrogen ions are bound and removed instead of water molecules.

References

Ophardt, C. E., "Cobalt Complexes in Equilibrium" (Tested Demonstrations), *Journal of Chemical Education,* 57, 6; 1980, p. 453.

Parry, R. W., et al.: *Chemistry: Experimental Foundations,* 1970. Prentice Hall, Englewood Cliffs, New Jersey, pp. 536–537.

Peterson, C. R., "Chemical Equilibrium", *The Science Teacher,* 44, 1; January, 1977, p. 41.

Vernon, E. L., "Cobalt Ion Colours", *The School Science Review,* 49, 168; March, 1968, p. 558.

Woodburn, J. H., "Discover and Describe", *The Science Teacher,* 38, 9; December, 1971, p. 40.

Young, R. S.: *Cobalt: Its Chemistry, Metallurgy and Uses,* 1960. ACS Monograph Series, Rembold Pub. Corp., New York, p. 76.

10. Halogen to Halogen

Science Topics   Preparation of chlorine, reactions between halogens, covalent and polar bonds, equilibrium

Level   C:3–4   E:3   D:2   L:3–4

Overview

This activity involves the preparation of chlorine from solid materials, its reaction with iodine and the equilibrium between these elements and their interhalogen compounds. It is presented in the form of a guided inquiry exercise and deals with a relatively large number of important chemical concepts. One or more portions of this activity demand extreme caution in handling potentially dangerous material.

Materials

Small test tube	Rubber stopper
One-hole rubber stopper	U-delivery tube
Solid iodine	Sodium chloride
Potassium permanganate ($KMnO_4$)	
Spatula	Alcohol burner
Granular anhydrous sodium hydrogen sulfate ($NaHSO_4$)	

Suggested Activities

Both chlorine and iodine are familiar elements in the home, chlorine in bleach and iodine in antiseptics. In both cases the elements are in solution: chlorine in aqueous sodium hydroxide and iodine in alcohol. In this inquiry you will have the opportunity to observe the free elements at room temperature.

Do halogens react with each other? Specifically, does chlorine (Cl_2) react with iodine (I_2)? Explain your hypothesis based on your knowledge of chemical bonds.

Sketch an apparatus for carrying out the possible reaction between chlorine and iodine. Label the various parts of the apparatus and the materials to be used.

Explain the steps in your proposed procedure for carrying out a reaction between chlorine and iodine. Be ready to present and discuss your experimental design in class.

- -

In your inquiry into a reaction between chlorine and iodine, the following procedure with a simple apparatus is recommended:

1. mix $KMnO_4$, NaCl and $NaHSO_4$ in a mass ratio of 1:3:6 in a mortar and transfer the mixture to the small test tube;
2. the U-delivery tube is connected to the test tube and a crystal or two of solid iodine is dropped into the bottom of the U-delivery tube using a thin spatula;
3. the solid mixture is heated until Cl_2 passes over the I_2 in the U-tube [forming first a brown liquid and then a yellow solid];
4. the U-delivery tube is detached, the test tube quickly stoppered, and the U-tube held upside-down *below* the table level; [the excess chlorine escapes, the yellow solid disappears and brown liquid reforms].

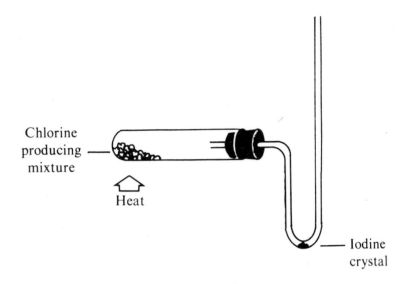

Chlorine is a poisonous gas. It is best prepared in small quantities by warming a mixture of the three solids: sodium chloride (NaCl), sodium hydrogen sulfate (NaHSO$_4$), and potassium permanganate (KMnO$_4$).

What kind of reaction must take place when the solids react if chlorine gas is to be one of the products? (You need *not* write the equation for the reaction.)

What is the function of potassium permanganate (KMnO$_4$) in the reaction?

Before proceeding with the experiment, read the more complete procedure outlined in the following paragraphs.

Weigh the following quantities of the three solids (to the nearest 0.1 gram), taking proper care in the use of the balance: 1g KMnO$_4$, 3g NaCl, 6g NaHSO$_4$ (crushed anhydrous). [These quantities are sufficient for three groups of students.]

Prepare a uniform mixture of the three solids by grinding them together in a small mortar and then transfer most of the mixture to the test-tube. Immediately stopper the tube with the U-delivery assembly.

Now use the thin spatula to transfer a crystal or two of solid iodine to the bottom of the U-delivery tube. *Warning! Iodine must not come in contact with your skin or clothing!*

Gently warm the solid mixture in the tube with an alcohol burner, so that chlorine gas is slowly produced. *Warning! You must not breathe chlorine vapor!*

Carefully observe and record your observations of the changes in the appearance of the iodine crystals as the chlorine passes over them. Do *NOT* warm the test tube more than necessary. Remove the burner as soon as you observe a change in the material in the U-tube.

Carefully placing your fingers on the U-tube, determine whether the reaction between iodine and chlorine is exothermic or endothermic.

Remove the delivery assembly from the test tube. Carefully place the delivery tube on the desk, and *immediately* stopper the test tube containing the solid mixture.

Now hold the delivery tube assembly vertically below the level of your workbench and slowly invert it so that the long straight arm of the U-tube points downward.

Observe and record all changes in the appearance of the material in the delivery tube.

Summarize the evidence for the reaction between chlorine and iodine.

Reconnect the delivery tube to the "chlorine-producing mixture" in the test-tube and try to repeat the entire experiment. Upon completion of this task, stopper your test-tube, leaving it and the delivery tube on your workbench.

Observe carefully.

[If the "chlorine-producing mixture" is not heated too rapidly, the solid iodine is seen to become a dark brown liquid on reaction with chlorine. As an excess of chlorine passes through the U-tube the brown liquid becomes a yellow solid.]

Careful experimentation supports the following hypothesis. Two reactions occur:

  1. $I_2(s) + Cl_2(g) \rightleftharpoons 2ICl(l)$
                         brown liquid

  2. $ICl(l) + Cl_2(g) \rightleftharpoons ICl_3(s)$
                           yellow solid

Based on the regularity in the boiling points and colors of the halogens in the series chlorine, bromine, iodine, explain the color and room temperature state of ICl. [ICl is isoelectronic with Br_2.]

The reaction between chlorine and iodine is exothermic. Explain this fact in terms of the kind of bonding in the two halogens (I_2 and Cl_2) and in the interhalogen compound formed (ICl). [Polar bonding in ICl, non-polar bonding in I_2 and Cl_2.]

ICl, a liquid, and Cl_2, a gas, react spontaneously to form ICl_3, a solid. Based on these facts, predict whether this reaction is exothermic or endothermic, giving the reason for your prediction. [Decrease in entropy, therefore decrease in energy.]

Explain your observations on the inverted U-tube in terms of the principles of chemical equilibrium. [Removal of Cl_2 shifts equilibrium.]

Safety Precautions

The solid mixture contains $NaHSO_4$ which is a strong acid; prevent contact with skin!

The chlorine-producing mixture becomes active upon mixing the ingredients. Prepare it fresh for each trial and *avoid inhaling near it!* Use a fume hood. Keep iodine off skin. This activity should be performed by the teacher or by advanced students under close supervision.

Comments

The first phase of this activity (planning the experiment) should involve time for class discussion. Such discussion is useful in the latter phases of processing the experiment as well. This activity can be carried out by students in the laboratory because of the convenient method of preparing chlorine gas by heating a mixture of solids. The $NaCl$, $NaHSO_4$ mixture replaces the HCl used in the traditional method for preparing chlorine.

This activity provides an excellent opportunity for students to interpret observations in terms of some basic concepts of bonding and equilibrium.

Reference

Swan, R. J., "The Chemistry of Halogens—Practical Notes", *The School Science Review,* 55, 191; December, 1973, p. 320.

11. A Halloween Reaction

Science Topics   Reaction rate, solubility product, complexes, clock reaction

Level   C:3–4   E:1   D:1   L:3–4

Overview

This reaction is a modification of the Landolt iodine "clock" reaction. Students can speculate about a plausible explanation for the "clock" color changes observed: colorless ⟶ orange (precipitate) ⟶ blue-black. The sophistication of their explanations will, of course, depend on the concepts they can bring to bear on the problem: oxidation-reduction, reaction mechanism, solubility product. One or more portions of this activity demand extreme caution in handling potentially dangerous material.

Materials

Solution A: Potassium iodate, KIO_3 (aq) (15g/liter)
Solution B: Sodium bisulfite, $NaHSO_3$ (aq) (15g/liter) + 3 grams soluble household starch per liter of solution.*
Solution C: Mercuric chloride, $HgCl_2$ (aq) (3g/liter)
*Make a paste of the starch and add to 500 ml boiling water; after cooling, add 15 g $NaHSO_3$

Suggested Activities

In this activity you will examine a very interesting "clock reaction".
Mix equal volumes of C + B + A in that order in a beaker.
What kinds of reactions might be taking place?
What causes the orange color?
What causes the black color?
Make some predictions and test them:
Will the order of mixing the solutions affect the results?
What will happen if the concentration of solution A is increased? Solution B? Solution C?
Does the hydrogen ion concentration affect the times between the color changes?
Does the temperature affect the times between color changes?
What other variables might affect the times between color changes?
Suggest a mechanism to explain the abrupt formation of the orange color, followed by the black color.
Which reactions are relatively slow and which are very fast?

Safety Precautions

Mercury compounds are poisonous; handle solids and solutions carefully!

Comments

In this inquiry students can be encouraged to ask for specific information about the behavior of the substances in the system and to use this information in constructing their explanation. Group discussion will be helpful, and competing explanations can be examined in terms of the validity of the chemical principles involved.

1. The oxidation reduction reactions involved are;
   iodate oxidizes bisulfite to sulfate and iodide ion,
   (1) IO_3^- (aq) + $3HSO_3^-$ (aq) $\longrightarrow$ I^- (aq) + $3SO_4^{2-}$ (aq) + $3H^+$ (aq)
   iodate oxidizes iodide to iodine,
   (2) IO_3^- (aq) + $5I^-$ (aq) + $6H^+$ (aq) $\longrightarrow$ $3I_2$ (aq) + $3H_2O$
   bisulfite reduces iodine to iodide
   (3) I_2 (aq) + HSO_3^- (aq) + H_2O $\longrightarrow$ $2I^-$ (aq) + SO_4^{2-} (aq) + $3H^+$ (aq)
2. The color reactions involve iodide ion and iodine.
   (4) I_2 + starch $\longrightarrow$ blue-black complex
   (5) Hg^{2+} (aq) + $2I^-$ (aq) $\longrightarrow$ HgI_2 (s)
3. As iodide is produced by reactions (1) and (3), its concentration increases until the K_{sp} of HgI_2 is exceeded, at which time the orange mercuric iodide precipitates.

4. Reaction (3) is much faster (nearly instantaneous) than reactions (1), (2), and (5). This means that the iodine formed in (2) will be converted to iodide and will not form the black-complex with starch. Once all of the bisulfite is consumed, the I_2 formed in (2) will immediately react with the starch to form the blue-black complex.

5. The concentrations are chosen so that the bisulfite is exhausted before it can oxidize all of the iodine formed in reaction (2).

References

Alyea, H. N., "The Old Nassau Reaction", *Journal of Chemical Education*, 54, 3; 1977, pp. 167–168.

Cotton, F. A., Darlington, C. L., Lynch, L. D., *Chemistry: An Investigative Approach*, Revised Edition, 1973. Houghton Mifflin Co., Boston, pp. 611–615.

12. The Blue Bottle

Science Topics   Chemical kinetics

Level   C:3–4   E:2   D:1–2   L:3–4

Overview

Shaking a colorless liquid in a stoppered flask causes the liquid to turn blue. On standing the blue liquid turns colorless. Shaking initiates a further bluing then de-bluing cycle. The activity provides opportunities for careful observation, for formulating both elementary and sophisticated hypotheses and for performing simple experiments to test hypotheses.

Materials

A solution containing: 20 grams NaOH, 20 grams glucose, and about 0.5 ml of 1% alcoholic methylene blue per liter of water (exact quantities are not critical)

Large flask

Clean rubber stopper

Suggested Activities

Here is a flask containing a colorless liquid. Notice what happens when it is shaken and then stands undisturbed. Try to find out as much as you can about what is happening here and why. Try to justify your explanation by your own observations and your knowledge of chemical systems.

Observe the bluing-debluing cycle carefully [A very thin blue layer forms about the colorless solution.]

How does the rate of de-bluing depend on the intensity and on the shaking time?

How many cycles of bluing-debluing occur without removing the stopper?

What happens when the stopper is removed?

What mechanisms might explain what you have observed? [Possible hypotheses may include: there is a colored material on the stopper; shaking warms the solution, initiating an endothermic reaction which is reversed on cooling; two layers are mixed when the flask is shaken, they separate out on standing; shaking mixes a gas (above the liquid) with the liquid and the gas then separates from the solution.]

Design experiments to test your hypotheses.

Comments

Each of the hypotheses listed in the preceding section can be refuted by observing the results of simple manipulations of this system; for further details consult the Campbell reference.

An extensive discussion of this phenomenon as an inquiry activity is found in the reference.

This is a particularly appropriate activity for large group discussion of alternative hypotheses and ways to test them. If the materials are used only as a demonstration, be certain that all students have thorough opportunity to observe the reaction closely.

Reference

Campbell, J. A., "Kinetics, Early and Often", *Journal of Chemical Education,* 40, 11, 1963, pp. 578–583.

13. Fast Foods and Slow Foods

Science Topics   Rate of reaction, catalysis, enzymes

Level   C:2–3   E:2   D:1   L:2–3

Overview

Foods contain catalase, an enzyme which catalyzes the decomposition of hydrogen peroxide to water and oxygen. Cooking generally destroys the activity of enzymes. Students can investigate variables affecting enzymatic action using common household materials: foods and hydrogen peroxide.

Materials

Paper cups	Manganese dioxide (MnO_2)
Medicine dropper	Wood splint
Crushed foods (or the juice from crushing)	
3% hydrogen peroxide (fresh)	

Suggested Activities

Demonstrate evolution of oxygen from hydrogen peroxide when a pinch of MnO_2 is added; compare with control. Home food stuffs contain chemicals that originate in plants and animals and that help or hinder digestion. Cooking sometimes changes these biochemical compounds.

Find out at home if food stuffs contain a catalyst that will act like MnO_2 to speed up the decomposition of hydrogen peroxide.

How would you set up your home experiment? What variables should be controlled? [temperature, quantity of food, quantity of peroxide, acidity. . . .]

How will you measure the activity of the foods in decomposing hydrogen peroxide? [observe rate of evolution of bubbles. . . .]

How could you make your experiments more quantitative?

What factors in food processing may affect the nature of the ingredients and their properties? Test your predictions where you can.

What differences do you find between fresh and cooked foods?

What differences do you find between canned and frozen vegetables? . . .

Why are home grown vegetables blanched before they are frozen?

Catalase is an enzyme in food which catalyzes the decomposition of hydrogen peroxide to water and oxygen. Design and carry out experiments in the laboratory to quantitatively measure the effects of variables such as substrate concentration, temperature and acidity on the decomposition of peroxide by catalase. Compare your conclusion about the conditions for optimum activity with those found in the literature.

Comments

Hydrogen peroxide is an intermediate metabolism product which is always decomposed by the catalase present in all cells.

References

Biological Sciences Curriculum Study, *Biological Science: An Inquiry Into Life, Teachers Edition,* 1980. Harcourt, Brace, Jovanovich, New York, pp. 65–67.

*Brown, W. C., "Home Experiments for High School Chemistry", The *Science Teacher,* 40, 7; October, 1973, pp. 45–46.

14. A Chemical Freezer

Science Topic   Spontaneous endothermic reaction, energy, entropy

Level   C:3–4   E:2   D:1   L:3–4

Overview

This striking demonstration of energy transfer from surroundings (water) to system (reaction mixture) provides the setting for an analysis of energy and entropy changes to "explain" observations.

Materials

Dry stoppered Erlenmeyer flask (150ml) containing 32 grams $Ba(OH)_2 \cdot 8H_2O$. (Use a new jar, to be sure that it hasn't absorbed CO_2.)

Dry stoppered Erlenmeyer flask (250ml) containing 16 grams ammonium thiocyanate (NH_4SCN)

Block of wood, approximately 15cm × 15cm × 1cm

Suggested Activities

Pour 1–2ml of water on top of the wood block. Add the barium hydroxide to the ammonium thiocyanate and shake vigorously until the solid mixture begins to liquefy. Then place the flask in the pool of water. After 5–10 minutes, lift the flask; it should be frozen to the block of wood!

Note evidence of a chemical reaction. Is an acid-base reaction involved? [$NH_4^+ + OH^- \rightleftarrows NH_3 + H_2O$] Why does the mixture liquefy?

Write a plausible equation for the reaction into flask. Have the surroundings undergone an exothermic or an endothermic change? What evidence do you have? [$H_2O_{(\ell)} \rightleftarrows H_2O_{(s)} + energy$]

Has the system undergone an exothermic or endothermic change? Explain. Do the observations confirm or refute the hypothesis that systems change spontaneously to a state of lower energy? How is energy conserved in the changes you observed? What factor, other than internal energy, changes in the system? [degree of disorder]

Interpret spontaneous change in terms of "drive" to greater entropy.

Comments

The chemical reaction in the system is:

$$Ba(OH)_2 \cdot 8H_2O(s) + 2NH_4 SCN(s) + energy \rightarrow Ba(SCN)_2(aq) + 2NH_3(aq) + 10H_2O$$

The reaction between citric acid and sodium bicarbonate, two common household materials, is also spontaneous. Careful addition of 12.6 grams (0.15 mole) $NaHCO_{3(s)}$ to a solution of 10.5 grams (0.05 mole) citric acid in water, causes a temperature drop of about 20°C. For further details, see the Britton reference.

Safety Precautions

Avoid skin contact with the solids; do not bring the mouth of the flask close to the nose; do not waft the ammonia vapor with hand movement.

References

Britton, G. G., et al., "Endothermic Sherbet", *The School Science Review,* 60, 210; (September), 1978, pp. 99–100.

Hambly, A. N., "A Spontaneous Endothermic Reaction", *Journal of Chemical Education,* 46, 1, 1969, p. A55.

15. Correlating Properties of Ions with the Behavior of Their Salts

Science Topics   Ionic radius, ionic charge, heat of solution, deliquescence

Level   C:4   E:1   D:2–4   L:2–4

Overview

Students observe regularities in the deliquescence of metal chlorides and they hypothesize about the effects of relevant variables on the phenomenon.

Materials

Pairs of test tubes, one stoppered and one unstoppered, each about half full of one of the following chlorides: LiCl, NaCl, KCl, $MgCl_2$, $CaCl_2$, $BaCl_2$, $AlCl_2$, $SrCl_2$

Suggested Activities

In this activity, you will examine the deliquescence (spontaneous absorption of water) of some metal chlorides and search for explanations of your observations.

Initiate the inquiry by displaying eight pairs of test-tubes, one stoppered and one unstoppered, containing the metal chlorides. The pairs of tubes may be hooked to a display board, in a periodic table array:

LiCl

NaCl $MgCl_2$ $AlCl_3$

KCl $CaCl_2$

                        $SrCl_2$

                        $BaCl_2$

Ask students to observe the tubes at convenient intervals (over some weeks or months, depending on atmospheric conditions).

What can you observe?

What may be a possible pattern in the deliquescence phenomenon?

What are the variables probably responsible for the pattern?

Based on what you know about probable mechanisms and on what you find in the literature regarding ionic charge and structure, predict the factors that make the deliquescence process spontaneous.

What interactions are responsible for the energy of this process, the heat of solution?

What interaction is responsible for a negative value for the heat of solution; a positive value?

What variables are responsible for the differences in the heats of hydration of the metal ions?

What are the values of these variables?

How can the pattern in the observations be explained by the pattern in the values of the variables responsible for the heats of hydration?

Comments

After an appropriate time, it will be found that the open tubes containing LiCl, MgCl$_2$, CaCl$_2$, and AlCl$_3$ deliquesce until only a concentrated solution remains. The tubes may be displayed after they have stood for an appropriate time, showing visually which salts have dissolved in the absorbed water.

This activity presents opportunities to identify relevant variables and to explain a pattern.

Many ionic salts deliquesce (spontaneously absorb water), to the extent that they dissolve in the water that they absorb. The spontaneity of this process should be due to the negative heat of solution (ΔH solution), since the solution of a salt involves an increase in entropy. A negative heat of solution, in turn, must be due to the hydration energy of the ions since the lattice energy value is always positive. Differences in the hydration energies of the metal chlorides will be due to the differing hydration energies of the metal ions. The hydration energy of a metal ion, due to its interaction with dipolar water molecules, is dependent on two factors:

1. ionic radius (the smaller the ion, the greater its charge density)
2. ionic charge

The following table gives the metal ionic radius, ionic charges and molar heats of solution for some metal chlorides:

	Ionic radius (A)	Ionic Charge	ΔH soln (Kj/mol)
Li	.60	+1	− 37.2
Na	.95	+1	+ 3.9
K	1.33	+1	+ 17.2
Mg	.65	+2	− 155
Ca	.99	+2	− 82.9
Sr	1.13	+2	− 52.0
Ba	1.35	+2	− 13.2
Al	.50	+3	− 332

Students should be asked to search for the relevant data in the literature, if the literature is accessible to them.

Reference

Luke, D., "The Relationship Between Hydration of Metal Ions and the Ionic Radii and Ionic Charge", *The School Science Review*, 56, 197; June, 1975, pp. 768–769.

Molecular Structure and Interactions

1. Molecular Size
2. How Does Your Crystal Grow?
3. Flowing Cakes
4. Curving Streams

5. The Paper-Disc Puzzle
6. Iodine of Many Colors
7. Sparkling Copper
8. The Tartaric Acid Problem and Mirror Images

1. Molecular Size

Science Topics   Molecular models

Level   C:2–3   E:2–3   D:1–3   L:2–4

Overview

An "oil" drop spreads out dramatically when dropped on a water surface. If the quantity of oil is sufficiently small, the extremely thin film formed by the drop will stop spreading before reaching the edges of its container. Why does the drop stop spreading? Pursuing the inquiry enables students to roughly estimate the number of molecules in a cubic centimeter and the molecular mass . . . with remarkably simple tools!

Materials

One tray (minimum—40cm × 40cm)—a cookie pan or lunchroom tray
One graduated cylinder (sensitive to .1ml)
Medicine dropper   Meter stick
Fine chalk dust or lycopodium powder
0.5% oleic acid in alcohol solution
Water
Aluminum foil (for lining pan to avoid contamination and extra cleaning)—optional

Suggested Activities

1. Student prepares or is given .5% solution of oleic acid in alcohol.
2. Fill large *clean* tray with a layer of water, then dust the surface lightly with fine powder.
3. Allow one drop of oleic acid solution to fall onto the water surface.

Why does the oil drop stop spreading?
Does a drop of pure alcohol behave similarly?
What are the effects of the powder or other indicator on the size of the film?
Can the layer be stretched and made thinner?
Is it uniformly thin?
Will a film made from two drops cover twice the area as a film made from one drop?
Estimate the maximum thickness of an oleic acid molecule by determining the thickness of the layer.
If oleic acid molecules were approximately cubic, how many molecules would occupy a one cubic centimeter space?
What would be the mass of one molecule? (The density of oleic acid is 0.898 g/cm³).

Using this information and the knowledge that oleic acid has a molecular weight of 282, make a rough estimate of Avogadro's number from your experimental data.

How much error was there in your estimate of Avogadro's number? To what major experimental procedures and assumptions do you attribute this error?

- -

Can you use this experimental method to estimate the thickness of other films or molecules?

Can you notice any interesting color effects when light reflects from your thin film, "mono-layer"? Does the color of the light make a difference? How can these observations be explained?

How can your estimates and techniques in this experiment be improved?

Does the temperature of the water make a difference?

Comments

The "oil" used in this activity is a solution of oleic acid in alcohol.

For good results in this activity, it is essential that the tray and water be clean.

This activity can be used at an introductory level to introduce some notions about molecular models. The inquiry questions can be discussed with students and they can be tested by individuals or by the group in response to alternative procedures that may be suggested.

Since the layer must be at least one molecule thick, measuring the thickness of the layer enables a person to determine the maximum thickness of the molecules [$\sim 10^{-9}$m], and older students can make such measurements.

$$\text{Volume} = \text{Area} \times \text{Thickness}$$

Thus, knowing the volume of oleic acid in the drop and measuring the cross-sectional area of the layer ($A = \pi r^2 = \pi \frac{d^2}{4}$) permits an estimate of the thickness of the layer of oil.

References

Boys, C. V.: *Soap Bubbles,* 1959. Doubleday, Anchor Books, Garden City, New York.

Debye, P. J. W., "How Giant Molecules are Measured", *Scientific American,* September, 1959, pp. 90–97.

Physical Science Study Committee, *Physics Laboratory Guide,* 1965. D. C. Heath, Englewood Cliffs, New Jersey, p. 10.

Physical Science Study Committee, *Teacher's Resource Book,* Part 1, 1967. D. C. Heath, Englewood Cliffs, New Jersey, I–6 (1–2).

2. How Does Your Crystal Grow?

Science Topics   Crystals, solubility

Level   C:2–3   E:2–3   D:1–2   L:2–3

Overview

Crystal growing is fun. To make it an inquiry activity, we suggest that students be challenged to find the conditions necessary for growing the largest and best shaped crystals.

Materials

Solids which yield good crystals (see references—ionic salts, salol, thymol, sulfur, napthalene)

Balance	Beakers
Covered jars	Petri dishes
Burner	

Suggested Activities

"Solid crystals are characterized by definite geometric shapes, as you can see in this large crystal of copper sulfate. Do all crystals have the same shape? Here are some solids we can use to grow crystals."

What methods do you suggest using?

Heat a solution of the solid to evaporate the solvent? Melt the solid and allow it to cool? Others? Test some crystal growing methods.

What can we do to get larger, better shaped crystals?

[In addition to sharing ideas, suggest that one or more students review references on this question in the literature. Two methods suggested are:

a. use an open saturated solution with a seed crystal;
b. use a covered supersaturated solution with a seed crystal.]

Test the new methods and compare results.

- -

Measure angles between faces of several large crystals of the same substance and between faces of crystals of different substances.

Study optical effects on transmitted light . . . Electrical effects.

Interpret crystal structure in atomic-molecular terms.

Comments

Background readings for *Suggested Activities* are presented in Chapters IV and V of Holden and Singer. Chapters VI and VIII are relevant to the extension activities (below the dashed line) relating to crystal structure.

More elementary activities can be developed using the Hoehn and Novick references.

References

DeVito, A. and Krockover, G. H. *Creative Sciencing,* 1976. Little Brown & Company, Boston, pp. 11–12.

Hoehn, R. G., "Crystals in a Minute!", *Science Activities,* 12, 2; March/April, 1975, pp. 14–15.

Holden, A. and Singer, P.: *Crystals and Crystal Growing,* 1960. Doubleday and Co., Garden City, New York.

Novick, S., "Growing Large Crystals", *The Science Teacher,* 44, 2; February, 1977, p. 39.

3. Flowing Cakes

Science Topics   Intermolecular forces

Level   C:2–4   E:1   D:1   L:1–4

Overview

In this activity, students propose hypotheses to explain shape retention in granular materials.

Materials

Polystyrene coffee cups
Paper towelling
Powdered or granular materials in the home and surroundings (e.g., powdered sugar, granular sugar, starch, flour, fine sand, baking soda)

Suggested Activities

Here are some free-flowing materials in these cups. Suppose I wanted to present them as cakes by carefully inverting and removing the cups. I wonder if the solids would retain their shapes.

Predict which materials will retain their shapes and which will fall apart. Why did you make these predictions?

Observe carefully what happens when the cups are slowly removed after being inverted on paper towelling.

Invent one or more hypotheses to explain these properties.

Can you interpret the results in terms of the forces between particles or molecules? [Particle size, interparticle distance, molecular structure. . . .]

What can we do to "non-sticky" solids to help them retain their shape? [Pack them tight, add water, . . .] Explain why this might make a difference in terms of your hypotheses.

Why does wet sand retain its shape while neither sand *nor* water alone will do so?

Comments

This activity presents an excellent opportunity for students to develop creative hypotheses in attempting to explain the properties of materials.

The ability of common powdered solids to retain their shape when lightly packed can be interpreted in terms of factors related to the strength of intermolecular forces.

Reference

Orlando, A., "Sand Castles", *The Science Teacher,* 46, 6; September, 1979, p. 46.

4. Curving Streams

Science Topics   Polar and non-polar liquids

Level   C:3–4   E:1   D:1   L:2–4

Overview

This activity examines the effects of positive and negative static charges on polar and non-polar liquids. One or more portions of this activity demand extreme caution in handling potentially dangerous material.

Materials

Two beakers   Two burettes
Water   Carbon tetrachloride (CCl_4)
Acetate strip and piece of silk
Other polar and non-polar liquids as suggested by students
Vinyl strip and wool or equivalent materials for producing positive and negative charges

Suggested Activities

Electrostatic interactions between positively and negatively charged objects are familiar phenomena in the study of electricity. Can liquids also show the effects of static electrical charge? Create some electrostatic charges by rubbing plastic strips with pieces of cloth. Examine the effects of a negatively charged strip and a positively charged strip near burette streams of water and carbon tetrachloride. See Activity C1. [The stream of water from the burette is attracted by both the positively and the negatively charged strips; the carbon tetrachloride is undeflected.]

Suggest an explanation for your observations.

Test other liquids and observe; can you notice any patterns?

Why is a stream deflected by two kinds of charge or not at all?

How are the deflections related to the molecular structure of the liquids?

Could a neutral molecule become polar in an electric field? Explain.

Safety Precautions

DO NOT inhale odor of CCl_4 or other volatile liquids; avoid skin contact. In case of spillage, wash with soap and water. There should be NO flames.

Comments

This activity is based upon a well-known demonstration, appearing in the CHEM Study film, "Shapes and Polarities of Molecules". It is best conducted *after* students have learned about polar and non-polar molecules. Whether the behavior of the liquids can be considered experimental evidence for the polarity or non-polarity of molecules is a worthy subject for discussion. Students may be able to offer other interpretations of the phenomena they observe.

The leaves of an electroscope repel or attract each other. In this inquiry we have another application of electrostatic interaction. In this case both negatively and positively charged objects attract, illustrating the dual behavior of a dipole in being attracted to both positive and negative charge. The deflection is probably due *both* to the permanent dipolar structure of the liquid molecules, *and* to the polarizability of the molecules (Kempa and Auld).

Students will suggest many liquids to test; have as many of these available as possible.

References

CHEM Study Films: *Shape and Polarities of Molecules.* Modern Learning Aids, New York.

Kempa, R. F. and Auld, J., "An Examination of the Deflection Method for the Study of Molecular Polarity", *The School Science Review,* 55, 193; June, 1974, pp. 716–724.

Robbins, R. and Kerr, B., "Polarity of Liquids—A Student Experiment", *The Science Teacher,* 41, 8; November, 1974, p. 53.

Thiemann, T., "Investigating the Polarity of Molecules", *Chemistry,* 38, 5; May, 1965, p. 24.

5. The Paper-Disc Puzzle

Science Topics   Polar and non-polar interactions between liquids and paper

Level   C:3–4   E:1–2   D:1   L:2–4

Overview

This activity is an excellent introduction to the study of molecular structure and its relationship to polar and non-polar interactions. Alternatively it can be performed after students have conceptualized these ideas, in which case they could apply them in explaining the immiscibility of polar and non-polar liquids and the regularity in the orientation of the paper discs at the interface between two immiscible liquids. One or more portions of this activity demand extreme caution in handling potentially dangerous material.

Materials

250 ml flasks

Distilled water

A supply of small paper discs (about 1/2 cm diameter) blackened on one side with carbon-based ink or pencil graphite

Two rubber stoppers

Carbon tetrachloride (CCl_4)

Suggested Activities

Give each student or group a stoppered flask containing equal volumes of two immiscible liquids, water and carbon tetrachloride, and about ten paper discs—black on one side and white on the other. Students shake the flask and allow it to stand for a minute or so.

Is there regularity observed in the orientation of the discs?

Is the regularity observed by all groups participating in this inquiry?

How could any observed regularity be explained? [A relationship between composition of black and white sides of paper relative to composition of liquids; black "likes" the heavier liquid; an interaction between the liquids at the interface. . . .]

What is the chemical nature of the white paper and the black graphite from the pencil? How are they different?

What is the chemical nature of the two liquids? How are they different? Why don't they mix together?

Why do the paper discs line up the way they do? How can the explanations be tested?

Try shaking discs with water alone and with carbon tetrachloride alone.

Shake discs with water and a liquid that settles on *top* of the water (such as heptane).

Shake discs with a variety of single liquids and mixtures of liquids, miscible and immiscible: alcohols, acetone, ether, glycerol, . . .

Which explanation fits the largest number of observations?

What would happen to the discs if a few drops of detergent were added and the mixture shaken?

Suggest additional experiments using the given liquids and others in order to support your hypotheses. There is also opportunity to use a handbook in seeking relevant information (density, dipole moment).

Safety Precautions

Avoid contact with carbon tetrachloride (CCl_4), and carbon disulfide (CS_2).

Flasks should be stoppered tightly when shaking and should *not* be removed.

During the inquiry there should be *no* flames in the vicinity.

Comments

The discs are easily prepared by blackening one side of a white file card with a "lead" pencil and the cutting into discs about $1/2$ cm in diameter.

The paper disc orientation between two immiscible liquids is an excellent analogy to the orientation of soap molecules between water and a non-polar medium.

The kind of polar and non-polar interactions which explain the phenomenon in this inquiry also explain many others: the action of detergent molecules in the cleaning process, formation of oil-water emulsions, the structure of biological membranes (lipid-protein interactions), the tertiary structure of proteins (polar and non-polar side groups of amino acid residues) are a few examples.

References

Woodburn, J. H., "Discover and Describe", *The Science Teacher,* 38, 9; December, 1971, p. 40.

6. Iodine of Many Colors

Science Topics   Solvation, polar and non-polar interactions

Level   C:4   E:3   D:2   L:4

Overview

A solution of iodine in carbon tetrachloride is violet, the color of iodine vapor. Aqueous solutions of iodine are brown. A reasonable explanation of the difference can be given in terms of solvation of iodine molecules. One or more portions of this activity demand extreme caution in handling potentially dangerous material.

Materials

Test tubes	Iodine crystals
Stirring rods	
A variety of solvents:	

    Water   Alcohols
    Acetone   Carbon tetrachloride
    Chloroform   Diethyl ether
    Concentrated hydrochloric acid
    Concentrated nitric acid
    Liquid alkanes (heptane, petroleum ether)

Suggested Activities

Add equal volumes of ethanol (polar) and carbon tetrachloride (non-polar) to a crystal of iodine in each of two test tubes.

Why are the colors different?

Test your tentative explanations by preparing and observing iodine solutions with other solvents.

How can you change the color of an iodine solution? By adding a different solvent? By changing concentration? By changing temperature?

How can you explain the observed color changes (or absence of change)? Be as explicit as you can. What explanations are provided in the literature?

Safety Precautions

Carbon tetrachloride should be dispensed with care, avoiding skin contact and vapor inhalation. *No flames* should be present when working with flammable solvents. Avoid skin contact with solid iodine. Many of the solvents in this inquiry are explosive, poisonous, and/or corrosive. Investigations should take place only in a fume hood and under the direct supervision of a teacher.

Comments

It is thought that in carbon tetrachloride solution, as in the gaseous state, there are free I_2 molecules interacting with light to produce the violet color. In aqueous solution, the I_2 molecules are somehow bound to water molecules. These solvated molecules are thought to be in equilibrium with a relatively small concentration of free I_2 molecules. The color of iodine in other solvents supports this theory. In general, polar solvents produce brown iodine solutions and non-polar solvents produce violet iodine solutions.

Evidence for the polar solvation of iodine by certain solvents is given by dipole moment values. Iodine has a dipole moment of 1.2 D in benzene (solution is reddish brown) and a dipole moment of 0 in cyclohexane (solution is violet). The familiar household iodine antiseptic is of course a solution of iodine in ethanol. For that reason students commonly picture iodine as brown. Adding a few drops of ethanol to a solution of iodine in carbon tetrachloride causes a color change; adding a few drops of carbon tetrachloride to a solution of iodine in ethanol does not produce a color change. This can be interpreted in terms of the equilibrium:

$$I_2 + \text{alcohol} \rightleftharpoons I_2(\text{alcohol})$$

Higher temperature favors the breaking down of the solvation complexes. A solution of iodine in ethyl stearate changes color from brown to violet at about 80°C. A solution of iodine in gasoline changes color from violet to brown at −50°C (in solid CO_2).

This activity highlights the fact that solutions are not always simple mixtures and that there are definite interactions between solvent and solute particles.

References

Cotton, F. and Wilkinson, G.: *Advanced Inorganic Chemistry,* 1962. Interscience Publishers, New York, p. 441.

*Holman, J. S., "The Colour of Iodine in Solution", *The School Science Review,* 56, 195; December, 1974, pp. 325–326.

7. Sparkling Copper

Science Topics   Catalytic dehydrogenation (oxidation) of alcohols

Level   C:2–3   E:2   D:1   L:2–4

Overview

In the dehydrogenation of methanol vapor on the surface of hot copper oxide, the repeated change in the copper color from shiny orange to black is visual evidence for the roles of copper and oxygen in the oxidation of methanol to methanal. Careful observations lead to a description of chemical reaction. Using some additional data, students can suggest a balanced equation which can be compared with the equation suggested in elementary organic chemistry texts. One or more portions of this activity demand extreme caution in handling potentially dangerous material.

Materials

20 cm length of stiff copper wire
150 ml Erlenmeyer flask
Tongs
Methanol
Gas burner
Wood test-tube holder

Suggested Activities

Heat to redness in a burner flame a stiff copper wire which has been previously wound into a spiral around a pencil. Then insert it just above the level of some methanol in a flask (see figure). Raise the spiral into the air and quickly insert it again. Repeat this until no change is observed.

Repeat the entire procedure a second time. What do you observe? [The hot copper repeatedly sparkles above the methanol and turns black when removed into the air; after a time the copper no longer sparkles. The process can be repeated with the same copper wire. A very pungent odor (like formaldehyde), different from that of methanol is detected at the mouth of the flask.]

Can you find a chemical explanation for these changes? Why does copper "sparkle"?

What is the composition of the "sparkling copper"? the "black copper"?

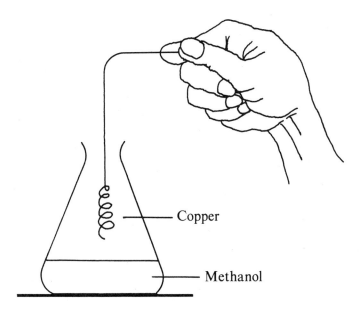

[Copper oxide loses oxygen over methanol, becoming copper metal. The methanol reacts with the oxygen lost by the copper oxide. (In air, heated copper does not lose oxygen when removed from the flame and this observation serves as a "control" in this inquiry.) The pungent odor is due to the formation of methanal (formaldehyde), thus its characteristic odor is present.]

If methanal (formaldehyde) (CH_2O) and water are formed, write equations for the reactions.

[$2Cu + O_2$ ——— $2CuO$
$CH_3OH + CuO$ ——— $CH_2O + H_2O + Cu$]

Try the technique with some other metals and observe. A platinum foil, warmed with a match and hung over a wire above the methanol, will glow red as the methanol is converted to methanal continuously.

Do oxidizing agents (e.g., dichromate or permanganate ions) in solution have the same effect on methanol as do the hot metals?

Safety Precautions

Copper wire should be held by tongs or test tube holder. Methanol is *flammable*. It may ignite if the copper spiral is brought too close to the liquid. Simply cover the mouth of the flask to extinguish the nearly colorless flame.

Avoid direct inhalation of methanol vapors; they are *toxic*. Methanal (formaldehyde) has an extremely pungent odor. Students should smell with care by wafting the vapors toward the nose by hand.

Comments

This phenomenon presents a good opportunity for interpreting observations in terms of elementary notions of chemical change and the atomic-molecular model. It can be presented in an introductory study of chemical reactions or in a unit on carbon compounds.

Molecular models of methanol and methanal will help students to deduce the reaction. The role of copper is essentially catalytic. This is concretely demonstrated by the observation of the repeated reduction of copper oxide to copper and reoxidation of the copper to copper oxide.

If platinum foil is available, the *continuous* catalytic dehydrogenation of methanol can be simply demonstrated.

This activity may be conducted using ethanol instead of methanol. The advantage of using ethanol is that the vapors (ethanol and ethanal) are not as toxic as those of methanol and methanal. The advantage of using methanol is that the molecular structures involved are simpler (no isomers).

Reference

Alyea, H. N. and Dutton, F. B., *Tested Demonstrations in Chemistry,* 1962, Journal of Chemical Education, Easton, PA, p. 106.

8. The Tartaric Acid Problem and Mirror Images

Science Topics   Optical isomers, organic molecules

Level   C:4   E:1   D:2   L:3–4

Overview

After students have acquired the concept of the asymmetric carbon atom and can explain the existence of optical isomers in terms of nonsuperimposable mirror images, they are invited to seek a solution to the tartaric acid problem posed by Mitscherlich and solved by Pasteur about a hundred years ago.

Materials   Ball-and-stick molecular model set

Suggested Activities

Consider the following simplified extract from a paper presented by E. Mitscherlich to the French Academy of Science in 1814:

> Two pure sodium ammonium salts of tartaric acid have been prepared (tartaric acid is a dihydroxycarboxylic acid whose molecular formula is $C_4H_6O_6$). They have the same chemical composition, the same density, the same index of refraction. But in solution one of the substances deflects the plane of polarized light, while the other has no effect on polarized light. Nevertheless the nature of the atoms, their arrangement and their distances are the same in the substances compared.

If you had been present at Mitscherlich's lecture in 1814, what possible explanations might you have proposed?

Based on your knowledge of optical isomers, how could you use molecular models to seek a solution to the tartaric acid problem? Try to build one model of tartaric acid which has a non-superimposable mirror image and another model which does *not* have one. Which structure would be optically active and which would be optically inactive? Explain.

Comments

This activity is appropriate for advanced secondary science students and for some college students. The ideas are usually presented in textbooks as a "rhetoric of conclusions" (using Schwab's terminology). The activity described here is intended to pursue a "narrative of inquiry". Whether or not students rediscover Pasteur's solution (the inactive meso form of tartaric acid), grappling with the problem should give them some awareness of the spatial thinking involved in its solution.

The model building can be done individually or in small groups. When all students have completed the model building exercise, the solution should be discussed with the entire group.

References

Mickey, C. D., "Optical Activity", *Journal of Chemical Education,* 57, 6; 1980, pp. 442–444.
*Wood, G. N., "Rediscovery in a Course for Non-Scientists", *Journal of Chemical Education,* 52, 3; 1975, p. 177.

X Special Resources

1. **A Graphical Method to Determine the Power of an Exponential Relationship**
2. **Exploring an Activity, Device, or Phenomenon**
3. **Ideas for Further Inquiring and Problem-Solving**
4. **General References for Further Activities**

1. A Graphical Method to Determine the Power of an Exponential Relationship

In attempting to learn more about the world around us we gather information as precisely as we can. We control variables wherever possible in order to learn how one variable affects another. In the process, we often graph the data to get a visual representation of the relationship. Often we discover that such relationships between two variables in the physical world are relatively simple; sometimes we find direct linear relationships.

One example of a graphed linear relationship is shown in Figure A in which the area of a rectangle is plotted vs. its length. From a graph of the data a student who had no knowledge of the relationship could develop a mathematical formula relating the variables. The general form of a linear relationship, as written in most algebra books is:

$y = mx + b$

Where m is the "slope" and
b is the "y-intercept".

In this example then:

$A = m \cdot \ell + 0$

or

$A = w \cdot \ell$

A

Frequently the physical relationship being examined is simple but *not* a linear, first power relationship. Often the simple relationship between the two variables is exponential, having the general form:

$y = kx^a$

Where k is a constant of proportionality and a is an exponent.

If you suspect this kind of exponential relationship exists among the variables you are studying, there is a relatively simple graphical technique you can use to check your prediction and to learn the value of the exponent (a) or "power" of the equation. The exponential equation above can be written in another form:

$\log y = \log k + a (\log x)$

or

$\log y = a (\log x) + \log k$

[Refer to an introductory algebra text for a discussion of logarithms, if you need to review that topic. Also, note that this new logarithmic equation has the general form of a linear relationship with slope a.]

Plot the data for the variables you are studying on special logarithmic (log-log) graph paper, or determine the values of log y and log x (with the help of log tables, slide rule, or calculator) and plot them on standard graph paper. If your prediction of an exponential relationship was valid, the graph will turn out to be a straight line and the slope of the line will be the value of the exponent (a).

2. Exploring an Activity, Device, or Phenomenon

Science Topic   All topics

Level   C:1–4   E:1–4   D:1–4   L:1–4

Overview

Individual students select a familiar activity, device, or phenomenon, analyze physical principles that underlie its use and answer interesting questions about its behavior. Inquiry should include the gathering of empirical data from experimentation with the device or activity, but it need not be limited to that. Students should be encouraged to review literature references that comment on the scientific concepts that are embodied in the device or activity.

Materials

A vast array of devices may be examined, but students will generally supply their own.

Items of laboratory equipment available in the lab may be used by students to pursue specific aspects of their inquiries.

Access to library references and journals can be an important part of this activity for some students.

Suggested Activities

In this activity you are to select an activity, device, or phenomenon of real interest to you. You will answer questions about its behavior and analyze physical principles that underlie its use. It might be efficient to select a device, activity, or phenomenon with which you are already familiar, but that is *not* essential. Your inquiry may include a review of relevant scientific and technical literature that you can acquire, but if possible it should also include a study of some empirical data you have gathered while working with the activity, device, or phenomenon.

As you look around the world in which you live there are many *things you do* and *devices you use* that function on a basis of scientific principles. Look around, be creative, and select a question to investigate that will give you new insights into something you do or use and the science on which it is based.

To begin your inquiry you should formulate a question of interest about your activity, device, or phenomenon and then design a scientific method to gather relevant data. You will subsequently analyze your data in an effort to answer your question. Or instead, use your device or activity to provide evidence of an underlying scientific principle or law. Your objectives, probable activities, material needs, method of reporting and target dates for this activity should be outlined as early as possible to facilitate effective planning.

- -

Were you able to answer the question you initially intended to examine?

How are your results consistent with and how do they differ from scientific principles, as you understand them. . . ?

How could you get more accurate and better data—if you had more time and resources?

What new questions and hypotheses has your inquiry suggested?

Based on your study formulate some recommendations for the design and use of your activity, device, or phenomenon.

CONTRACT

NAME _____   DATE _____

PROJECT TITLE _____

MAJOR QUESTION TO BE INVESTIGATED _____

OBJECTIVES TO BE ACCOMPLISHED:

PROPOSED ACTIVITIES AND DEADLINES FOR COMPLETION:

SAFETY PRECAUTIONS:

RESOURCES TO BE USED:

FORM OF REPORT:

PROBLEMS/QUESTIONS:

(Additional pages may be used if needed.
The final negotiated contract will be signed by student and instructor.)

Figure 1. Sample contract form.

Comments

This activity is best run as an extended project with outside class activity. Students will work individually or in small groups on different activities of their own choosing. To facilitate teacher input and monitoring, it is recommended that students be required to prepare and subsequently update contracts for the inquiry they plan to conduct. A sample student contract form is shown in Figure 1. Teachers are encouraged to solicit the support of persons with relevant technical expertise to supervise projects for a small number of students.

References

How Things Work, 1967. Simon and Schuster, New York.

Summerlin, L. R., *Chemistry of Common Substances,* 1979. Silver Burdett, Morristown, N.J.

Walker, *The Flying Circus of Physics,* 1977, John Wiley and Sons, New York.

3. Ideas for Further Inquiring and Problem-Solving

The activities in this sourcebook elaborate a number of interesting phenomena that can provoke questioning and a search for understanding and solutions. Yet, the world that surrounds us contains multitudes of phenomena, technology, and issues that have the potential to provoke questions and to stimulate and motivate people in the study of science. One of the tasks of science teachers is to help students see and contemplate phenomena, technology, and issues in their world.

Science teachers can help students identify ideas about which to wonder; they can also help them formulate interesting questions to investigate. This section contains a number of issues, not elaborated in detail in Part I, that can serve as alternative starting points for inquiring and problem-solving activities.

Survey and classify chemicals found in your community.

Investigate chemical and physical properties in soils, foods, cosmetics, water, . . . Study pH, proteins, fats, saturated and unsaturated lipids. . . .

Study ways to reduce the "hardness" of water.

Conduct an "energy audit" of homes, public buildings, your school, . . . Prepare practical recommendations on how energy costs can be reduced.

Examine materials used in building construction in your community.

Investigate sewage/effluents over a period of time for composition, environmental effects. . . .

Study engineering publications and/or public documents shedding light upon geological, technological, environmental, . . . issues.

Examine aerial photographs to study geological and environmental factors in your community.

Study the history of energy consumption in your community, region, . . . Make future projections. . . .

Design and construct a wind or water powered generator and measure energy input/output as a function of other factors like water volume, velocity. . . .

Make and test solar panels, fuel cells. . . .

What area would be needed to supply the energy requirements of your community or home from solar energy?

Examine contemporary solar powered devices such as water heaters and evaluate their design.

Study/measure the efficiency of different methods of energy conversion.

Survey the raw material and energy sources consumed by nations or regions; examine trends, identify problems and ways for their resolution. . . .

Examine the physical principles underlying a sporting activity.

Investigate the efficiency of specific machines (simple and/or complex), tools, engines, appliances, . . .

Design a container that will prevent damage to its contents when it is dropped.

Design a good paper airplane, . . . a more efficient bicycle, . . .

Test stresses in materials or in structures (real and/or models). . . . .

Investigate methods for measuring the velocity of fluids, . . .

Study the effects of various "streamlined" designs, . . . wings, . . . on friction, turbulence, lift, . . .

How many ways can you think of to measure the height of a tall building, a mountain, . . . ? Measure the height of an object using several methods and examine their accuracy and utility. . . .

Plot the motion of planets or satellites from photographs or naked-eye observations.

What ways can you use to determine the weight of a heavy object (like an automobile . . .). Compare the accuracy and utility of these methods.

Examine the heating effects of electric currents.

Compare the effectiveness (energy efficiency, utility, . . .) of various heating devices, systems, . . .

Measure terminal voltages and internal resistances of batteries and investigate how these change in various charge-discharge conditions.

Using an oscilloscope and other electrical instruments, examine the electrical characteristics of various electrical devices . . . when used with variable frequency alternating current, direct current, . . .

Study the uses and limitations of various electrical measuring instruments, . . .

Naturally falling snowflakes or raindrops are often charged. Study the factors affecting the amount of charge that is present.

Design an electrical device that will signal when rain is falling.

Design a "resistance-meter" to show the pressure of subsurface objects such as rocks, water, artifacts, . . .

Study the acoustical effects of various rooms and surroundings (reverberation time, effects of curtains, rugs, screens, . . .)

Study the effects of various loudspeaker or microphone designs on high and low frequency response, sound quality, . . .

Survey your school and/or community for "noise pollution".

Study limits of human hearing.

Study the sound characteristics of musical instruments.

Study the effectiveness of different kinds of radio and TV antennas.

Study the effectiveness of different systems of noise reduction (in engines, . . .).

Examine the effects of windows on transmission and filtering of sound. (Size, shape, materials, layering, thickness, . . .)

Examine the characteristics and effectiveness of various camera systems and components, lenses, range-finders, lightmeters, filters, lighting, speed, . . .

Compare the characteristics of contact lenses with those of conventional eye glasses.

Photograph interesting phenomena such as high speed motion, diffraction patterns, mirages, . . . ?

Examine the polarization of light in the sky. Does it vary with direction, position of the sun, time of day, time of year, . . . ?

Conduct a scientific study of optical illusions.

Explore the resolving power of telescopes, microscopes, the human eye, . . .

Study one or more aspects of the chemistry that underlies modern photography.

Study the strength of materials: hair, threads, papers, wires, . . .

Examine the effects of temperature on length, volume, density, elasticity, . . . of specific materials.

Study the "tearing" or liquid absorption properties of fabrics, papers, . . . What are the effects of perforations? temperature? chemical treatments? rubbing?

Study the effects of oil films between sliding surfaces.

Study the effects of temperature on the flow of motor oils or other fluids, on the motion of ball bearings falling in oil, . . .

Examine the color effects of films. . . .

What are the effects of length, material, diameter, shape, . . . on vibration frequency. . . .

Study the properties of drops and/or bubbles for various liquids and gasses.

Examine the effects of water waves on a beach.

Examine the optical properties of various minerals (diffraction effects, refraction, dichroism. . . .)

When an onion is sliced some people cry. Are these effects dependent on temperature or humidity or other factors?

Study the "popping" of popcorn. What mass changes occur if any? What are the effects of cooking oil? What are the effects of piercing the unpopped kernel?

Examine the background radiation in various locations. Is it uniform? random? Can you observe effects due to altitude?

What are the effects of driving, temperature, altitude, . . . on the pressure of an automobile tire? Are your observations consistent with your predictions and "theoretical models"?

Study the fuel consumption and efficiency of engines, vehicles, . . . under various conditions (speed, load, . . .)

Investigate the effects of the media in influencing public opinion or a specific issue or problem in science and/or technology.

What has humankind gained or lost through scientific and technological progress throughout human history?

4. General References for Further Activities

a. Books

DeVito, A. and Krockover, G. H. *Creative Sciencing*. 1980. Little Brown, and Co., Boston, Massachusetts.

Elementary Science Study (ESS). [Many titles], 1962–1973. McGraw-Hill Book Co., New York.

Fuller, H. Q., Fuller and Fuller, Laboratory Manual: *Physics Including Human Applications*, 1978. Harper and Row, Publishers, New York.

How Things Work, 1967. Simon and Schuster, New York.

Individualized Science Instructional System (ISIS), [Many Titles], 1980, Ginn & Co., Lexington, MA.

Interdisciplinary Approaches to Chemistry, *The Delicate Balance*, 1973 Harper and Row, New York.

Piel, E. J., and Truxal, J. G., *Man and His Technology: Problems and Issues,* 1973. McGraw-Hill, Inc., New York.

Rutherford, F. J., et al. *The Project Physics Course Handbook,* 1978. Holt, Rinehart, and Winston.

Summerlin, L. R. *Chemistry of Common Substances,* 1979. Silver Burdett Co., Morristown, N.J.

Walker, J. *The Flying Circus of Physics,* 1977. John Wiley and Sons, New York.

Walker, J. *The Physics of Everyday Phenomena,* 1980. The Scientific American, New York.

b. Periodicals.

The Journal of Chemical Education, American Chemical Society, Washington, D.C.

The Physics Teacher, American Association of Physics Teachers, Stony Brook, New York.

The School Science Review, Association for Science Education, College Lane, Hatfield, Herts AL109AA, England.

Science Activities, Heldref Publications, Washington, D.C.

Science, American Association for the Advancement of Science, Washington, D.C.

Science 8, American Association for the Advancement of Science, Washington, D.C.

The Science Teacher, National Science Teachers Association, Washington, D.C.

Scientific American, Scientific American, Inc. New York.

Part II

Implications for Science Education

A Suggestions for Teaching

Teaching Guidelines
Evaluation
Two Sample Inquiries
References

In the complex world of human learning, there is little doubt that diverse teaching strategies can be appropriate. In fact, excessive dependency upon one good mode of instruction may well result in less than optimal interest and attention while a careful blend of teaching strategies may enhance interest and attention and be more responsive to the needs of different learners. To meet certain instructional goals, it is appropriate to have students perform structured laboratory activities in which they develop manipulative skills, observe phenomena, and verify relationships that have been outlined earlier. While this kind of didactic instruction has a place in science teaching, it will not be discussed in this sourcebook, for contemporary teachers' guides and laboratory handbooks support that effort fairly well. This sourcebook does provide resources for one of the more important strategies useful for teaching scientific concepts as well as for communicating the image of *science as inquiry*. That strategy involves students in *learning through inquiry*.

Exploration is an important first phase of scientific and technological research. Scientific research starts with questions about phenomena and technological research starts with the identification of a problem to be solved. An important part of science education is to use teaching methods which increase a student's ability to generate questions about his or her natural and technological environment. In a healthy inquiry-oriented environment, students explore, raise questions, and feel free to wrestle with competing ideas. Their ideas are accepted openly and examined by their peer group and teacher with sensitivity in the light of data and logical analysis. They come to recognize that simple scientific models can be very helpful, but that as students grow and get more information, their understanding and these mental models also grow and evolve. A classroom environment can be developed where students raise questions and offer conjectures without the hesitation that results from the fear of being judged "wrong" or "right". They can be helped to recognize how to test their conjectures in the light of data they have gathered. Learning through inquiry can facilitate the attainment of many of the goals outlined for introductory science teaching and thus is one especially important strategy for the science teacher.

Emphasis. The amount of time dedicated to learning through inquiry should depend in large measure on the goals of science instruction thought to be most important. When students are actively manipulating materials or ideas, the probability that meaningful learning is occurring is greater than when they are passively observing or listening. As a result, some teachers have inferred that an intensive array of activities is best for learners in introductory science. However, a random walk through myriad unconnected activities does not guarantee that meaningful learning will occur. In fact, a random walk may be counterproductive. While student action on objects and ideas *is* helpful, an adequate amount of time must be invested in discussing, questioning, and explaining, thus helping students to interpret and to integrate the results of class activity with concepts they already understand.

Though time and care must be devoted to inquiry activities for meaningful learning to occur, with proper planning these activities can occur in a series of single class periods. While extended class periods can be helpful at times, they are not essential and will even result in problems with students who have relatively short attention span. Appropriate inquiry activities can occur over an interval of several days or even weeks. Some of these activities may be performed by an entire class while others may be individually assigned to selected groups of students or individuals.

Format. Teaching strategies should be varied for the sake of interest and efficiency. Sometimes it is appropriate to begin a unit with a stimulating inquiry-oriented class demonstration, asking for predictions about what will happen and following with discussion of observations and results. Sometimes it is helpful for a class to process the data gathered in such a demonstration, from a film, or from "scientists somewhere else". Often it is appropriate for an entire class to process data that has been gathered in small groups and then pooled, scrutinizing the information, developing generalizations, raising questions about sources of errors, speculating about inferences and applications of data. . . . Teachers who want to encourage learning through inquiry may vary the format of inquiry teaching and learning in order to capitalize upon special interests and opportunities available in selected topics and in order to increase the attractiveness of science topics over an extended period of time.

Joseph Schwab has proposed the use of "Invitations to Enquiry" as outlined in *The Biology Teachers' Handbook*[1]. These invitations written for biology teachers present data gathered in scientific investigations to be used in an attempt to see relationships, to seek explanations, to identify assumptions, to search for implications, and to raise new questions. This kind of inquiry is also appropriate for teachers in the physical sciences and material for such "invitations" can be gathered from journal articles, books, or from investigations conducted by students. Even brief newspaper articles on relevant topics in the physical sciences can be gathered by students and processed in this way. When using newspaper articles, students can be asked to look for assumptions or biases of the author, for errors, or even for missing information.

The inquiry/problem-solving activities in this sourcebook are another good resource with which to stimulate meaningful student inquiry. Prior to introduction of a course topic, they can be used to raise questions and to stimulate discussion of ideas relevant to that topic; in essence, they can be used to introduce the study of selected topics. At other times, they can be used to build upon and to elaborate topics introduced earlier. For example, Activity *B11* can be used to stimulate the search for variables affecting the motion of pendulums that are not included in classical study of pendulum motion. Activity *D8* on interference can stimulate the search for interference patterns in wave media (sound, water, light, or microwaves) that are different from the one studied in formal class work. Activity *F1* on the effects of insulating materials can take the students beyond the formal study of a science concept to look for applications that have relevance in energy conservation and the heating of buildings. It is one of several in this sourcebook examining applications of scientific concepts and phenomena.

Inquiry into products for the consumer can provide a large number of meaningful extensions of science topics for individual students or groups. Such an inquiry normally includes a description of the needs of the consumer, identification of performance criteria, design of experiments to examine the product, assessment of the product in terms of the criteria, and finally a comprehensive judgment about which product is best or acceptable, in terms of the criteria. *What's Best for Heartburn,* Activity *A8,* assessing the best buy in terms of product characteristics, consumer needs, and cost is a good example of such an inquiry. *Batteries and the Traveling Lady,* Activity *C5* is another such example outlined in this sourcebook.

Teaching Guidelines

Action on materials and ideas increases the probability that learning will occur. Random activity, however, may merely increase the noise level, both figurative and real! The guidelines for teaching that follow should increase the probability of *meaningful learning* through inquiry. We do not view them as sequential rules, but rather as suggestions that can enhance learning.

---

1. Mayer, W. V.: *BSCS Biology Teachers Handbook,* 1978. John Wiley and Sons, Inc., New York, pp. 299–487.

Planning

1. Identify important goals and objectives for the instructional unit.
2. Identify skills and interests students bring with them to the unit of instruction.
3. Identify the materials and resources available in the school or in the community to support the instructional goals you have selected.
4. Design lessons and activities for students that are consistent with the goals, student experiences, and materials and recourses available.
5. Select activities, major parts of which students can accomplish with the materials available in an appropriate period of time.
6. Have some challenging expectations, but do not expect students to do unrealistic amounts of work in a class session or in a semester.
7. Plan with both long term goals and short term objectives in mind.

Motivation

1. Stimulate interest and curiosity in the activity by beginning with an interesting demonstration, puzzle, or question.
2. Show the relevance of the inquiry or topic to the student's world and experiences.
3. Indicate that students may be able to pursue different aspects of an activity in topics that are of greatest interest to them. For example, in Activity *D8* on interference, students with special interests in music might examine interference in sound waves; students with special interest in art might examine interference in lights of different colors; students who have special interests in electronics might investigate interference in microwaves.
4. Provide opportunities for students to explore issues at the interface of science and society. Activity *A1, Searching for Soft Energy* is one example of this kind of activity.
5. Encourage students to pursue excursions of special interest to themselves that go beyond normal classwork; grant proper credit for such special projects and find ways for students to discuss their findings with others.

Management

1. At the beginning of each activity, clearly explain the purpose of the activities, your expectations, and criteria for evaluation and credit.
2. Carefully prepare written handouts outlining organizers for the activity such as important questions to be asked, potentially useful practices, safety considerations and general expectations.
3. Specify how materials are to be procured and returned. Involving students in aspects of this responsibility may be helpful.
4. Clearly specify how the student is to report results.
5. Initiate inquiry with a pre-lab discussion. Through such discussion, questions to be investigated can be outlined and predictions can be made. Subsequently, methods to test the predictions and to investigate the questions raised can be discussed. Alternatives for experimental design can be discussed and, if appropriate, different groups within the class can be assigned different aspects of the inquiry.

Structure

1. Arrange the amount of teacher guidance provided throughout each inquiry to reflect the goals of instruction and the skills of students in the class. The science topic to be studied is another important variable in the decision about the amount of structure that is appropriate. Some topics are more appropriate for highly structured inquiry while others are appropriate for less structured teaching. Highly structured inquiry may be appropriate for elaboration of certain

science concepts, but it is not necessarily an efficient way to teach students how to identify problems or how to design experiments. These skills can sometimes best be developed through the right kinds of discussions interspersed with relatively low structured experimentation.

2. If a highly structured approach is intended, be certain that the problem, procedures, and questions to be examined are clearly defined and understood by students before proceeding.

3. If an activity with low structure is desired, be certain that students can identify the problems to be investigated, the general goals of the activity, and the general procedural requirements under which they are operating.

4. Use written *contracts* when possible to assist in the management of inquiry activities that have low structure. Contracts provide a way in which students can develop the ability to plan, to organize, and to become more independent while documenting important information that will facilitate interaction with the teacher and others about the appropriateness of plans. Contracts provide one mechanism through which teachers can encourage individual students to pursue activities that are appropriate for their own interests and level of development. Better students can get credit for doing work that goes beyond required basic topics while slower students can work on more central basic skills.[2] (A sample contract form is pictured in Part I, Section X2, Figure 1.)

Teaching During Inquiry

1. Model the use of inquiry skills. Observe carefully, raise logical and relevant questions, and show real interest in the phenomena being studied.

2. Serve as "research director".[3] That role involves discussing problems and progress with individuals and groups of students, raising questions about their observations and work, discussing procedural alternatives, and helping them search for relationships, interpretations, explanations, and applications.

3. Raise questions that are appropriate for the particular skills and level of development of individual students. Focus upon the development of lower level skills, such as manipulating and observing, for the less sophisticated students; provide greater challenges and higher level thinking, such as encouraging the development of hypotheses and ways to test them for the more sophisticated students. In general, *divergent questions* necessitating *extended answers,* explanation, and elaboration, are more consistent with the goals of student inquiry than are more convergent questions.

4. Ascertain that students are responsible for carrying their share of the load in small group work. Raise concerns about the effectiveness of group behaviors with all members of a group. Discuss and encourage improvement in group effectiveness and behavior.

5. Respond honestly to questions, but do not "give answers" to questions you really want students to wrestle with themselves. Occasionally, ask how an answer to a question raised by a student could be found.

6. Let students explore without excessive correction. Give them a reasonable amount of time for this without burying them in questions and details.

7. Recognize that in the time available most students will not have the opportunity to explore everything. Encourage them to explore a limited number of questions carefully and to identify questions they have not been able to investigate properly.

8. Push for verbalization of observations, inferences, and possible explanations from all students.

9. Through questions and discussion help students relate what they are doing to concepts and topics studied earlier and to technological and societal applications.

10. Encourage students to identify new questions and problems arising from their activities which can serve as a basis for further investigation.

2. For more details see: Romey, *Inquiry Techniques for Teaching Science,* 1968. Prentice-Hall, Englewood Cliffs, New Jersey, pp. 77–86.
3. Romey, W. D.: *Inquiry Techniques for Teaching Science,* 1968. Prentice-Hall, Englewood Cliffs, New Jersey, p. 26.

Post-Lab Discussion

Even when students have not partitioned responsibilities for a particular inquiry, it is helpful to have them share and communicate the results of their inquiries. Results of different student groups should be contrasted and discussed to see how procedures and results differed. Differences in results should be scrutinized by the group to ascertain probable cause. It is also appropriate in post-lab discussion to compare results with those obtained by researchers using more sophisticated techniques and equipment. Once again, there should be some speculation about the reasons for different procedures and for differences observed between results. The discussion should elicit questions that still need to be investigated and possible ways to do so. It should also result in the development of hypotheses to explain relationships that were observed and ways to test those hypotheses. In post-lab discussion encourage small groups of students to discuss and to support their own findings and interpretations.

There are many differences among students, so do not assume when one student responds to a question that all others understand the response! Give students time to think and respond, to raise questions, and to offer explanations. Avoid implying that there is one "right" question, one explanation, one way of testing it. . . . As in all discussions, the good moderator waits for individuals to respond and there is open acceptance of all ideas that are suggested; these ideas are weighed on the basis of logical analysis of what is known about the phenomenon. Inevitably there will be unanswered questions, and one of the important parts of understanding the scientific process is to recognize that uncertainty is one part of scientific reality. Uncertainty stimulates experimentation and further analysis that generally leads in time to more complete understanding. Once again, students should recognize that as more information is obtained, models and understanding may well develop and change.

An important role for the post-lab discussion, in addition to helping students pull their ideas together, is to communicate ways to continue the search for information and understanding. The conversation can occasionally take students out beyond the simplicity of the science laboratory to problems in the world that are more complex and value laden. Some students may subsequently pursue further inquiry on such topics. An activity like *A1,* for example, involves students in a search for alternative sources of energy in their community. In that inquiry the issues are complex and some of the variables difficult to control.

Evaluation

Grading systems reflect the real goals that teachers have for student learning, and for many students the grading system plays a major role in identifying efforts to be emphasized. If inquiry is to be emphasized in student learning and if the development of problem-solving skills is an important part of science learning, those skills should be nurtured and evaluated with care. Test items can assess the ability to make inferences from data, to explain, and to design tests of hypotheses. "Practical" exams with laboratory materials can also be used to assess the student's ability to communicate and to function effectively in inquiry activity. Laboratory notebooks can be evaluated. Most important, however, behaviors that are related to inquiry can be observed and assessed by the teacher or by the students themselves. Possible criteria and rating scales for the assessment of inquiry behaviors and skills are outlined in Figure 1. Teachers can distribute a skills assessment record card like the one shown in Figure 2 to their students and ask them to rate themselves on these criteria after completion of each inquiry activity or at the completion of a unit of study. The teacher can then review each student's own assessment and challenge it or agree with it.

OBSERVATIONAL ASSESSMENT CRITERIA

SKILL AREA	CRITERIA	SCORE
A. Planning and Design	Able to present a perceptive plan for investigation. Plan is clear, concise, and complete. Able to discuss plan for experiment critically.	9–10
	Good, well-presented plan, but needs some modification. Understands over-all approach to problem.	7–8
	Plan is O.K., but some help is needed. Not a very critical approach to problem.	5–6
	Poor, ineffective plan needing considerable modification. Does not consider important constraints and variables.	3–4
	Little idea of how to tackle the problem. Much help needed.	1–2
	No opportunity to use these skills.	X
B. Manipulative Skills	Good general ability to carry out full range of skills. Appreciates precision of apparatus. Quantitative results within expected range. Can carry out plan in a reasonable time, modifying it creatively and effectively when appropriate.	9–10
	Good general ability but limited in certain skills. Can assemble materials and make modifications.	7–8
	Routine worker who does not always appreciate delicacy of apparatus. Needs help in putting plan into operation.	5–6
	Rather careless in handling apparatus. Sometimes fails to perform important steps. Runs out of time. . . .	3–4
	Careless in handling apparatus. Quantitative results outside acceptable range. Much help needed in carrying out plans.	1–2
	No opportunity to use these skills.	X
C. Observations and Recording of Data	Correct observations specified; unexpected results noted. Errors and possible inaccuracies are not ignored; results lying outside expected range noted. All relevant information accurately recorded in an appropriate form.	9–10
	Good presentation of data but little attention to errors. Description good but lacking in fine detail.	7–8
	Adequate presentation of data. Some essential features omitted from descriptions.	5–6
	Poor presentation of data. Many omission of essential features in descriptions.	3–4
	Very poor presentation of data; only part of data reported. Observations inaccurate. Relies upon other students.	1–2
	No opportunity to use these skills.	X

Figure 1. Reprinted with additional details and permission from: V. Lunetta, A. Hofstein, and G. Giddings, "Evaluating Laboratory Activities", *The Science Teacher,* January 1981, p. 24.

Figure 1. Continued.

SKILL AREA	CRITERIA	SCORE
D. Interpretations of Data and the Experiment	Good appreciation of data, appreciation of error and limitations of experiment. Knows when to search for additional information. Good analytical approach. Good appreciation of apparatus required, scale of experiment, etc. Ability to calculate accurately results from experimental data. Good written/oral appreciation of results and variables. Ability to relate the whole practical experience to particular problems.	9–10
	Data appreciated. Adequate understanding of procedure and analysis of error. Method of calculation correct but minor errors occur frequently.	7–8
	Data appreciated. Some help required in handling data and calculations.	5–6
	Little understanding of the relevance of data. Difficulty in handling data and carrying out calculations. Requires assistance in interpreting results and applying experience.	3–4
	Needs much help; little is understood.	1–2
	No opportunity to use these skills.	X
E. Responsibility/ Initiative/Work Habits	Self-reliant, able to work with little supervision. Willing to tackle problems. Can work as part of a team as well as on own. Safety conscious. Willing to help in running of laboratory if asked. Consistent and perseveres. Tackles practical work with enthusiasm.	9–10
	Works well and with enthusiasm within the context of what is expected. Shows consideration for others.	7–8
	Works reasonably well but with little initiative or enthusiasm.	5–6
	Poor persistence.	3–4
	Inconsiderate of the needs of others. Work constantly needs to be checked. Relies on the contributions of others when working with a group. Easily distracted. Often engages in "childish" behavior.	1–2
	No opportunity to use these skills.	X

Laboratory Skills Assessment

NAME _____   COURSE _____

Experiment/Unit Assessed	Date	A. Planning & Design	B. Manipulative Skills & Conduct of Experiment	C. Observations & Recording of Data	D. Interpretations of Data & the Experiment	E. Responsibility/ Initiative/Work Habits

Figure 2. Adapted with permission from: V. Lunetta, A. Hofstein, and G. Giddings, "Evaluating Laboratory Activities," *The Science Teacher*, January 1981, p. 25.

Two Sample Inquiries

An Inquiry Discussion

The dialogue that follows is a sample of a portion of a class discussion conducted by a chemistry teacher based upon activity *G11*. It is included to show one way among many that a guided inquiry discussion might be conducted as an introduction to a new concept, in this case, oxidation.

T   What do you think will happen when a metal like copper is heated in a hot flame?
S_1 It will burn up.
T   What are some other possibilities?
S_2 It might melt.
S_3 It might glow.
T   Anything else?
S_4 It might break down or something.
T   Explain what you mean, Kathy.
S_4 Well, like when you heat sugar and it turns black, there is a chemical reaction.
S_5, S_6 . . . [offer other suggestions]
[All ideas are written on the blackboard as they are suggested.]
T   Here's a piece of copper wire. Hold it with a pair of tongs and observe what happens when you hold it in the Bunsen flame; then remove the wire and let it cool. Be careful not to touch the hot wire.
[One or more students heat a copper wire.]
T   Well, now, what did you find out . . . Mark?
S_7 The copper glowed red in the flame.
T   Anything else?
S_7 Well, it looks sort of black after it cooled.
T   Does anyone have anything to add to John's description? . . . OK. What do you think made the copper turn black?
S_4 It's like I thought; the copper breaks down.
T   Do you mean it loses something?
S_4 Yes, I think so.
T   Can anyone think of another explanation?
S_6 I think the black stuff is probably soot from the flame. You know, like the black stuff under the pot when you cook on the stove.
T   Any other ideas?
S_1 It could be that the heated copper combines with something and that makes it black.
T   Where could that something come from?
S_2 Maybe the air—maybe it's like rusting, but you need more heat with the copper.
[All hypotheses are listed on the blackboard as they are suggested.]
T   We have three explanations or hypotheses so far. Any others?
[After other hypotheses are offered, the teacher canvasses the students for their opinions as to the "best" hypotheses and there is some discussion.]
T   Now, we're going to break into small groups. Each group will adopt one of these hypotheses and it's up to that group to suggest some specific experiments that would tell them if their hypothesis was right or wrong. We'll give each team about eight minutes to talk it over and come up with some suggestions.
[The experiments are suggested and discussed. Ways to improve the experiments and limitations are also suggested.]

This class as a whole was not asked to pursue this inquiry further. However, two students did pursue some of the experiments as a special extra-class project.

EXCERPTS FROM EXPERIMENT I
Keeping Heat Together
Student Instructions

Introduction

At home we often heat liquids such as water for tea or coffee. Sometimes we are in a hurry and our tea or coffee is too hot to drink. We then try to cool it by stirring or blowing. At other times we want to keep our coffee warm as long as we can, and we put some kind of cover on our coffee pot or use a thermos bottle. In a series of activities we are going to invent some methods to cool liquids or to keep them warm, and we are going to see how well these methods work.

[A materials list and notes on safety precautions are included here.]

Experiment I

Use your Bunsen burner or alcohol lamp to heat water in the large beaker (about ¾ full) to about 80°C. Then turn off the burner and carefully use tongs or insulated gloves to pick up the hot beaker and pour water into the cups. Use equal amounts of water and fill two identical cups until each is ½ full. Put a thermometer in each cup and record the temperature of each cup every 30 seconds for eight minutes. Record your data in the following table.

Data:

The Cooling Rate of Cups of Water

Time (Minutes)	Temperature of cup A(°C)	Temperature of Cup B(°C)	Time (Minutes)	Temperature of cup A(°C)	Temperature of cup B(°C)
0			4		
½			4½		
1			5		
1½			5½		
2			6		
2½			6½		
3			7		
3½			7½		
			8		

Questions

1. Do the cups cool down equally fast? Why, or why not?

2. To answer question 1, could you only use the initial and final temperatures rather than all data? Could you only use the final temperature? Why or why not? Why is it useful to record the temperature every half minute?

3. If we fill cup A so that it is full and cup B so that it is half full, which one will cool most quickly? Why?
   (If you have time left, do this experiment to check your prediction.)

Figure 3

A Series of Investigations

This sample series of investigations based upon Activity *F1* will be described as used with one average ninth grade class. The sample consists of student instructions for a series of three "experiments" interspersed with commentary about class activities and about a fourth experiment in the series.

This version of the activity is structured in the sense that what needs to be done is made very clear to students in the printed instructions. Yet, a fair number of decisions regarding how to execute the clearly defined tasks and how to solve the problems posed is left for the students, providing them with ample opportunity to use certain inquiry skills. As the activity proceeds the experiments become less structured; students design the last two experiments themselves. As they progress, the students can handle greater openness since they have learned the necessary basic techniques, and they can then concentrate on bigger questions.

For students who have more advanced competencies, more emphasis can be placed upon Experiments III and IV and other extensions. Note that this version of Activity *F1* is only one of many ways to work out the activity. Teachers will probably want to write their own versions of student instructions to reflect their own priorities and the special needs of their students.

Excerpts from the student instructions for Experiment I are included in Figure 3.

The main purpose of Experiment I is to teach techniques to be used in later investigations (heating water, reading and recording temperature and time) and to sensitize students to some of the parameters of the experiment through direct experience. The format of the data tables has been included here although that need *not* be done for experienced students who need to learn to organize and tabulate data in a format of their own. (Group discussion about the organization of data may be very appropriate.)

Questions 1 and 2 have been included because some students at first think that the final temperature is the criterion variable instead of the difference between the initial and final temperatures. For example, some students say that cup B cools fastest because its final temperature after eight minutes is lower than that of cup A. They neglected to note that the initial temperature had been lower too and that the measured drop in temperature is the same for both cups.

In small or experienced classes one may choose to omit question 3 and let students work through the problems that result if they do not control the amount of water used. The teacher may also want to require that students test the prediction in question 3 rather that to keep it optional.

Instructions for Experiment II are shown in Figure 4 and leave more decisions to the student. They have to design the experiment themselves, yet the data table suggests a design including the use of one cup for a control. Checking the student's design provides the teacher with an opportunity to encourage students to clearly describe a design for the experiment and to think plans over before performing them.

In a post-lab discussion students can present the results of their experiments. Differences between the results obtained by different students and differences between *expected* and actual results can be used to initiate discussion of the effects of variables and aspects of experimental design. For example, the effect of stirring on the cooling rate of the water may be dependent on the diameter of the beaker or cup, the rigor of stirring, the amount of water used, or the kind of stirring utensil. At this point differences between the ways student experiments were carried out may be so chaotic as to prevent generalizations other than the importance of attention to experimental design and control of variables. The need for controlling variables which can so easily confound results will be apparent and can be input for Experiment III. Also, if the stirring experiment has generated interest in some students, there is nothing wrong with repeating the experiment under better controlled conditions. [Stirring with a thermometer does not seem to have much influence on the cooling rate in a 500 cc beaker.]

Student instructions for Experiment III are considerably less structured and are shown in Figure 5. They think of imaginative ways to insulate hot water and keep it warm. They take into account some of the experimental variables (a lid on top of the cup, limiting drafts around the cup using wool or other textiles, etc.) and design an experiment using basic design and control techniques learned in Experiments I and II. The questions are intended to reinforce the ideas that relevant variables need to be controlled.

EXCERPTS FROM EXPERIMENT II
Student Instructions

Does stirring speed up the cooling of a cup of water? Design an experiment to check whether stirring accelerates cooling. Check your plans with the teacher and perform your experiment. (You may carefully stir with your thermometer.)

Describe your experiment here:

Data:

The Influence of Stirring on Cooling Rate of Water

Time (Min.)	Temp. cup A (°C)	Temp. cup B (°C)	Time (Min.)	Temp. cup A (°C)	Temp. cup B (°C)
0			4		
½			4½		
1			5		
1½			5½		
2			6		
2½			6½		
3			7		
3½			7½		
			8		

Cup A—stirred

Cup B—not stirred

Questions

1. Why is it best to use an unstirred cup for comparison here?

2. Will the kind of stirring rod make a difference? Will stirring with a spoon give different results than stirring with the thermometer? (If there is time, do this experiment to check your predictions.) How can your results be explained?

Figure 4

This investigation with the ninth grade class was followed by further group discussion. The teacher then presented four mechanisms for heat transfer: convection, conduction, radiation, and evaporation. After some discussion and brainstorming regarding ways to reduce each of these four kinds of heat loss, Experiment IV was introduced. Students were asked to: "Design a method to keep water warm in which you try to limit heat losses through convection, conduction, radiation, and evaporation." The instructions were similar to those in Experiment III. Alternatively, a teacher and students could plan a systematic class investigation of the four mechanisms in which groups of students conduct experiments investigating different variables. The results could subsequently be pulled together to form the basis for more wide ranging generalizations. Time permitting, the teacher should discuss experimental design with as many

EXCERPTS FROM EXPERIMENT III
Student Instructions

In previous experiments we investigated cooling of two cups of water and the influence of stirring on cooling of hot water. In this experiment we are going to invent ways to keep hot water warm as long as possible. Think of a way to keep hot water and describe an experiment to test your method. Check with your teacher before performing your experiment.

Outline your experiment here.

Record your data in an appropriate table.

Questions:

1. If you used two cups, was the temperature drop the same for both cups?

2. Did your way of keeping water warm longer work?

3. If someone wanted to copy your experiment and placed one cup close to an open window and the other away from the window, would that be a fair experiment? Why or why not?

4. Why is it better to use one cup which you do not insulate in addition to the cup which is insulated in this experiment?

5. Explain your experimental results.

6. What are the sources of error in this experiment? How could these sources of error be controlled if you were to modify your experiment and do it again?

7. What new questions has this experiment raised in your mind?

8. Describe the ways that heat energy leaves your cups to explain why the temperature falls. What mechanisms or models can you identify that can help us understand how heat travels away from the cups causing the temperature to drop?

Figure 5

student pairs as possible. In the discussion with each student pair, the teacher should ask how they prevent each of the four kind of heat loss, thus reinforcing the link between theory, assumptions, hypotheses, and experiment. Ideas about the mechanisms of heat transfer should guide the students' thinking about ways to prevent heat loss. Within the framework of Experiment IV, students may perform a number of experiments depending on the time commitment the teacher decides to make and on the skill and efficiency of student pairs. A thermos bottle or a joulemeter (formerly called a calorimeter) provides an excellent example of an apparatus in which heat losses through convection, conduction, radiation and evaporation are reduced, and in the summary or in a test, students may be asked to look at a thermos bottle or joulemeter and to describe the functions of various parts in preventing heat loss.

Possibilities for extending this activity are numerous. In an academically oriented physics course one may continue with the joulemeter and introduce definitions of specific heat and heat capacity. In a more general course one might continue with a consumer investigation of thermos bottles and the insulating properties of various kinds and brands of such bottles. Related investigations might be conducted into cooling experiments using liquids other than water and examining the effects of heat capacity and specific heat. Investigations into domestic heating systems and insulation and into cooking conditions and devices could also be pursued. (What are the effects of pan or kettle shape, size, material, location, method of use. . . ?) In this kind of applied investigation into relevant, consumer related questions, there is much opportunity for students to develop skills in performing and assessing experiments they have designed themselves.

An Inquiry Template

The sample activities outlined in the preceding series of investigations were based upon Activity *F1*. They enable students to practice and develop many inquiry skills as shown by the skills template that follows. It provides examples of specific inquiry skills used by students in Activity *F1*.

SKILL	*EXAMPLE*
1.0 Planning and design of Experiments	
1.1 Formulates question or problem to be investigated	[Generally *not* done by the students in these examples.]
1.2 Predicts results	Students individually predict results in their versions of Exps. III and IV.
1.3 Formulates hypothesis	[A metal screen will reduce heat loss due to radiation.]
1.4 Designs observation or measurement procedures	Provided in Exp. I, but developed by students in Exps. III and IV.
2.0 Performance	
2.1 Observes/measures	Measures time and temperature simultaneously, volume of water used; observes cup characteristics and variables thought to be relevant to the experiment.
2.2 Manipulation	Lighting Bunsen burner, heating water, using a thermometer, pouring hot water.
2.3 Records results, describes observations	Records temperatures in tables provided.
2.4 Calculates	$t_{initial} - t_{final}$
2.5 Explains or makes decisions about experimental technique	Student decides about major aspects of experimental techniques in Exps. III and IV, what insulation material to use, how to prevent radiation and convection heat losses.
2.6 Works according to own design	The basic technique of time-temperature measurements are provided by teacher in Exp. I, but in Exps. III and IV, student *does* make decisions and follows own design.
3.0 Analysis and Interpretation	
3.1 Transforms results into standard form	Teacher requires time-temperature graphs or asks students to find a way to graphically display the rate of cooling; students prepare their own data table in Exps. III and IV.

SKILL	EXAMPLE
3.2 Determines relationships	Qualitative relationships between stirring and cooling, lid and no lid on cup, normal and draft-free air layer around cup.
3.3 Discusses accuracy of data	Teacher asks some students to estimate accuracy of time-temperature measurements, to estimate the error in the criterion variable $t_i - t_f$, and to estimate error in the equivalence of volumes in control and experimental conditions.
3.4 Discusses limitations/assumptions	Same environmental conditions for both cups (drafts, temperature, table contact, effects of breathing on water cooling, etc.)? In Exps. III and IV students carefully examine and discuss sources of experimental error and mechanisms of heat loss.
3.5 Formulates generalizations	Heat radiation is reduced by metal objects/foils; metals are heat conductors, paper and many plastics and textiles are not.
3.6 Explains relationships	Cooling rate is affected by the amount of water, surface area, evaporation, insulation materials, etc., in the following ways. . . .
3.7 Formulates new questions/problems	Effects of other liquids, other materials, container shapes and design, initial temperature?

4.0 Applications

4.1 Predicts based on results of investigation	Predictions for extension experiments such as heat loss in cooking, home heating systems (fireplaces, furnaces, stoves. . . .)
4.2 Formulates hypotheses	Evaporation is a source of energy loss; a container of . . . design will be more efficient than my coffee cup in retaining heat. . . .
4.3 Applies technique to new problem or variable	Consumer investigation of thermos bottles, home heating systems or devices, home insulation materials. . . .

References

Connelly, F. M. *Enquiry Teaching in Science,* 1976. The Ontario Institute for Studies in Education, Toronto.

Feldhusen, J. F. and Treffinger, D. J. *Creative Thinking and Problem Solving in Gifted Education,* 1980. Kendall/Hunt Publishing Co., Dubuque, Iowa.

Mayer, W. V. *BSCS Biology Teachers Handbook,* 1978. Joon Wiley and Sons, Inc., New York.

Patterson, J., Prescott, J., "Self-paced Freshman Physics Laboratory and Student Assessment," *American Journal of Physics,* 48(2), February, 1980, pp. 163–167.

Pavelich, M. J. and Abraham, M. R. "Guided Inquiry for General Chemistry Students", *Journal of College Science Teaching,* Sept. 1977, 23–26.

Prescott, J., Anger, C., "Removing the "Cook Book" from Freshman Physics Laboratories". *American Journal of Physics,* Vol. 38, No. 1 January, 1970, pp. 58–64.

Reif, F. and St. John, J. "Teaching Physicists' Thinking Skills in the Laboratory", *The American Journal of Physics,* Nov. 1979, 950–957.

Robinson, M., "Undergraduate Laboratories in Physics: Two Philosophies," *American Journal of Physics,* 47(10), October 1979, pp. 859–861.

Romey, W. D. *Inquiry Techniques for Teaching Science,* 1968. Prentice-Hall, Englewood Cliffs, New Jersey.

Rowe, M. B. *Teaching Science as Continuous Inquiry,* 1978. McGraw-Hill Book Company, New York.

Rutherford, F. J. "The Role of Inquiry in Science Teaching", *Journal of Research in Science Teaching,* 2, 1964, pp. 80–84.

Sund, R. B. and Trowbridge, W. *Teaching Science by Inquiry in the Secondary School,* 1973. C. E. Merrill, Columbus, Ohio.

B Theoretical Perspectives

The Nature of Inquiry
Implications
References

"To communicate the spirit of science and to develop people's capacity to use its values should . . . be among the principal goals of education. . . ."

These values are: (1) Longing to know and understand, (2) Questioning all things, (3) Searching for data and their meaning, (4) Demanding verification, (5) Respecting logic, (6) Considering premises, (7) Considering consequences.[1]

A major goal for education today is to help students become successful in a world of changing and unknown dimensions. One very important reason for young people to study science is to learn how to approach their world objectively and how to develop solutions to complex problems.

As new information is identified and as old facts are interpreted anew, people trained for a stable, fact-centered science will have difficulty adjusting to the fast-changing world around them. (Some students are still forced to memorize the "fact" that an atom consists of three particles early in their study of science!) Models and facts are useful, but they are not static, and science teachers should make this clear in their teaching.

Many contemporary scientists and philosophers see sciences as dynamic with evolving models and systems of explanation. Science is a conceptually organized body of knowledge about the material universe, but it is more than that. It is more than a collection of facts, concepts, and principles; it is also a process used by humans to reveal relationships in the universe and to invent explanations for them. Effective science teaching integrates the notions of science *as information* and science *as the search* for information and understanding.

Science teachers have multiple responsibilities. They must help students learn some of the important accumulated discoveries of humankind, as well as to acquire skills for the acquisition and discovery of new information, and for problem solving and communication.

National Assessment results, however, confirm that large numbers of 13 and 19 year old students are deficient in higher order inquiry and problem-solving skills such as the ability to *analyze* and to *synthesize*,[2] and visits to science classrooms frequently reveal students engaging in activities that are not consistent with the broad goals outlined in Figure 6. Laboratory activities generally prescribe detailed instructions that lead the student to the "right" answer. Students often are expected to listen attentively as "the word" is delivered by the teacher or by the textbook. Certainly, textbooks and teachers have a very important role to play, but the message often communicated is that using creative ingenuity is unnecessary and may very well lead to the "wrong" answer. Students learn that listening to authority or following directions is the best way to succeed in science. Joseph Schwab[3] calls this kind of didactic instruction presenting science as a "rhetoric of conclusions". Do science teachers want to convey the notion that science is best done by listening to authority rather than by asking questions, making observations, analyzing data, and wrestling with explanations and interpretations?

A student's involvement in appropriate inquiring and problem-solving activities can promote understanding of science as both a system of concepts and theoretical constructs and an active knowledge-creating and problem-solving process. Schwab characterizes this kind of science teaching as a "narrative

1. Educational Policies Commission. *The Spirit of Science,* 1966. National Education Association, Washington, D.C., p. 15.
2. National Assessment of Educational Progress, Science Technical Report Summary, 1977. NAEP, Denver, Colorado.
3. Schwab, J. J. *The Teaching of Science as Enquiry,* 1962. Harvard University Press, Cambridge, Massachusetts, p. 24.

SELECTED GOALS FOR SCIENCE TEACHING

PROMOTE INTELLECTUAL DEVELOPMENT
ENHANCE THE LEARNING OF SCIENTIFIC CONCEPTS
INCREASE UNDERSTANDING OF SCIENCE AND SCIENTIFIC METHOD
DEVELOP SKILLS IN PROBLEM-SOLVING
DEVELOP SKILLS IN PERFORMING SCIENCE INVESTIGATIONS
DEVELOP SKILLS IN ANALYZING DATA
DEVELOP SKILLS IN COMMUNICATING
DEVELOP SKILLS IN WORKING WITH OTHERS
ENHANCE ATTITUDES TOWARD SCIENCE
PROMOTE POSITIVE PERCEPTIONS OF ONE'S ABILITY TO UNDERSTAND AND TO
AFFECT ONE'S ENVIRONMENT

Figure 6. Adapted with permission from: V. Lunetta, A. Hofstein, and G. Giddings, "Evaluating Laboratory Activities," *The Science Teacher,* 48:1, January 1981, p. 22.

of enquiry." In particular, inquiry activities provide ways for students to become involved in the development of scientific thinking and problem-solving skills while increasing their understanding of particular scientific concepts. Student inquiry should also extend beyond the boundaries of the science classroom into the technological, economic, and social milieu. Some students will find that such experiences make science instruction more relevant and interesting to them.

Effective science teaching embodies goals developed from the world of science, from expectations of the society and students, and from an understanding of how people learn. One necessary condition for acquiring an understanding of science is involvement in aspects of scientific activities. Inquiry activities like those included in this sourcebook provide one means to that end.

The Nature of Inquiry

Novak[4] has defined scientific inquiry broadly as the "total configuration of behaviors involved in the struggle of human beings for reasonable explanations of phenomena about which they are curious." The behaviors include systematic investigation and thinking based upon a thorough knowledge of a particular discipline.

People have used the term *inquiry* in different and sometimes conflicting ways. An important distinction should be made between inquiry in the teaching and learning of science and scientific inquiry as a mode for extending the frontiers of scientific understanding.

Perceptions of the nature of science have changed over the years as science and as the philosophy of science have developed. At times there has been emphasis upon empirical observation, upon description and classification; at other times there has been emphasis upon intuition, rational thought, and abstract constructs. Science is now perceived as an experimental discipline in which general theories are developed to explain and relate phenomena that can be observed. When new information is uncovered revealing an inadequate explanatory system, explanations and models are revised.

Schwab[5] has described two kinds of scientific inquiry: *stable* and *fluid.* In stable inquiry the scientist works within the framework of a discipline's conceptual structure, which guides him or her in identifying research problems and in conducting deductive investigation. Stable inquiry leads normally to the interpretation of new phenomena in terms of a particular discipline's currently accepted conceptual structure. At the same time, in the continuing effort to increase the validity of the conceptual structure by extending the range and depth of phenomena which it can successfully explain, anomolous findings are uncovered.

4. Novak, A. "Scientific Inquiry", *BioScience,* 14, 10; October 1964, p. 26.
5. Schwab, J. J. *op. cit.,* p. 15.

These eventually bring original assumptions and conceptual schemes into question. Inquiry then becomes fluid. Methods of fluid inquiry are not clearly defined and involve much creative insight. Fluid inquiry leads to a redefinition of a discipline's conceptual structure, the development of new concepts, and to the definition of new kinds of research problems for conducting stable inquiry. Stable and fluid inquiry are thus two complementary aspects of scientific inquiry.

"Scientific literacy", a frequently stated goal for introductory science teaching, includes the notion that students will understand and even use modes of scientific inquiry and problem-solving as well as some of the concepts and facts of science. In science education the term, problem-solving, has commonly been used to mean the application of scientific knowledge to resolve problems in the world of people and technology. This use of the term goes well beyond more precise definitions outlined by psychologists conducting research into the problem-solving process. However, just as methods of fluid inquiry have not been clearly defined by researchers, neither have methods for scientific problem-solving been thoroughly elaborated at this time.[6] Certainly, however, problem-solving involves a complex array of skills and abilities.[7] (These skills involve much more than the ability of find discrete solutions to numerical problems in which the algorithm is known!) Jerome Bruner has written that "Problem solving strategies may be considered for purposes of simplification as essentially two processes: (1) hypothesis generation and (2) hypothesis testing."[8] More recent research by Jill Larkin and other indicates that physical intuition and expert problem solving involves a sizeable body of organized knowledge and some complex processes they are currently studying. Their studies provide information that "enables us to begin to explore the learning processes needed to acquire suitable knowledge and problem-solving processes".[9]

The way people have understood the philosophy and structure of science has influenced their beliefs about how to teach science. The image of *science as inquiry* can be communicated in a variety of ways that do not necessarily involve students in the process of solving problems or even in the manipulation of materials. The image of science as inquiry can be communicated verbally as well as through a variety of media. The process of *learning through inquiry* is a different matter and has been justified based upon psychological models of learning that go well beyond the effort to communicate the nature of science. Teachers who intend to use inquiry generally hope to involve the learner in identifying questions for investigation, designing experiments, manipulating materials, making observations, interpreting data, and explaining relationships. . . . Figure 7 presents a more complete outline of inquiry skills that can be used as an operational definition of student inquiry.

In recent times, science educators have come to recognize the importance of helping students develop the higher cognitive processes on which much of science is based. They have tended to move away from an emphasis upon laboratory activities in which students merely illustrate, demonstrate, or verify known concepts and laws. While it clearly is impossible to have students "discover" all the information and relationships they ought to assimilate in their schooling, many contemporary educators believe that learning science through inquiry and developing inquiring and problem-solving skills are especially important aspects of the science teaching-learning process.

Morine and Morine[10] have described modes of "discovery" which differentiate three kinds of inquiry. *Inductive discovery* involves collecting, organizing, and interpreting data to arrive at new generalizations. It is often present in descriptive activities in science teaching. *Deductive discovery* involves using general ideas to arrive at specific statements. One form of deductive discovery especially relevant to science has been termed *hypothetico-deductive discovery*. This mode of deductive thought involves explaining relationships in terms of abstract concepts; specific results based on the relationships or theories can then be predicted and examined experimentally. It requires the ability to control variables and to use other

6. Champagne, A. B. and Klopfer, L. E. "A Sixty-year Perspective on Three Issues in Science Education: . . .(III) Reflective Thinking and Problem Solving", *Science Education*, 61:4, 1977, pp. 431–452.
7. Merrifield, P. R., Guilford, J. P., Christensen, P. R., and Frick, J. W. *The Role of Intellectual Factors in Problem Solving*. Psychological Monographs, 1962, 76, No. 10.
8. Bruner, J. S. *The Process of Education*, 1963. Vintage Books, New York.
9. Larkin, J., et al. "Expert and Novice Performance in Solving Physics Problems", *Science*, 208, June, 1980, p. 1342.
10. Morine, H. and Morine, G. *Discovery: A Challenge to Teachers*, 1973. Prentice-Hall, Englewood Cliffs, New Jersey.

STUDENT INQUIRY SKILLS

1.0   PLANNING AND DESIGN

1.1   Formulates a question or defines problem to be investigated

1.2   Predicts experimental result

1.3   Formulates hypothesis to be tested in this investigation

1.4   Designs observation or measurement procedure

2.0   PERFORMANCE

2.1a   Carries out qualitative observation

2.1b   Carries out quantitative observation or measurement

2.2   Manipulates apparatus; develops techniques

2.3   Records result, describes observation

2.4   Performs numeric calculation

2.5   Explains or makes a decision about experimental technique

2.6   Works according to own design

3.0   ANALYSIS AND INTERPRETATION

3.1a   Transforms result into standard form (other than graphs)

3.1b   Graphs data

3.2a   Determines qualitative relationship

3.2b   Determines quantitative relationship

3.3   Determines accuracy of experimental data

3.4   Defines or discusses limitations and/or assumptions that underly the experiment

3.5   Formulates or proposes a generalization or model

3.6   Explains a relationship

3.7   Formulates new questions or defines problem based upon result of investigation

4.0   APPLICATION

4.1   Predicts based upon result of this investigation

4.2   Formulates hypothesis based upon results of this investigation

4.3   Applies experimental technique to new problem or variable

Figure 7. Adapted from P. Tamir, V. Lunetta, S. Novick, and M. Fuhrman, Laboratory Structure and Task Analysis Inventory, reported in V. Lunetta and P. Tamir, Matching Lab Activities with Teaching Goals, *The Science Teacher,* 46:5, May 1979, p. 23. Printed with permission.

"formal operational" logical skills. The third mode of discovery with relevance to inquiry activities has been labelled *transductive discovery*. Piaget has defined transductive thinking as the relating of sets of data in non-logical ways[11]. While transductive thinking is typical of the "pre-operational" stage of cognitive development, it is also present in older persons and is responsible for imaginative constructions that do have logical constraints. This kind of thinking might result in novel models and explanations. Through inquiry activities some students may make creative and imaginative leaps in the development of explanations and models.

Educational philosophers such as Pestalozzi and Dewey also have had impact on the development of inquiry teaching strategies. These educators suggested departures from memorizing and reciting which were so widely used in nineteenth century schools. They encouraged the use of more relevant student experiences proceeding from work with materials to abstract ideas. In more recent times, psychologists including Jean Piaget and Jerome Bruner have stressed how important it is for students to have direct experience and independence in conducting their own explorations and inquiry in order to create meaningful mental structures appropriate for their own development and prior experiences. Piagetian studies indicate that young children pass through a stage of "concrete operations" between the ages of approximately seven and fourteen years. In that stage of development, children have special need for a broad variety of experiences with different kinds of objects. In fact, if they do not have such experiences during early years, their intellectual development may be inhibited. It even may be detrimental to try to force students to think abstractly before they have a strong foundation in direct experience with objects. Piaget also has observed that development leads to a stage marked by the appearance of "hypothetico-deductive"

11. Flavell, J. H. *The Developmental Psychology of Jean Piaget,* 1963, Van Nostrand, Princeton, New Jersey.

reasoning based upon the logic of combinations. The level of development of the student will affect the kinds of inquiry activities appropriate for that student. At the same time, development can be facilitated by the right kinds of inquiry/problem-solving activities. These activities can also facilitate the formation and understanding of scientific concepts and knowledge.

Implications

An effective science program must provide intellectual challenge and the possibility of success for students of many different backgrounds and experiences. Even college students enter a class with a great array of individual differences in their science experiences, in their reading, mathematical, communication, and science skills, and in their interest and intellectual development. Thus, responsive teachers provide activities for students that are appropriate for their particular interests, skills, and intellectual capacities. They provide activities that are neither excessively easy (boring) nor excessively difficult (impossible) for individual students. If a student has not developed the logical structures necessary for controlling variables, for example, a sensitive teacher will not involve that student in an activity where he or she must control large numbers of variables. A student who is ready to develop that skill and has the necessary prerequisite structures, however, may indeed develop the ability to control variables through appropriate activities. In the same investigation, students at lower levels of logical development may be encouraged to develop more basic skills such as observing and organizing data. Similarly, if a student has limited reading skills, he or she can still engage in science activity that does not demand excessive reading and research in the written literature. Good curriculum materials and class activities provide varied opportunities and experiences for students with diverse interests, skills, and needs. Also, students need to receive more than facts and information from their teachers; they should be confronted with challenging problems appropriate for their individual levels of development. Use of inquiry/problem-solving activities like those in this sourcebook provide one mechanism through which diverse students can be challenged with new experiences that are at various levels of sophistication; in most of the inquiries, activities can be found that are appropriate for a variety of student developmental levels.

One of the important questions raised about learning through inquiry involves the amount of structure and guidance to be provided by the teacher. In highly structured inquiry, the student is explicitly directed by the teacher or a laboratory guide in all aspects of the inquiry activity. In an inquiry with low structure, the teacher or guide may make an initial statement or suggestion or raise a question, but the design and conduct of the experiment is, for the most part, left to the student. Activities having low structure are often described as "inefficient" by teachers concerned about teaching specific science concepts. However, low structure activities provide students with opportunities to increase skill in organizing and in making decisions about experimental procedure. While highly structured inquiry activities may be more efficient in helping students observe specific concepts and relationships, they do not provide opportunities for students to develop some higher order skills such as organizing, controlling variables, or designing experiments. At the same time, students often seek structure and guidance for a variety of reasons and prefer not to have to make all decisions for themselves in a laboratory activity. While one of the tasks of the science teacher is to help wean students from dependency on the authority of the teacher, certainly some guidance and structure are appropriate. Unguided inquiry (child abandonment) may very well result in high frustration, misunderstanding of scientific concepts, and a distorted view of scientific inquiry. For students whose logical skills are not well developed, the understanding of principles and concepts through unguided inquiry may very easily be buried amid large quantities of irrelevant and sometimes erroneous information. Yet, analyses of contemporary curriculum materials and teaching practice generally imply that the majority of students can operate *only* within a highly structured instructional environment. Data from students, however, indicate that excessive teacher imposed structure is as ineffective as unguided inquiry for attaining instructional goals. The sensitive teacher should ascertain the amount of guidance appropriate for attainment of a wide array of instructional goals. This guidance should almost certainly vary to meet specific goals of instruction and to match the student's level of development.

Effective teachers motivate students and stimulate their curiosity. One of the ways science teachers arouse interest is to provide activities that students find relevant and fun to perform. Interest and curiosity in science often can be stimulated by observing and exploring discrepant events. (A discrepant event is one which observers normally find to be intriguing, contrary to expectation, and in which the explanation for the event is not immediately obvious.) The inquiring and problem-solving activities in this sourcebook often include discrepant events that can increase interest and curiosity.

Experiences with "new" curriculum projects have taught that effective introductory science curricula must include an appropriate mix of theoretical and applied experiences and ideas. Science curriculum projects of the early 1960's generally eliminated applications of science in order to emphasize concepts and structures which seem more consistent with "pure" science. For example, writers of the first edition of *PSSC Physics*[12] were reluctant to include commentary on telescopes because that seemed too *applied* and not sufficiently *pure*. Young students, however, tend to be most interested in topics they consider relevant to their own lives. The movement away from applied topics toward a more theoretical orientation in the 1960's caused special problems in motivating many students and may have contributed to a subsequent decline in enrollment in the physical sciences. In addition, effective science curriculum materials and teaching strategies enable students to make connections to their everyday lives. They include experiences with applications of science as well as with the concepts of science. The inquiry/problem-solving activities in this sourcebook include many relevant applications of science.

In short, science curricula and teaching strategies should be consistent with instructional goals and with what is known about science and about how people learn, and teachers have a very important role to play in selecting and using appropriate curriculum materials and teaching strategies. To that end, this sourcebook contains materials and ideas that can facilitate learning in the physical sciences.

References

Bingham, R. M., ed. *Inquiry Objectives in the Teaching of Biology,* 1969, Mid-Continent Regional Educational Laboratory, Kansas City, Mo.

Bloom, B. S. *Taxonomy of Educational Objectives: Handbook 1: Cognitive Domain,* 1956. David McKay Co., Inc., New York.

Bruner, J. S. *The Process of Education,* 1963. Vintage Books, New York.

Champagne, A. B. and Klopfer, L. E. "A Sixty-year Perspective on Three Issues in Science Education: . . . (III) Reflective Thinking and Problem Solving", *Science Education,* 61:4, 1977, pp. 431–452.

Conant, J. B. *Science and Common Sense,* 1951. Yale University Press, New Haven, Connecticut.

Flavell, J. H. *The Developmental Psychology of Jean Piaget,* 1963. Van Nostrand, Princeton, New Jersey.

Hurd, P. D. *Theory Into Action,* 1964. National Science Teachers Association, Washington, D.C.

Larkin, J., et al. "Expert and Novice Performance in Solving Physics Problems", *Science. 208,* 20 June 1980, pp. 1335–1342.

Morine, H. and Morine, G. *Discovery: A Challenge to Teachers,* 1973. Prentice-Hall, Englewood Cliffs, New Jersey.

Nagel, E. *The Structure of Science,* 1961. Harcourt, Brace & World, New York.

Robinson, J. T. "Science Teaching and the Nature of Science", *The Journal of Research in Science Teaching,* 3:1, 1965, pp. 37–50.

Schwab, J. J. *The Teaching of Science as Enquiry,* 1962. Harvard University Press, Cambridge, Massachusetts.

---

12. Physical Science Study Committee, *PSSC Physics,* 1960. D. C. Heath, Boston, MA.

Science Topic Index

NOTES